# SUBMARINES

# SUBMARINES

## Antony Preston

BISON BOOKS

First published in 1982 by

Bison Books Ltd.
176 Old Brompton Road
London, SW5
England

ISBN 0 86124 043 X

Printed in Hong Kong

Reprinted 1985

# CONTENTS

# FIRST STEPS

For centuries designers have dreamed of submarines but the first practical design did not appear until 1578, when the Englishman William Bourne wrote of a submersible boat in *Inventions and Devices*. There is no evidence that Bourne ever built one but his description leaves us in no doubt that he had grasped the essentials of a workable craft. A simple boat-shaped hull was to be decked over and sealed to make it watertight, while leather bags were built into the bilges to act as ballast tanks by admitting sea-water through holes in the wooden hull.

As the bags filled with water the positive buoyancy would be destroyed and the boat would submerge. To come to the surface the operator would turn two screw presses and squeeze the water out of the leather bags.

Bourne had mastered a concept which eluded many later submarine designers, by providing a simple mechanical means of varying the boat's total weight displacement. He also solved the lack of fresh air by providing a hollow mast, but there is no record in his description of any form of propulsion, nor of any pur-

pose, peaceful or otherwise, for his boat. Obviously he was content to provide a solution to the chief technical problem of getting a boat to submerge below the surface of the water. Other problems, however, would have prevented his ideas from working. Even with an air-mast an oarsman would soon become exhausted, and of course the lack of means of attacking an enemy ship robbed this submarine of any value as an instrument of war. Its application could only have been for peaceful use; the diving bell was already well-known as a means of working under-

water, and the submarine was an obvious development. If it is useful to be able to work underwater in a fixed position it is much more so to be able to move around.

England was an expanding maritime power in the late sixteenth and early seventeenth centuries, so it is not surprising that the next submarine inventor, although not English, took his ideas to that country. The Dutch physician Cornelius van Drebbel went a step further than Bourne, and in 1624 built two different-sized submersibles. Van Dreb-

bel relied on oars to force his boat below the surface, and did not, as far as we know, provide any means of increasing the displacement. The problem with this method was that great exertions were needed merely to maintain depth, and since there was only a limited air-supply inside the hull the rowers would tire quickly and the boat could do little more than crawl. However, van Drebbel was an astute publicist, and is reputed to have persuaded King James VI to travel in his boat, despite that monarch's reputation for a certain reluctance to risk his neck. The contemporary claims that the boat was rowed at a depth of 12–15 feet for *several hours* can be dismissed as an example of over-enthusiastic sales promotion – something which was to afflict other submarine-inventors to a similar degree.

*Below: The Turkish Nordenfelt submarine* Abdul Hamid *(1887) in Constantinople. The bow torpedo tube can be seen to the left. A machine gun is also carried.*

Very little is known of van Drebbel's submarines, but we can assume that they were, like Bourne's, based on the shape of an ordinary rowing boat but decked over. The design probably differed little from Bourne's conception but van Drebbel encased the hull with greased leather to make it watertight. One of the problems of tracing the history of all the early submarine inventions and ideas is that the details were so sparsely described, but in 1747 the *Gentlemen's Magazine* published the first drawing of a submarine, the dream-child of an inventor called Symons. It appears to profit from the ideas of both van Drebbel and Bourne, with the oars of the Dutchman's design and leather air-bags for taking on water ballast.

The purpose of submarines up to this point seems to have been restricted to salvage or construction work on the sea bed, in other words an extension of the diving bell's capability. In 1653 a Monsieur de Son took the first step in the long process of subverting the submarine to warlike purposes. At Rotterdam he built a boat which he claimed, 'Doeth undertake in one day to destroy an hondred ships,' would have the speed of a bird and would be immune to fire, storm and bullets, 'unless it please God.' The boat was a big catamaran with a clockwork engine driving a paddle wheel between its twin hulls. De Son's enthusiasm had run away with him for the clockwork engine proved too weak to move the boat, which was larger than the submarines built in the early years of the twentieth century. The 72-feet-long wooden monster embodied sound principles, and because of its size contained enough air to keep two or three men alive for some time, but there was still no suitable means of propulsion and the submarine would have to wait for over 200 years before a solution was found to this problem.

The Russians claim that Czar Peter the Great ordered a submarine at the beginning of the eighteenth century, and it was reported to have been launched in

1729, during the reign of Peter II. Virtually nothing is known of this submarine, apart from the fact that it was no more successful than any of the others.

A ship's carpenter called Day experimented around 1773 with a diving machine, and converted a small sloop by building an air-chamber amidships. Day's contribution to the art of submarine design was the idea of detachable ballast in the form of large boulders hung from external ring-bolts. The inventor achieved one successful dive in Plymouth Sound but on 20 June 1774 a second dive proved disastrous; the pressure at 22 fathoms (132 feet) probably crushed the wooden hull. The First Lord of the Admiralty, Lord Sandwich, was visiting Plymouth at the time, and personally authorized the use of Royal Navy ships in the first attempted submarine rescue in history. But all efforts failed, as they were doomed to with only one exception in the following 140 years.

Almost coinciding with Day's unfortunate attempt to defeat nature was the highly successful endeavor of David Bushnell in America. This intelligent young Yale graduate had previously been fascinated by the idea of the submarine but the outbreak of the War of Independence in 1775 gave him the incentive to produce a weapon which would break the British naval blockade of the colonies. We are fortunate that Bushnell wrote in 1787 to Thomas Jefferson, then Minister Plenipotentiary for the United States in Paris, giving him a full description of his invention:

'The external shape of the sub-marine vessel bore some resemblance to two upper tortoise shells of equal size, joined together; the place of entrance into the vessel being represented by the opening made by the swell of the shells, at the head of the animal. The inside was capable of containing the operator, and air sufficient to support him 30 minutes without receiving fresh air. At the bottom opposite to the entrance was fixed a quantity of lead for ballast. At one edge which was directly before the operator who sat upright, was an oar for rowing forward or backward. At the other edge was a rudder for steering. An

aperture at the bottom, with its valve, was designed to admit water for the purpose of descending; and two brass forcing pumps served to eject the water within, when necessary for ascending. At the top there was likewise an oar for ascending or descending, or continuing at any particular depth. A water gauge or barometer determined the depth of descent, a compass directed the course, and a ventilator within supplied the vessel with fresh air when on the surface.

'The entrance into the vessel was elliptical, and so small as barely to admit a person. This entrance was surrounded with a broad elliptical iron band, the lower edge of which was let into the wood of which the body of the vessel was made, in such a manner as to give its utmost support to the body of the vessel against the pressure of the water. Above the upper edge of this iron band there was a brass crown or cover, resembling a hat with its crown and brim, which shut watertight upon the iron band; the crown was hung to the iron band with hinges so as to turn over sideways when opened. To make it perfectly secure when shut, it might be screwed down upon the band by the operator, or by a person without.

'There were in the brass crown three round doors, one directly in front, and one on each side, large enough to put the hand through. When open they admitted fresh air; their shutters were ground perfectly tight into their places with emery, hung with hinges and secured in their places when shut. There were likewise several small glass windows in the crown for looking through and for admitting light in the daytime, with covers to secure them. There were two air pipes in the crown. A ventilator within drew fresh air through one of the air pipes and discharged it into the lower part of the vessel; the fresh air introduced by the ventilator expelled the impure light air through the other air pipe. Both air pipes were so constructed that they shut themselves whenever the water rose near their tops, so that no water could enter through them, and opened themselves immediately after they rose above the water. The vessel was chiefly ballasted with lead fixed to its bottom; when this was not sufficient, a quantity was placed within, more or less according to the weight of the operator; its ballast made it so stiff that there was no danger of oversetting. The vessel, with all its appendages and the operator, was of sufficient weight to settle it very low in the water. About two hundred pounds of the lead at the

bottom for ballast, would be let down forty or fifty feet below the vessel; this enabled the operator to rise instantly to the surface of the water in case of accident.

'When the operator would descend he placed his foot upon the top of a brass valve, depressing it, by which he opened a large aperture in the bottom of the vessel, through which the water entered at his pleasure; when he had admitted a sufficient quantity he descended very gradually; if he admitted too much he ejected as much as was necessary to obtain an equilibrium by the two brass forcing pumps which were placed at each hand. Whenever the vessel leaked, or he would ascend to the surface, he also made use of these forcing pumps. When the skilful operator had obtained an equilibrium he could row upward or downward, or continue at any particular depth, with an oar placed near the top of the screw, forming up on the principle of the screw, the axis of the oar entering the vessel; by turning the oar one way he raised the vessel, by turning it the other way he depressed it.

'A glass tube eighteen inches long and one inch in diameter, standing upright, its upper end closed and its lower end, which was open, screwed into a brass pipe, through which the external water had a passage into the glass tube, served as a water-gauge or barometer. There was a piece of cork with phosphorus on it, put into the water-gauge. When the vessel

*Above: The tiny French submersible* Gymnote *in 1899 after her second rebuilding.*

*Left: The Confederate submersible* H.L. Hunley *on dry land shortly before her attack on the USS* Housatonic *in 1864.*

descended the water rose in the water-gauge, condensing the air within and bearing the cork with its phosphorus on its surface. By the light of the phosphorus the ascent of the water in the gauge was rendered visible, and the depth of the vessel under water ascertained by a graduated line.

'An oar formed upon the principle of the screw was fixed in the forepart of the vessel; its axis entered the vessel, and being turned one way rowed the vessel forward, but being turned the other way rowed it backward; it was made to be turned by the hand or foot.

'A rudder, hung to the hinder part of the vessel, commanded it with the greatest ease. The rudder was made very elastic and might be used for rowing forward. Its tiller was within the vessel at the operator's right hand, fixed at a right angle on an iron rod, which passed through the side of the vessel; the rod had a crank on its outside end, which commanded the rudder by means of a rod extending from the end of the crank to a kind of tiller, fixed upon the left hand of the rudder. Raising and depressing the first mentioned tiller turned the rudder as the case required. A compass marked with phosphorus directed the course, both above and under the water, and a line and lead sounded the depth when necessary.

'The internal shape of the vessel in every possible section of it verged toward an ellipsis, as near as the design would allow, but every horizontal section, although elliptical, yet [was] as near to a circle as could be admitted. The body of the vessel was made exceedingly strong, and to strengthen it as much as possible a firm piece of wood was framed, parallel to the conjugate diameter, to prevent the sides from yielding to the great pressure

of the incumbent water in a deep immersion. This piece of wood was also a seat for the operator.

'Every opening was well secured. The pumps had two sets of valves. The aperture at the bottom for admitting water was covered with a plate, perforated full of holes to receive the water and prevent anything from choking the passage, or stopping the valves from shutting. The brass valve might likewise be forced into its place with a screw if necessary. The air pipes had a kind of hollow sphere fixed round the top of each to secure the air-pipe valves from injury; these hollow spheres were perforated full of holes for the passage of the air through the pipes. Within the air-pipes were shutters to secure them, should any accident happen to the pipes or the valves on their tops.

'Wherever the external apparatus passed through the body of the vessel the joints were round, and formed by brass pipes which were driven into the wood of the vessel. The holes through the pipes were very exactly made, and the iron rods which passed through them were turned in a lathe to fit them; the joints were also kept full of oil to prevent rust and leaking. Particular attention was given to bring every part necessary for performing the operations, both within and without the vessel, before the operator [i.e. within his reach] and as conveniently as could be devised, so that every-thing might be found in the dark, except the water-gauge and the compass which were visible by the light of the phosphorus, and nothing required the operator to turn to the right hand or to the left to perform anything necessary.

'In the forepart of the brim of the crown of the submarine vessel was a socket, and an iron tube passing through the socket; the tube stood upright and could slide up and down in the socket, six inches. At the top of the tube was a wood-screw fixed by means of a rod which passed through the tube and screwed the wood-screw fast upon the top of the tube. By pushing the wood-screw up against the bottom of a ship and turning it at the same time it would enter the planks; driving would also answer the same purpose. When the wood-screw was firmly fixed it would be cast off by unscrewing the rod which fastened it upon the top of the tube.

'Behind the sub-marine vessel was a place above the rudder for carrying a large powder magazine; this was made of two pieces of oak timber, large enough when hollowed out to contain one hundred and fifty pounds of powder, with the apparatus used in firing it, and was secured in its place by a screw turned by the operator. A strong piece of rope extended from the magazine to the wood-screw above mentioned and was fastened to both. When the wood-screw was fixed and [ready] to be cast off from its tube, the magazine was to be cast off likewise by unscrewing it, leaving it hanging to the wood-screw; it was lighter than the water, that it might rise up against the object to which the wood-screw and itself were fastened.

'Within the magazine was an apparatus constructed to run any proposed length of time under twelve hours; when it had run out its time it unpinioned a strong lock resembling a gun lock which gave fire to the powder. This apparatus was pinioned that it would not possibly move, till, by casting off the magazine from the vessel it was set in motion. The skilful operator could swim so low on the surface of the water as to approach very near a ship in the night, without fear of being discovered, and might if he chose, approach the stem or stern above water with very little danger. He could sink very quickly, keep at any depth he pleased, and row a great distance in any direction he desired without coming to the surface, and when he rose to the surface he could soon obtain a fresh supply of air, when if necessary he might descend again and pursue his course.'

If nothing else was known about Bushnell, this lucid explanation of his submarine and its mode of operation would stamp him as a skilled and far-sighted engineer. His little *Turtle*, as it was

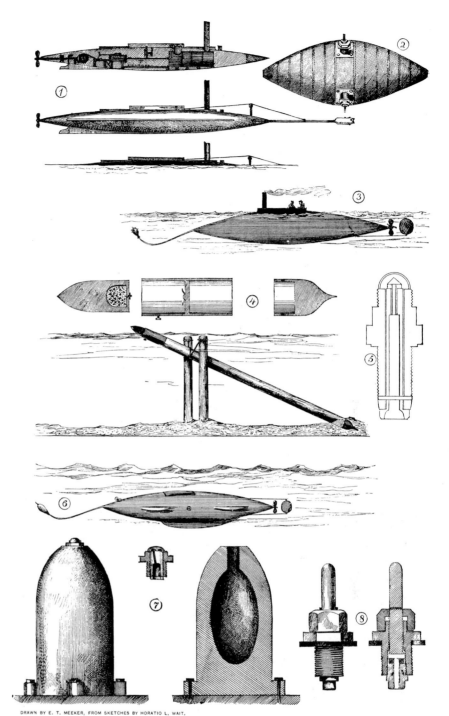

DRAWN BY E. T. MEEKER, FROM SKETCHES BY HORATIO L. WAIT.

1. CONFEDERATE TORPEDO-BOAT "DAVID." 2. CONFEDERATE TORPEDO. 3. CONFEDERATE TORPEDO-BOAT, AS DESCRIBED BY A REFUGEE. 4. CONFEDERATE SPAR-TORPEDO. 5. FUSE OF A BARREL-TORPEDO FOUND IN THE ST. JOHN'S RIVER. 6. CONFEDERATE SUBMARINE TORPEDO-BOAT, AS DESCRIBED BY A REFUGEE. 7. CONFEDERATE VOLCANO-TORPEDO. 8. CONFEDERATE TORPEDO-FUSE.

called from its double shell configuration, had features unknown for another hundred years: the depth-gauge, the snorkel breathing-tube and a detachable explosive charge complete with time-fuze. The attention to detail was matched by careful thought about the purpose of his submarine, and Bushnell conducted a series of trials to test the *Turtle.* He first proved that the explosive charge and its mechanism were reliable and then tested the strength of the hull by submerging it in deep water by means of ballast. Only when he was satisfied with the *Turtle's* inherent soundness did he allow his brother to take her down, and only then with a strong line attached until the drill had been perfected. Bushnell even made his brother practice against a moored vessel until he was quite familiar with the problems.

At this stage Bushnell came up against a problem which even his methodical and skilled preparations could not defeat. His brother fell ill during the trials in 1776, and from what we know today we can assume that his prolonged dives in the *Turtle* had seriously affected his physical wellbeing. Nobody connected his illness with the extended program of trials but it was reported that he never fully recovered his health. It therefore became necessary to train another operator as fast as possible, and the Army was asked to provide three 'volunteers.' The most skilled of the three soldiers was a Sergeant Ezra Lee, to whom goes the credit of carrying out the first submarine war mission in history.

On the night of 6 September 1776 Lee climbed into the *Turtle* and was towed down the Hudson River by two rowing boats to a point not far from the British squadron under Admiral Lord Howe lying off Governor's Island. Here the rowing boats slipped their tow and left the current to carry the little egg-shaped submarine down-river. What followed must have seemed like a nightmare, for Lee found that the tide was sweeping him rapidly past the enemy anchorage, so far that it took him two hours to work the *Turtle* upstream again. Bearing in mind Bushnell's own estimate of only half an hour's air-supply we can assume that the submarine was trimmed down but not fully submerged for most of the time, but even so the sheer physical exertion involved was tremendous. Despite the current Lee was eventually able to submerge under the hull of the British flag-

ship, the 3rd Rate 64-gun ship *Eagle*, but when he tried to operate the screw to fix the explosive charge to her hull he found that it would not penetrate. After trying again he realized from the dim light filtering through the windows that dawn was breaking, and decided that it was time to make his escape.

This time the tide was in his favor, and he made good progress. In the early morning a British guard-boat sighted the conning-tower and gave chase, but Lee had his wits about him and jettisoned the powder-charge to gain more speed, not forgetting to set the clockwork fuze. The resulting explosion disconcerted the pursuers and allowed Lee to escape.

Bushnell was most anxious to find out from Lee what had caused the failure, and he was rightly sceptical of the theory that the screw had been blunted by the copper sheathing which had just been introduced to protect the bottoms of British men-o'-war. He felt that Lee had given up too easily, and that he had merely struck iron fastenings in the vicinity of the sternpost. In the light of modern diving knowledge we can understand the problems more easily; Ezra Lee was tired and probably suffering from a lack of oxygen, which would tend to make him dispirited. Maneuvering in total darkness under what to him would be the massive hull of the *Eagle*, he would

quickly lose all sense of direction, and would hardly know which end of the ship he was at. Whether he did strike an iron fastening or merely gave up too soon cannot be known for certain, but he did not strike copper sheathing; documentary proof exists to show that HMS *Eagle* did not have her hull coppered until after the war was over. But the most important factor militating against success was that the *Turtle* was far too complicated for one man to operate, as he would have to steer with one hand, pedal furiously to stem any current, be ready to adjust ballast, and presumably find a spare pair of hands to force the vertical screw into thick timbers! All that in an atmosphere becoming saturated with carbon dioxide.

The *Turtle* was, despite her problems, the world's first submarine to complete a war mission and survive. She is said to have been used again in two attacks, also without success, but after she was lost on board a frigate which ran aground her inventor turned his talents to the equally fascinating hobby of designing underwater mines. A copy, or at least a very similar boat, may have been built in the War of 1812 between the United States and Great Britain, for in July 1813 the 74-gun ship HMS *Ramillies* reported that she was attacked by a 'diving-boat' which succeeded in piercing her copper sheathing before the screw broke.

Another American, Robert Fulton, took the submarine a step further, but in a more circuitous manner. Although a prolific inventor he was also an ardent pacifist who conceived the idea of a submarine to destroy navies and thus rid the world of expensive and repressive armaments. Although he later denied doing so, there is some evidence that he may have discussed his ideas with David Bushnell, but in any case his submarine

ideas were considerably different. Like so many republicans and libertarians of the day he regarded the French Revolution as a great force for freedom, and he emigrated to France to offer his ideas in the service of Mankind. On 13 December 1797 he wrote to the Directory, the committee which ruled France, to offer them a 'mechanical engine' for the annihilation of the Royal Navy, which was currently strangling French commerce by its close blockade. Fulton suggested that he build his submarine at his own expense and be rewarded if it succeeded; 4000 francs per gun for every British ship sunk carrying more than 40 guns, and half that amount for smaller ships.

There was only one drawback to this scheme; the near-bankrupt Directory could not have afforded the sort of victory that Bushnell promised. A ship-of-the-line such as HMS *Victory* would have cost them 400,000 francs, a cool million pounds or more in modern terms! Even a modest run of successes would have brought France to her knees, and the Directory soon began to quibble at the price. First they cut the price and then on the advice of the Minister of Marine, refused to grant commissions to crew-members, thus ensuring that the British would hang prisoners as pirates. Disgusted, Fulton went to Holland but the thrifty burghers were even less inclined to invest in a submarine on these terms. Two years later the American idealist was back in France, and this time the ruler of France was not a committee of nonentities but the dynamic Napoleon Buonaparte, then known as First Consul. Napoleon was eager to find a weapon to offset British naval superiority, and he authorized the payment of 10,000 francs to Fulton to allow him to build his submarine.

*Above: The Reverend Garrett's* Resurgam, *with the inventor, his young son and two helpers, in the builders yard in December 1879.*
*Below: Profile, plan and section of the* Resurgam *redrawn from the builders' plans in the Glasgow Museum of Transport.*

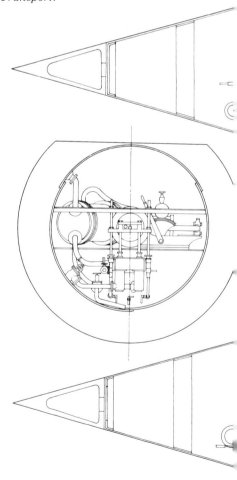

Work began in the winter of 1799 and by the spring of 1800 the boat was ready to be launched as the *Nautilus*, a name which would make submarine history again 150 years later. She was cylindrical in shape, with a copper hull on iron frames, and like modern submarines she had a conning tower and diving planes. She was much bigger than the *Turtle* and could accommodate three men; she also relied on a detachable powder-charge which could be left attached to the underside of an enemy ship. Like the *Turtle* she was propelled by a hand-operated screw but a kite-shaped sail could be used on the surface to take some of the strain off the operators. The first trials of the *Nautilus* were carried out in the River Seine in the spring of 1800, opposite the Hôtel des Invalides, when Fulton took her down to 25 feet. After several successful dives she was sent to try her paces in the open sea, but once she reached Brest she ran into political trouble. It was the

old question of commissions for the crew-members of the *Nautilus*, as the Maritime Prefect of Brest could not bring himself to sanction what he regarded as inhuman methods of waging war. The ensuing story of the *Nautilus* is a tale of unsubstantiated claims to have attacked British warships and squabbles over money, and one can understand why the French came to talk of *le charlatan Americain*. With the French admirals making no secret of their dislike of his infernal machine Fulton had a hard time convincing anybody of its worth, but in the end it was his patron Napoleon who finally killed off the scheme. The First Consul was hoping to negotiate a ceasefire with England, and news of a submarine would certainly jeopardize the plan. The French also suspected that their enemies had learned about the *Nautilus*, and that they had made better offers to her inventor to sell his secrets.

It was true that Robert Fulton's

idealism had become tarnished, but who would blame him? In 1804 he arrived in England, where the Prime Minister, William Pitt, received him as cordially as Napoleon had four years earlier. A committee including the inventor of the war-rocket, Major Congreve, was appointed to study the problem. Despite a convincing demonstration off Walmer in which a brig was blown up, or possibly because of it, the Royal Navy wanted nothing to do with the *Nautilus*. In a phrase which still thunders its disapproval Lord St Vincent denounced Pitt as 'the greatest fool that ever existed to encourage a mode of warfare which those who commanded the sea did not want, and which, if successful, would deprive them of it.' It is easy to dismiss that as crass stupidity but St Vincent was right; the submarine was nowhere near ready to take its place in any navy. With nothing but hand-propulsion available and only the crudest of close-range weapons

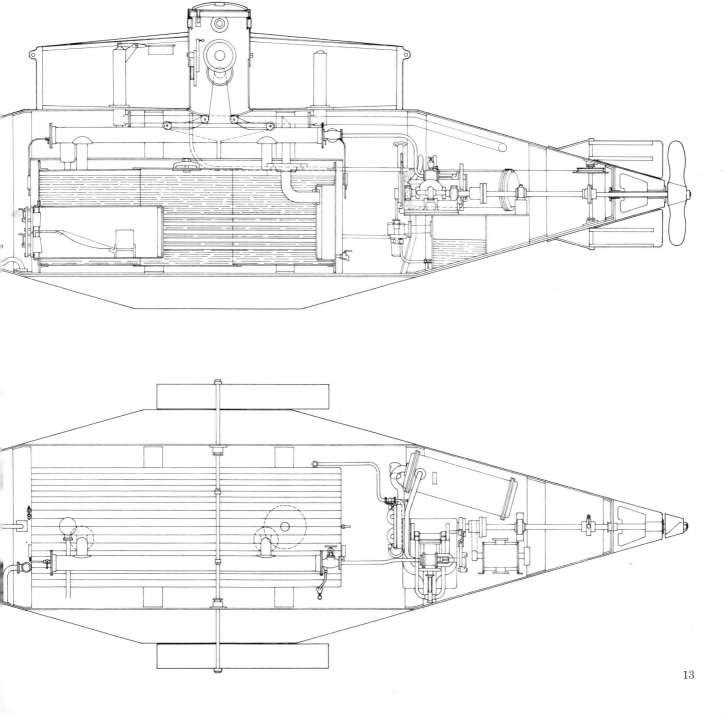

it was still nothing more than a toy.

Inventors of submarines seem to have remained quiet for nearly half a century after Fulton's experiments, possibly because the civilized world was at peace after the Napoleonic Wars and expending its energies in other directions. However in 1850 war broke out between Prussia and Denmark. The powerful Danish fleet blockaded the German coast, and for much the same reasons that Bushnell and Fulton had turned their minds to the design of submarines, a Bavarian artillery sergeant called Wilhelm Bauer produced his own ideas on how to drive off the Danish ships. His submarine was called the *Brandtaucher* or 'Fire Diver', and was virtually a sheet-iron rectangular tank driven by a hand-wheel. Water ballast was admitted to destroy buoyancy, but the diving angle was created by winding a heavy weight backwards and forwards.

The principal failing of the *Brandtaucher* was the weakness of her hull, as the rectangular box form was not ideal for maintaining structural strength at any considerable depth. The first voyage in December 1850 was successful, for the Danes were forced to withdraw their ships from Kiel, but little more than a month later the *Brandtaucher* suffered a disastrous accident. While she was diving in Kiel Harbour the plating at the stern collapsed under the pressure of 50 feet of water. Bauer kept his head, and told the two seamen to allow the boat to flood so that the pressure of air could force open the hatches, but the two men grew panicky. After a desperate argument he was able to convince them that he could save them, and five hours later all three reached the surface, the first submariners ever to escape from a damaged boat.

Bauer was not discouraged by this setback, and after he returned to Bavaria he produced a number of other designs for underwater craft. After an unsuccessful attempt to sell his ideas to the Emperor Maximilian he traveled to Britain. The Crimean War had begun and the Prince Consort introduced Bauer to influential naval officers in the hope that his ideas could be used against the Russians. What follows is a mystery, for although the rumors persist about 'Lord Palmerston's Submarine' virtually no concrete evidence has survived as to where it was built or even what happened to it. All that is known is that the well-known British naval architect Scott Russell produced a design for a submarine after long discussions with Bauer, and that the Prime Minister, Lord Palmerston, sanctioned the expenditure of £7000 for building a prototype. Admiral Sir Astley Cooper-Key remembered it as being 'merely a large diving bell' capable of accommodating two men, but this does not sound like any of Bauer's existing ideas. The Victorians were obsessed with technological progress and published detailed descriptions of every type of equipment, even their latest warships and weapons, yet nothing has survived of this experiment. Even the Liverpool shipyard alleged to have built the boat never advertized the fact, which leads one to the reluctant conclusion that the whole thing could have been nothing more than a hoax to frighten the Russians. The idea was probably investigated in some detail, but the total absence of any paper evidence of ordering, payment or building, *anywhere* in British official papers indicates conclusively that the boat was not built, despite Cooper-Key's references to seeing it dive.

Bauer had more success with the

*Above: The second French submersible* Gustave Zédé *was much larger than the* Gymnote *but was still only suited for experiments.*

*Right: The French* Sirène *(1901) was steam driven, a development of Laubeuf's successful* Nautilus.

Russians in 1855 as he was allowed to build an improved 52-foot submarine called the *Seeteufel* or 'Sea Devil' (sometimes known as *Le Diable Marin*). On 6 September 1856, during the coronation of Tsar Alexander II the *Seeteufel* embarked several musicians at Kronstadt, so that they could strike up the National Anthem underwater while the fortress guns boomed out a salute overhead. This was the first demonstration of the distance that sound can travel through water.

The French were not lagging behind in the search for a workable submarine, and in 1858 the Minister of Marine called on various designers to submit proposals for a submersible to protect France's coastline, to meet requirements put forward by a Captain Bourgois. Five years later the *Plongeur* took the water at Rochefort, a 140-foot boat which bore a remarkable resemblance to French submarines built 40 years later. The submarine by its very nature makes big demands on technology, and the *Plongeur* showed how new developments in engineering could come to the aid of submarine designers. She had 23 reservoirs to hold compressed air for expelling water from the ballast tanks and for driving a four-cylinder engine. This was the biggest advance in submarine design for many years, but the reservoirs proved impossible to charge with air at any great pressure, and so

'blowing tanks' took some time. The other drawback was the recurrent one in all early submarines, the lack of a worthwhile weapon; it was no use building a highly complex vessel like a submarine and then equipping it with a suicidal weapon. The spar torpedo, all that was available, was a canister of explosive on the end of a wooden pole, which had to be poked against the side of an enemy ship.

The 'kamikaze' nature of the spar torpedo became even more obvious in the next series of submarines. These were the famous 'Davids', built in the American Civil War by the Confederate States to break the Federal blockade. The original 'David' (so-called because of its Goliath-killing potential) was hardly a submarine, rather a submersible torpedo-boat but she included a feature which was an important improvement, a steam engine. At least steam offered a relatively light propulsion unit, and although it was hardly ideal for underwater use it

did offer a chance to dispense with sheer muscle power. A 'David' could be trimmed down by filling her ballast tanks, leaving only a tall, slender funnel and a narrow superstructure above the water. On a dark night the funnel was hard to detect, and the 'David' would probably get within spar-torpedo range before she was spotted.

The first 'David' was swamped by the wash of a passing steamer but she was raised and manned by a fresh volunteer crew. On 5 October 1863, off Charleston, she damaged the Federal ironclad *New Ironsides*, but took nearly all her crew with her. Four months later a new type of 'David', named *H L Hunley* after its inventor, sank the steam sloop USS *Housatonic*, and the submarine could be said to have 'arrived' as a credible weapon of war. The *Hunley* was a proper submersible despite reverting to hand-propulsion, with eight men working a crankshaft. The cost of these successes

was exorbitant, however, two warships sunk and a third damaged in return for the loss of two submersibles (which had each sunk once before during training with the loss of their entire crews). The only other effort of the period was the *Intelligent Whale*, the North's answer to the 'Davids', which was built in New York. She was completed too late to see service, and was discarded in 1872. By a curious coincidence one of her backers was Cornelius S Bushnell.

In 1878 a Liverpool clergyman, the Reverend George Garrett, built a small egg-shaped boat, and a year later he embarked on a much more ambitious scheme. His second boat, christened the *Resurgam* was ordered from Messrs. Cochrane late in 1879, and was ready the following year. It was based on his prototype but was much longer (40 feet), and used steam on the surface. Before submerging a full head of steam was raised to provide latent heat in special storage tanks – a principle then in use in 'smokeless' locomotives for underground railways. Garrett's ideas were sound, but as a Victorian clergyman he naturally found difficulty in financing such an expensive scheme, and it was necessary to restrict the *Resurgam*'s size to keep the cost down. This meant that the 30-ton boat was very cramped, and Garrett had to enlist his 10-year-old son as a crewman because the boy could squeeze through the 12-inch spaces.

The *Resurgam* started trials in December 1879 but the following year she broke loose from her moorings while the crew were ashore and foundered off the Welsh coast. Just in time Garrett succeeded in attracting the attention of the Swedish arms manufacturer Thorsten Nordenfelt, and was saved from ruin. Nordenfelt put up fresh capital to allow the building of a new boat at Stockholm under Garrett's supervision. The prototype, known as *Nordenfelt No 1* was sold to Greece in 1883, which inspired Turkey to order two more in 1886. Despite the interest generated by these orders the Nordenfelt submarines were not a success. The propulsion system proved a big drawback as the slightest leakage from the smoke-box of the boiler allowed carbon monoxide fumes to seep into the boat. Nordenfelt's idea of providing vertical propellers did nothing to improve depth-keeping, and the big ballast tanks tended to produce a surge backwards and forwards. In one respect the Nordenfelts were successful, for they were the first to use the new Whitehead 'fish' or automobile torpedo. For the first time a submarine could attack a target from a safe distance.

Three more Nordenfelt submarines were built, one in Britain in 1887 and two

*Right: The French* Espadon *under construction in a dry dock in 1900.*

16

Above: The epoch-making Narval seen
before her torpedo drop-collars had been
installed. Laubeuf's principles
transformed the submarine from a
harbor-defense weapon into a seagoing
warship.

Right: The Italian midget submarine
B.1 and her sisters were built in 1915–16
for harbor defense. They were based on
a French design.

in Germany. The British one attracted a
lot of attention as she appeared at the
Golden Jubilee Review of the Royal Navy
in 1887 but was later lost while on passage to Russia. The German boats were
built at Kiel three years later, but little
is known of their subsequent fate.

The submarine now had a weapon, but
it still needed a workable means of underwater propulsion. The answer lay in the
electric motor, as it was completely independent of the outside atmosphere, but
early electricity generators were too
heavy. The accumulator battery was also
very heavy, but it did suggest a way
around the problem to a young Spanish
naval officer, Isaac Peral. He designed a
boat in 1886, powered by two 30-horse-
power electric motors using current from
420 accumulators but the Spanish Navy
was not in a position to exploit the lead
given to them by Peral. However, the
French, who had made a lot of progress
in electrical engineering, soon grasped

the implications. After a false start made
by Claude Goubet with his private ven-
ture boats the French Navy's great naval
architect Dupuy de Lôme started work
on a design of his own. On de Lôme's
death in 1885 his disciple Gustave Zédé
took over, and by November 1886 the
Ministry of Marine was ready to place
an order.

Many details still had to be worked
out; it was April 1887 before the submarine could be laid down, and she did
not begin her trials until the autumn of
the following year. Known as the Gymnote or 'Eel', she was 60 feet long and had
a cylindrical hull with a diameter of 5 feet

10 inches. Her armament was a single
14-inch Whitehead torpedo-tube mounted in the bow, and her electric batteries
drove her at a theoretical maximum
speed of 6½ knots.

There was never any intention to use
the Gymnote as anything but a test-bed,
and during the next decade she was
rebuilt twice. In 1892 she was fitted with
two sets of hydroplanes or diving rudders, forward and amidships to improve
her depth-keeping. At the same time a
small conning tower was added to provide a steering platform and to reduce
the risk of the boat being swamped by a
wave while running on the surface. In

1898 she was rearmed with 'drop-collars' for 14-inch torpedoes on either side of the hull below the conning-tower. The Drzewiecki drop-collar was much favoured in French naval circles as it enabled designers to dispense with the bulky internal torpedo-tube and its gear for compensating weight after the firing. Basically an external sling which held the torpedo and even allowed angled firing, the drop-collar proved liable to be damaged by seaweed and other flotsam. The angling mechanism was temperamental, and one delightful contemporary account talked of the 'suspense as to whether it will release at the exact angle' adding zest to the experience.

The *Gymnote* had no means of generating power and relied totally on her accumulator batteries, which had to be recharged by a generator ashore or in another ship. Her original electric motor was soon replaced by a more robust type developing only 33 shaft horsepower, but to achieve this she carried a 564-cell lead-acid battery weighing nearly a ton, and a motor weighing two tons – 10 percent of the displacement.

The next submarine ordered by the French Navy was much larger. Originally to be called the *Sirène*, she was renamed *Gustave Zédé* in honor of the designer, who had died while she was

power steam engine for surface running and an 80-horsepower electric motor for running underwater. Most important of all, the steam engine could also run a dynamo to recharge the accumulators, and so the effective range of the *Narval* was much greater than the all-electric boats. To distinguish her from them she was classed as a *submersible*, whereas the battery-driven boats were called *sousmarins*. This distinction still causes confusion, as today's submarines are divided in exactly the opposite way: 'submersibles' are the 'conventional' diesel-electric boats capable of limited underwater running, as against nuclear-powered 'true submarines' limited only by the endurance of their crews and the air supply.

The *Narval* had a double hull in which she could stow both oil fuel and water ballast, a feature which survives in one form or another to this day. She was stoutly built, with ¼-inch plating on her outer hull and ½-inch on the inner or 'pressure' hull – on one occasion she collided with and sank a tug but suffered no damage herself. When she came into service in 1900 she caused even more excitement than the *Gymnote* and *Gustave Zédé*, and four more similar craft were immediately ordered. She took nearly 20 minutes to dive, what with the

Despite the importance of Laubeuf his fame has been eclipsed by that of John P Holland, an Irish-American who had been designing submarines secretly since 1875. As a member of a Fenian secret society Holland wanted to destroy the power of the British by sinking their fleet, making him the last in a long line of idealistic submarine-inventors. As time passed Holland became less interested in striking a blow for Ireland and more interested in the creation of a workable submarine, and by 1893, when the US Navy announced a competition to choose a submarine design, he was an engineer pure and simple.

Only three inventors submitted designs, Holland, Lake and Baker. The Baker boat quickly dropped out of the competition and as Simon Lake had not completed his prototype the Ordnance Bureau awarded the contract to Holland. The boat was called the *Plunger* and was launched in 1897 after a number of changes and delays. So many changes were made against the designer's wishes that he withdrew from the contract, and ordered his Holland Boat Company to build a second submarine at his own expense. His faith was justified by the total failure of the *Plunger* to pass her trials; the boat was never accepted by the Navy and the contract was cancelled in 1900, four years after she had been built. The trials of the *Holland*, by comparison, were a great success and the attendant publicity forced the US Navy to buy her for $120,000 in 1900. A year later a further seven of similar type were building and the British had taken out a license to build five for the Royal Navy.

The *Holland*'s design differed from the French *Narval* in several ways. She also had a dual propulsion system, but used a 45-horsepower gasoline engine for surface running, giving more power for less weight as well as faster (if less reliable) starting and stopping. This produced two advantages, the boat could be smaller and it could dive faster than the French boat. It is interesting to compare the *Gustave Zédé* and *Narval* with the *Holland*.

building. Although she gave a lot of trouble she provided invaluable experience, and convinced the French that the submarine was worth developing as an operational craft. In February 1896 the Minister of Marine M Lockroy proposed an open competition to produce designs for a 200-ton submarine with a range of 100 miles on the surface, and no fewer than 29 designs were submitted from all over the world. The winner was a Frenchman, Maxime Laubeuf, who takes the credit for finally solving the basic problems of propulsion.

Laubeuf's remarkable boat, the *Narval* had *two* propulsion systems, a 220-horse-

*Above: The launch of* Holland No.1 *in 1901, the Royal Navy's first submarine. She was a copy of a US Navy design.*

need to damp down the boiler, fold down the funnel and close all the vents, but she established completely the submarine's need for a dual propulsion system, one engine on the surface to take her to her area of operation economically and fairly quickly, and a separate electric motor for submerged operation. Laubeuf's contribution to submarine design was the link between the late nineteenth century experimental boats and the far more advanced craft used in World War I.

|  | Surfaced/ Submerged Displacement | Surfaced/ Submerged Power and Speed |
|---|---|---|
| Gustave Zédé | 261/270 tons | 208/208 hp = 9¼/6½ knots |
| Narval | 117/202 tons | 250/280 hp = 12½/6.1 knots |
| Holland | 64/74 tons | 45/50 hp = 8/5 knots |

The American boat was 55 feet 9 inches long overall, making her nearly one-third of the size of the *Gustave Zédé* and half the size of the *Narval*. Instead of a double hull containing ballast tanks and fuel the Holland design had 'saddle tanks' outside a single hull, with the fuel stowed

A Lake submarine crossing the bows of
the battleship USS Kearsarge *during*
the 1905 review of the US Atlantic Fleet.

*Above: After the* Narval *the French Navy built a number of steam-driven submarines like the* Germinal *(1907) shown here.*

*Right:* U.6, *with smoke billowing from her Körting kerosene engine.*

inside the hull, and there was no attempt to provide a boat-shape to improve running on the surface. The Holland boats had short, fat, cigar-shaped hulls which handled badly on the surface, and they tended to 'porpoise' when diving or surfacing. However, their biggest failing was their petrol engine, which filled the boat with toxic and explosive vapor. Some early submarines even carried white mice as crude indicators of the presence of a dangerous level of carbon monoxide and petrol vapor. In spite of the number of explosions which occurred from time to time the petrol engine's good power-to-weight ratio made it better than the French steam plant, and the French Navy later compromised by introducing an auxiliary benzol motor to improve surface running performance in some submarines.

Simon Lake was not deterred by his failure to win the US Navy contract; in 1894 he built a wooden prototype and then formed a company which built the *Argonaut,* a 67-foot craft which displaced 157 tons on the surface. What made Lake's designs different was his view that the main purpose of a submarine was to travel on the bottom of the sea, from where she could send divers into enemy harbors to disable ships or to cut cables. Torpedo-tubes were fitted as in the Holland boats, but to allow his boat to run along the bottom he fitted her with three large wheels. This feature seems to have annoyed the US Navy, and although

they admitted that the design was sound they would not accept it unless Lake modified his design. His cussedness lost him the contract but the Russians bought her and renamed her *Ossetr*. Several more submarines were built for the Austrian and Russian navies but Lake was never able to catch up with Holland, whose designs became the basis for subsequent British and American developments.

The last independent designs put forward by Lake were in conjunction with the English firm of Thornycrofts, which was anxious to make a reputation in the submarine field similar to the one it already held as a destroyer-builder. In November 1909 the British Admiralty had asked Thornycrofts to produce their own designs, but had not taken the

*Left:* No.6, *the first submarine built for the Japanese Navy in Japan, was a derivative of the Holland design. She is seen here at Yokosuka in 1907.*

matter any further. Then in August 1911 the firm joined a syndicate to build submarines in collaboration with the Lake Company, in the hope that the Admiralty or another navy would be interested.

The first design submitted by Lake was in December 1912, and it was very similar to one of the original 1909 Thornycroft designs:

| | |
|---|---|
| Dimensions: | 161 feet × 13 feet |
| Submerged displacement: | 535 tons |
| Speed: | 14.7/10.1 knots |
| Armament: | Two bow TT, two twin revolving deck TT |

Two boats of this type had been built for the US Navy as the *Tuna (G.2)* and *Turbot (G.3)*, and the Russian *Alligator* Class were similar. The negotiations broke down because the Royal Navy's ideas about submarines changed by 1913, with the Admiralty asking for 800–900 ton designs. The final Lake design submitted was a 'submarine cruiser-gunboat' displacing 810 tons submerged and armed with four bow torpedo-tubes, a stern tube, four revolving deck tubes and two 3-inch

*Right:* U.4 *shows a broad flat casing typical of U-Boats.*

guns. The last comment in Thornycrofts' files in June 1913 notes that they are still waiting for a reply to an enquiry, and that the big submarine design ought to be pursued.

Thornycrofts were unlucky, and never completed a submarine for the Royal Navy, but the Lake Company built three 'L', four 'N' and three 'O' Class boats for the USN during World War I. The last group built entirely by the Lake Company were the 16 boats numbered *R.21-27*, *S.2*, *S.14-17* and *S.48-51*. The experimental *S.2* was launched and completed post-war, but apart from more powerful diesels she showed no great improvement over the rest of the 'S' Class, and was one of the first to be scrapped. The end of large-scale submarine-construction was also the end of the Lake Company's participation in submarine development.

*Above: The Greek submarine* Xiphias *(1912) was built in France to a design by Maxime Laubeuf.*

*Right: The Norwegian boats B.6, B.1 and B.5 (right) lying at Horten Dockyard.*

The Germans had the example of Bauer to inspire them and as we have seen they had already built two Nordenfelt boats in 1890. Nonetheless, of all the major naval powers they were the last to show an interest when the French and American developments became known, for Admiral Tirpitz saw submarines as a threat to his plans for a big battlefleet. The firm of Krupps built a small submarine called the *Forel* for Russia in 1902–03, and were then asked by the Russians to tender for three more boats. Almost immediately a spy-scare swept France, with the newspapers suggesting that the Germans had stolen the plans of their newest submarine, the *Aigrette*. Like most lurid news-stories this one had a basis of truth, for there was a tie-up between French and German designs. The *Aigrette* was powered by a new German type of motor, the diesel, which used compression-ignition to burn heavy oil. The diesel motor eliminated the prob-

*Below: The* Aigrette *(1904), first French submarine driven by a diesel engine. Note the external torpedo.*

lem of explosive fumes, and this proved to be the final development needed to make the twentieth century submarine workable. The German press was extremely cutting about the French Navy's need to 'buy German' but omitted to mention that the German Navy still had no submarines of its own.

At this time a French inventor, M d'Equevilley, had been trying without success to interest the Ministry of Marine in his design for an improved *Narval*. He moved to Germany and took a job with Krupps, who developed his ideas for the new Russian boats. These were known as the *Karp* Class, and a fourth unit, almost identical, became the German *U.1* in 1906. She had the double hull of the *Narval* but in place of the cumbersome steam engine she had a Körting kerosene engine. The Körting was safer than the gasoline engine of the Holland boats but it had one terrible drawback, it gave off dense clouds of smoke which betrayed the submarine's position. Despite the widespread belief that the Germans were the first to instal diesel engines in submarines, this is not so. After the French the Russians were the next to put a diesel in a submarine, the *Minoga* in 1906; the British followed with

*Above: The French* Mariotte *was known as the 'tooth brush' because of her unusual profile.*

the *D.2* launched in 1910, the Americans with the *Skipjack* in 1911, while the Germans trailed fifth and did not launch their *U.19* until 1912.

By 1904, therefore, the broad outlines of the modern submarine were settled. However much the boats of the various navies might differ in detail the main problems had all been solved. The three big advances, the electric accumulator battery, the diesel engine and the self-propelled torpedo were to be steadily improved as the years went by, but no other fundamental change was necessary for another 50 years. The submarines of 1904 were essentially the types that would revolutionize naval warfare in just 10 years' time, yet 10 years earlier in 1894 only two workable submarines existed. It had been a remarkably short period of gestation.

27

# HOW A SUBMARINE WORKS

A submarine can only remain submerged by altering its displacement, and thus increasing its own weight to overcome natural buoyancy. This was the principle of Bourne's boat as far back as the sixteenth century, and it remains true of the largest nuclear submarines today. There are three states of buoyancy:

1 *positive buoyancy*, when the submarine behaves like the boat which she is, and rises to the surface;
2 *negative buoyancy*, when she sinks because enough weight has been taken on board to overcome positive buoyancy; and
3 *neutral buoyancy*, a fine balance between positive and negative buoyancy, in which state the submarine can maneuver under power without any uncontrollable tendency to rise or sink.

Ingenious men have tried to find other ways to get submarines to submerge, but with little success. If there was only a small reserve of positive buoyancy a boat could be forced beneath the surface of the water, but this method is of limited value because it means that any slackening of propulsive effort allows the submarine

to return to the surface. As it was used chiefly with oar-propelled craft the crew rapidly became exhausted. Bauer's *Brandtaucher* relied on a hand-wheel to move a weight forwards and backwards to produce a series of dips, but even this method needed musclepower, and as the air-supply was limited the operators quickly exhausted themselves.

The first problem, therefore, was to provide a reliable form of mechanical propulsion to take the strain off the operators. Compressed air was used in Capitaine Bourgois' *Plongeur* in 1863, followed by the Reverend Garrett's idea of using latent heat to produce steam underwater. The first idea failed because it proved impossible to store compressed air at high enough pressures, while the second suffered from excessive heat and the danger of toxic fumes escaping into the boat. Not until the perfection of an electric motor powered by current stored in accumulator batteries was the problem solved, with a power source independent of the atmosphere.

Another obstacle to making the submarine an effective warship was the lack of a suitable weapon. None of the earliest

inventors of submarines seems to have shown much interest in the ultimate purpose of their boats – presumably because their time was taken up with far greater technical problems. The spar torpedo's essentially suicidal qualities were not conducive to any startling progress, and it is possibly significant that the success of the Confederate 'Davids' in the American Civil War did not result in a large fleet of Federal submarines.

The Whitehead torpedo, designed first as a surface weapon, proved to be the second great step forward in the submarine's evolution. By allowing the submarine to attack from a safe distance, the automobile torpedo gave the attacker greater freedom to select the right moment and even the best angle of attack.

The application of electric propulsion and the automobile torpedo set the submarine on a course of steady development and improvement which is still in progress. Nothing that has happened since the nineteenth century, not even nuclear propulsion or the guided missile, has changed the fundamental principles of submarine operation. A submariner of today might shake his head over the

*Below: The conning tower of U.26 about to vanish below the surface during a prewar training exercise.*

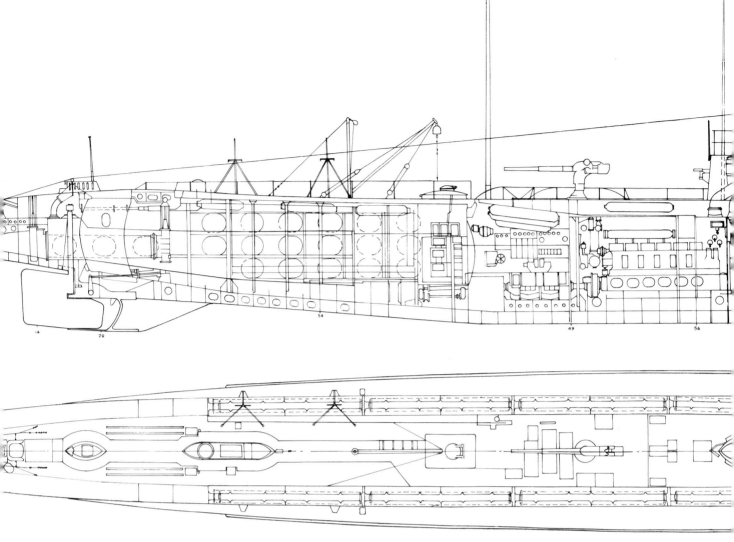

crudity of a submarine of 1914, just as a jet fighter pilot would quail at the idea of flying a Sopwith Camel, but he would immediately understand the layout and function of every piece of equipment.

To comprehend the submarines of the two World Wars it may be helpful to imagine oneself in a British 'U' Class boat of 1941. With a submerged displacement of 720 tons and an overall length of 191 feet the 'U' Class were not much larger than the run-of-the-mill U-Boats and British submarines of 1914–18, and as they were kept as simple as possible they retained many older characteristics.

Imagine a riveted steel hull with a circular section 16 feet in diameter, capable of resisting 70 pounds per square inch pressure; it is less than 190 feet long internally and is divided into six watertight compartments. It comprises an inner steel hull known as the *Pressure Hull*, with an external hull known as the *Casing*. The pressure hull is divided into six compartments by bulkheads fitted with watertight doors, and access is gained in only three places: the *Fore Hatch* leading to the *Crew Space* in the second compartment (through which torpedoes are also loaded), the *Upper* and *Lower Conning Tower Hatches* leading to the forward end of the *Engine Room*. An additional emergency *Escape Hatch* is fitted at the forward end of the Crew Space, but this can not be used for access. The compartments are linked by a star-board passage; although not normally closed when diving, the watertight doors would be closed at 'collision stations' or during a depth-charge attack.

In the foremost compartment are four 21-inch torpedo-tubes, the submarine's main armament. The tubes are loaded through hinged rear doors before the start of a patrol, with four spare torpedoes stowed in the Crew Space. The torpedoes, each weighing $1\frac{1}{2}$ tons, have to be manhandled with a hydraulic hoist from their racks into the tubes, and a reload takes as much as 20 minutes for each tube. The junior ratings live and sleep between the torpedoes and reloading the tubes or testing the torpedoes means their entire personal belongings, bunks and messtraps have to be cleared away.

The wartime complement of this type of submarine is 4 officers, 5 petty officers, 4 engine room artificers and 18 junior ratings. The officers and petty officers have separate messes at the forward end of the *Accomodation Space*, and like the ratings their food is prepared in the *Galley*, which is at the after end of this compartment. The sanitary arrangements are simple; three WCs and three hand-basins for 31 men. To overcome the pressure underwater, the WCs have a specially-designed flushing system, and to avoid the risk of bubbles being sighted by aircraft, it is always necessary to have the Captain's permission to 'blow heads.' The luxury of a shower or bath has to be

*Above: Plans of the mine-laying U-Boat U.123. She was completed in 1918 and was armed with four torpedo tubes and two 10.5cm guns as well as up to 42 mines.*

*Above: An early submarine model intended for tank-testing by the Admiralty.*

*Above right: The giant U.153 lying interned at Harwich after the 1918 Armistice. Her profile is dominated by her two heavy guns.*

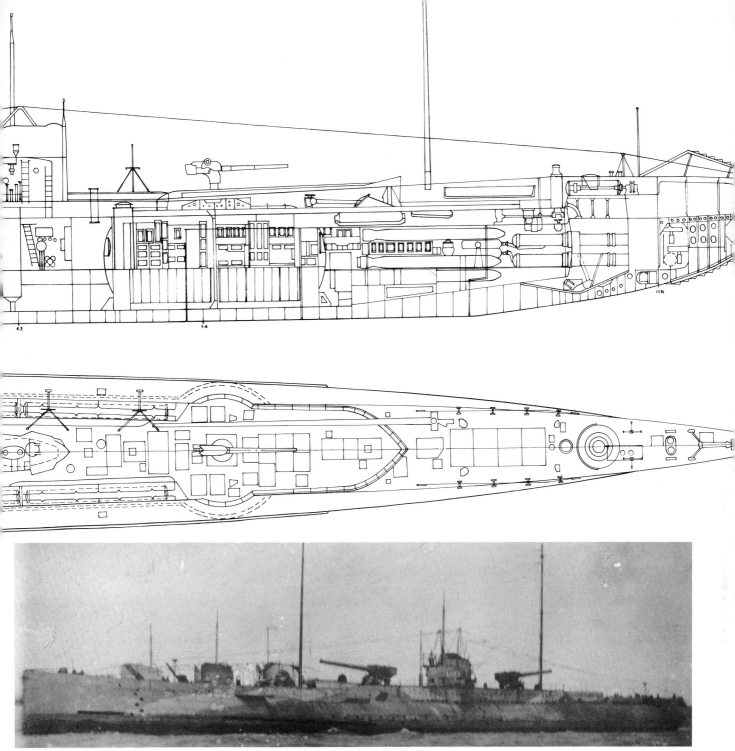

deferred until the end of the patrol.

Moving aft the third compartment is the *Control Room*, the fighting heart of the submarine. Here are two periscopes, fitted in tubes running up through the *Conning Tower* to give the Commanding Officer visual contact with the surface. He can use the *Search Periscope* to scan the horizon and sky or the *Attack Periscope* with its smaller head during the approach to the target. Both periscopes are fitted with high and low magnification. The diving of the boat is controlled from here by ratings on the hydroplane controls, changing the angle of the planes much as a pilot uses his ailerons to change the angle of ascent or descent. The hydroplanes are positioned outside the hull, two forward and two right aft.

Compartment No 4 is the *Engine Room* containing two 400 brake horsepower diesel generators which provide current to drive four electric motors, two coupled to each propeller shaft or to charge the batteries. When on the surface both generators can be used to drive the electric motors if maximum speed is required, or with the submarine stopped, both can be used to recharge the batteries at the maximum rate. Alternatively, one can provide propulsion and the other a charge. When submerged the submarine propels itself on both shafts if on passage, or very slowly on one shaft if in her patrol area. In either case the two electric motors draw their power from the 230-volt lead-acid accumulators that make up her battery. The *Main Battery* is made up of ½-ton cells and is capable of producing several thousand ampere-hours at 2.2 volts when fully charged. These are placed in compartments under the Control Room and Accomodation Space. Apart from the great weight of these lead-acid batteries they have one great drawback; seawater leaking into the cells will mix with the sulphuric acid to produce chlorine gas. The four Engine Room Artificers (ERAs) who run the main machinery live in a small mess at the forward end of the Control Room. The *Motor Room* contains the steering gear. Larger submarines would usually have one or two torpedo-tubes in this compartment but the 'U' Class are too small for this refinement.

Diving the submarine is achieved by taking on 90 tons of seawater ballast to convert her weight of 630 tons at which state she has positive buoyancy, to 720 tons, giving her slightly negative buoyancy, enough to take her down under control. As the 'U' Class and their later

Above: Diving stations in the engine room of a British submarine during World War II.

Left: The hydroplane operator on a British submarine watches the depth gauge, ready to begin a dive.

Below: Mice were carried aboard early submarines to detect concentrations of noxious fumes, a picture from a postcard produced about 1902.

Right: Four British 'A' Class submarines seen in Dover Harbor some time before World War I.

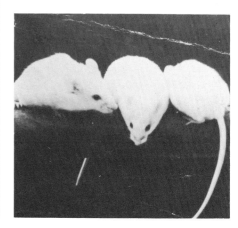

'V' Class half-sisters were odd men out, it is perhaps better at this point to explain the diving procedure in terms of the more usual arrangements found in the bigger 'S' and 'T' types.

The 'U' and 'V' Classes were different from their contemporaries in having internal main ballast tanks. In boats with external ballast tanks there was a single Kingston valve which would be left open on leaving harbor, allowing the tank to remain 'free-flooding'. These tanks were not part of the main strength of the hull, and were made of $\frac{3}{8}$-inch plate. With internal ballast tanks the Kingston valves on all internal MBTs were opened on leaving harbor. In other words, in *all* submarines, opening the vents at the top of the tank allows air to escape and the water floods in until the tank is full; this destroys buoyancy and allows the submarine to dive.

After diving and ensuring that the tanks have no air left in them, the commanding officer (CO) orders the main ballast vents to be shut. This allows air to be blown in at the top of the tank at a moment's notice, forcing the water out through the free-flooding vents at the bottom. Because of the danger of forcing high-pressure air at about 2400 pounds per square inch into a tank with the Kingston valve shut, and causing the tank to rupture, all 'kingston tanks' are connected to the low-pressure blower system. If, in an emergency the blower system failed, they could also be cross-connected and supplied from the high-pressure system.

In submarines with internal ballast tanks, of course the Kingston valves must be shut on diving, in order to preserve the integrity of the pressure hull. The forward and after ballast tanks were kept free-flooding at all times. In all submarines there is an additional 'Q' or quick-blowing tank, the only one with a Kingston valve *and* a direct HP 'blow'. As a safety measure it is fitted with an internal vent which lifts with a loud noise if pressure is accidentally put on with the Kingston shut. In older submarines the Kingston valves were hand-operated but by the Second World War most submarines had hydraulically operated Kingstons.

With all seven tanks full, hydroplanes set to a diving angle, and the submarine moving at about seven knots, she will now submerge. By blowing compressed air into the 'Q' or quick-blowing tank the submarine levels off at periscope depth (27 feet) or more if needed. The CO now has to 'trim' the boat by using compensating tanks throughout the hull to reach neutral buoyancy. Once that has been achieved the submarine will maintain a constant depth with minimum use of the hydroplanes.

To surface the CO has to reverse the procedure, using high-pressure air to blow water out of the forward and after ballast tanks and setting the hydroplanes to an upward angle. Low pressure blowers empty the remaining ballast tanks but in wartime most COs would keep the boat 'partially trimmed down' with main ballast tanks partially flooded to reduce diving time. Even so, a well-drilled crew would be able to get a boat in normal trim down in less than 25 seconds.

The external details of the submarine are comparatively simple. The *Conning Tower* provides a platform from which the boat can be steered while running on the surface. The *Casing* is simply a metal shell to the *Pressure Hull* providing a deck for the crew to work mooring wires and a platform for the deck gun. The gun in this instance is a 12-pounder (3-inch) weapon for use against small targets and the shells have to be handed up from below. In addition two .303-inch Lewis machine guns can be brought up from below and mounted on the conning tower. The *Jumping Wire* acts as a guard to prevent wires from fouling the periscopes, and also carries the radio aerial.

World War I submarines had been fitted with hydrophones for tracking propeller noises, but British submarines of World War II had a refinement, the Asdic. This sensor, taking its name from the *Allied Submarine Detection Investigation* Committee of 1918, could fix the position of another vessel by measuring high-frequency echo, much like a radar set. In a 'U' Class boat the Asdic set was at the forward end of the keel, with the controls in the control room. The other important piece of equipment which dis-

tinguished Second World War submarines from older boats was, of course,
radar and ultimately most submarines
were fitted with surface warning and air
warning radar aerials on the periscope
standards.

The main improvement in submarine
technology between the two world wars
was the introduction of diesel-electric
drive. This meant simply that in place of
the diesels driving the electric motors on
the surface, they drove electric generators which provided power for electric
motors. Although this arrangement occupied more space than the old system it
provided more flexibility. What had
proved very difficult was reversing, because it was necessary to stop the diesels
before reversing them, and the resulting
delay often led to collisions.

The primitive living conditions aboard
submarines made it necessary for the
crew to live ashore or in special depot
ships when in harbor. The depot ship
provided the room for recreation lacking

on board a submarine, and also provided
the workshops which were needed for
major repairs and maintenance of the
torpedoes, machinery and equipment.
Torpedoes need constant maintenance if
they are to run properly, and a submarine by her very nature dare not
attempt to dive if any of the valves and
vents are not fully reliable, so all equipment needs constant attention. In 1920
the French Navy studied a proposal to
replace their surface fleet entirely with
a force of 250 to 300 submarines. When
the details of the proposal were worked
out it was discovered that on a ton-for-
ton basis a submarine was as expensive
to build and maintain as a cruiser or a
battleship. To make matters worse the
submarine's effective life could be less
than that of a large surface ship, although in practice submarines like the
'H' Class of 1916 ran for 25 years. Modern
boats like the US *Balao* Class and the
British 'A' Class were in service for nearly
30 years but only after extensive rebuild-

*Above: The torpedo room of U.126, which
was operated by the Royal Navy after the
end of World War I from 1919–26.*

*Right: Engine room of a U-Boat. Note
the leather overalls used to protect
against grease, condensation and contact
with any hot or sharp-edged parts of the
machinery.*

ing. To run a squadron of submarines it is
necessary to have a very well-equipped
base with a large number of technicians;
even the building of submarines can only
be entrusted to specialized shipyards. In
the First World War two of the most
famous British shipyards, Yarrows and
Thornycrofts took so long to complete
one submarine each that the contracts
were cancelled and given to other firms –
yet both firms had begged the Admiralty
to allow them to build submarines!

The depot ship contained all the maintenance facilities of a base, but had the
advantage of mobility. The loss of a depot

ship in wartime, as when HMS *Medway* was torpedoed in the Mediterranean in 1942, could cripple the operations of a large number of submarines. The *Medway* was carrying a fresh supply of torpedoes on deck, and these were so desperately needed that a special salvage operation was mounted to recover them. This offset the loss of the depot ship to some extent, and the 1st and 10th Flotillas were able to continue operating from Beirut without too much difficulty. Within hours of the surrender of France in June 1940 the German U-Boat Command had loaded equipment ready for transhipment by road to the Bay of Biscay ports, and as a result the U-Boats were able to resume their campaign against British shipping in the Atlantic with little delay. The operational radius of a submarine is not merely a matter of fuel, and the more 'forward support' that can be provided the more time she can spend on patrol.

It is easy to talk of the 'special breed of men' who serve in submarines, a term which makes most submariners curl up with embarrassment. But obviously the nature of a submarine, the restrictions on space and the inherent dangers of underwater operating make special demands on her crew. Most landsmen and not a few sailors shudder at the very thought of serving in a submarine for the simple reason that Man was never designed to shut himself in a steel box underwater.

The first thing which makes submariners different from other sailors is the complexity of their job. The submarine has always been complicated, and has needed highly trained operators. Even Ezra Lee in 1776 had to be trained to handle equipment far more advanced than anything he would have encountered as an army sergeant. When the first modern boats appeared in the 1890s they were manned by hand-picked officers and men because the authorities wished to get the best results out of the new weapon. Everybody on board a submarine is to a greater or lesser extent a technician, for there is no room for 'extra' personnel who do not contribute to her running and operation. Today the West German Navy's new Type 206 submarines are manned by a crew composed entirely of officers and petty officers, all of them specialists.

The cramped quarters inevitably meant that the traditional gulf between officers and 'other ranks' was hard to maintain. The most that could be done in early boats was to give the CO a modicum of privacy by curtaining off his cabin, but in the British 'U' and 'S' Classes he still had to sleep on a bunk in the wardroom. Operationally there could be no privacy or seclusion, with the CO in the control room surrounded by officers and ratings watching his every move. Their lives depended on his decisions but equally his life depended on everyone doing his job promptly without question. This interdependence of the leader and led existed elsewhere but in a submarine there was only a small margin between success and failure, with awful penalties if anything went wrong. In the words of one submariner about his famous CO; 'You can tell when your CO is frightened by what he can see through the periscope – his hair rises. But his hair *never* stood on end.' Another CO claims to have worn long trousers to hide his shaking knees.

Personality plays an important part in the wellbeing of a submarine crew. Officers and ratings live so close together that any relatively innocuous habit or failing can become obnoxious to one's neighbors. Care has to be taken to avoid eccentricities which get on other people's nerves, but at the same time there is the need to avoid boredom. Today's submariners are carefully vetted for psychological quirks which could cause a breakdown under stress, but in the First World War and later it was only possible to run the roughest checks on mental stability. This is the reason for the constant stress on voluntary service in submarines, for it was felt that at least a volunteer would be less likely to be

harboring secret claustrophobia, for example. But in the stress of war it has been necessary to use conscripts, and during the later stages of the Second World War the German Navy even 'borrowed' officer-candidates from the Air Force to make good a lack of U-Boat officers. To do them justice many of these adopted submariners turned out to be first-class officers.

The living conditions aboard the earliest submarines were primitive in the extreme, and the crews only embarked when putting to sea; at other times they lived aboard the depot ship or ashore. The first improvement came with increasing size, for a larger submarine not only carried more fuel but tired her crew less quickly. Bigger crews meant more reliefs and more space meant more amenities. But life was still primitive by comparison with surface ships. In winter condensation dripped from the deckhead and in summer the steel hull became an oven.

The following description of a First World War submarine gives a graphic idea of the working details. The broad picture of cramped quarters and the arduous routine was common to all boats of the period:

'The boat that we were going over was lying tied up to the jetty. Before we crossed we examined the outside appearance. We saw a long, low-lying object, a little over one hundred feet in length, best described, perhaps, by that rather over-worked description, cigar-shaped; however, when in dry dock, and all the boat was visible, this cigar shape gave way to the impression of some huge fish, the head, tail and fins all being there, and the holes in the bow cap like two great goggle eyes. Almost in the centre of the boat, the conning tower rose up about ten feet above the casing, which ran nearly the whole length of the boat, and which was fitted on the hull. This casing was in no way connected with the inside of the boat, but merely formed a deck on which to walk, and provided a few lockers

*Above: The Norwegian* Kobben *(later A.1) surfacing during trials.*

*Left: A Type IX U-Boat schnorkelling at about $4\frac{1}{2}$ knots.*

*Right: The periscope of a modern British* Oberon *Class submarine with an ASW helicopter and a frigate in the background.*

for the stowage of lines and wires used in making the boat fast when in harbour. The top of the conning tower formed the bridge from which the boat was conned or navigated when cruising on the surface. Here were the wheel and telegraphs, a small mast for flag-signalling, and the two standards which supported the two periscopes, or 'look-sticks', as they were unofficially called. Before going down the hatch into the boat, we looked over the side, and saw, one on each side, and immediately opposite each other, two flat semi-circular plates of steel. These were the hydroplanes, and at the after-end of the boat, near the stern, was found a similar pair. These hydroplanes were nothing more or less than rudders, acting in exactly the same way in relation to the upward and downward movement of the boat as the vertical rudder did to port or starboard.

'We now entered the foremost compartment by descending the short steel ladder of the fore hatch. The boat was divided into three compartments by means of strong bulk-heads fitted with water-tight doors, the compartments comprising respectively, fore-ends, control room in the centre, and an after compartment consisting of engine-room, motor-room, and stern tube.

'First of all, we examined the fore-ends. Straight in front of us as we turned towards the bows of the boat were the two bow torpedo tubes, from which were fired the 18-inch torpedoes used by this particular class of boat. The 18 inches referred to the diameter of the torpedo at its thickest point, and when

it was considered that each torpedo, or "tin fish", as they were more often called, was about ten feet long, and that four of them had to be juggled with in this small compartment, about 20 feet by 12 feet, the amount of work entailed in getting two fish out of the tubes and back again was realised, especially when the two spare ones were being carried, under war conditions. Torpedoes, however, were another story, of which we should learn a little later on in the evening. There was little else of interest in this compartment, except for the fact that underneath the steel deck upon which we were walking were the fuel tanks, and right forward of the torpedo tubes was a locker where the emergency rations were kept, consisting of bully beef and biscuits, tea, ship's cocoa, sugar and milk. Incidentally, one needed to be in a condition where emergency rations were an urgent necessary before being able to get between the tubes to reach the locker!

'We now stepped through the doorway of the bulk-head into the control room. Our first impression was one of relief at getting out of the fore-ends, where it was necessary for even the very short to walk with bent head, and the tall with bent back. This centre compartment, at its highest point, was about eight feet, so that we could walk through in comfort; in fact, with the increased space and the electric lights switched on, reflecting their light in the highly-polished brasswork which is everywhere, we began to feel quite cosy. The first things we noticed were the bunks on the starboard side of the boat. There were two

*Below: The sail of a modern submarine bristles with more than periscopes. From left, whip aerial, snorkel mast, search radar, search periscope, attack periscope, electronic countermeasures mast.*

*Right: An* Oberon *Class submarine surfacing.*

*Far right: Commander Whetstone, captain of HMS* Repulse *at the periscope.*

that we can see, one ahead of the other, but when the rather large drawer under the foremost one was pulled out, it was seen that the supposed drawer was really another bunk. These, of course, belonged to the officers, and jutting out from the bunks at the top was a brass rail, upon which when at sea a curtain was hung, enclosing a space of about 12 feet long and 5 feet wide. This space was then dignified by the title of Wardroom, as it comprised the Officers' Mess, and as such was sacred ground.

'Opposite the officers' bunks, on the port side, was the switchboard. This was an attractive looking affair in black and red enamelled paint, with several rows of fuses and switches, each fuse-holder having brass ends brilliantly polished. The largest switch was the change-over switch, or "grouper", which was on a separate panel from the main switchboard. This switch enabled the change over from series at 220 volts, with the "grouper" up, to 110 volts with the "grouper" down, to be made, the battery then being in parallel. The battery was in a large tank underneath

in shallow water during the boat's trials by flooding or pumping out other and smaller tanks which were inside the boat. When the trim was once obtained, a careful note was taken of the amount of water in the various tanks, so that any variations in weight, or differences in the quantity of oil-fuel might be compensated for. The Kingston valves of the main-ballast tanks flooded direct from the sea, and in consequence they were large, heavy things, impossible to open quickly for rapid diving. For this reason, when once at sea these valves were opened and kept open. This might have suggested an involuntary dive, but consideration showed that it was perfectly safe, since there had to be an outlet for the air already in the tanks before water could enter. Over our heads in the control-room were eight small wheels, operating eight valves which opened the vent pipes of the tanks; thus all that was necessary on the order, "Flood main-ballast", was to open these small valves, an operation of a second with a man standing by each wheel. Our next objects of interest in the control-room were the depth-gauges. These were two large dials bearing figures from 0 to 100 feet, and in between them a smaller dial indicating the depth from 100 to 200 feet. There was no gauge beyond 200 feet, as the boat was only intended to stand the pressure as deep as 200 feet, which would be somewhere about 90 pounds to the square inch. At the bottom of these depth gauges was a spirit level, and it was the job of the men sitting one at each wheel in front of the diving gauges to keep the bubble perfectly central by turning the wheels which work the hydroplanes. When patrolling just beneath the surface in a choppy sea, this job called for a nicety of judgment and concentration quite out of proportion to its appearance. The only occasions when the boat was allowed to be out of the horizontal were in diving and in returning to the surface. The inclination was then only slight, usually about five degrees, and not a decided nose dive, or a sudden upward rush, as might have been thought. Next we saw the periscopes, which needed little explanation. Most boats had two periscopes, some three, the third being fitted with a lens so arranged as to enable those down below to keep a more efficient look-out for aircraft. These periscopes could be raised or lowered by means of a steel wire rope wound round a drum, which was operated by a small electric motor. Beneath each periscope was a small well, into which the periscope might be lowered so that no part of it projected above the top of the standards on the bridge, the object being, of course, to leave nothing that would give a hold to enemy sweeps when lying doggo on the bottom. One more thing remained to be seen in the control-room, and that was the Sperry Gyroscopic Compass. Owing to the amount of steelwork confined in a submarine, the ordinary magnetic compass was of little use (although one is kept at the top of the conning tower as a standby), so that some other kind of compass was necessary. Instead of indicating the Magnetic North, like an ordinary compass, the Sperry Compass pointed to the True North, which makes a difference of about 14 degrees. The gyroscope inside it made 8,000 revolutions per minute. Next to the Sperry Compass was the steering pedestal from which the boat was steered

the deck of the control-room, upon which we were walking. It consisted of 224 cells, each weighing about 7½ cwts, and was divided into four separate batteries, each of 56 cells. This battery supplied the electricity for the lighting and cooking facilities of the boat, and also for driving the motors by which the boat was propelled under the surface, and occasionally on the surface also.

These batteries were no exception to that rule that accumulators require attention. At intervals, owing to constant discharging and recharging, the electrolyte in the accumulator became used up, its level sank in the cells, and it became necessary to "top up", as it was called, with distilled water. After that was done the densities of the cells were taken and the cells wiped over before once more the battery boards were put down, the deck-cloth spread over the boards to keep out dirt, and the inside of the boat resumed its normal appearance. There was one other point worth noting in connection with the battery, and that was the system by means of which the hydrogen was given off by the

battery, particularly when charging, was sucked away by fans and drawn up the ventilators to the outside of the boat. When diving, these fans were stopped and the shafting from the outside to the inside of the boat was all shut off.

We next saw something of the boat's diving apparatus. At various points in the control-room on each side of the boat were large wheels – eight in all. These were the Kingston valves, by means of which the eight external main-ballast tanks were flooded. These eight external tanks formed the bulge in the middle of the boat, and assisted in giving that cigar-shape illusion to the eye. Their work, however, was much more important than that of imparting a symmetrical appearance to the boat. It was by flooding these tanks and going ahead on the motors, together with a slight downward tilt of the hydroplanes, that the submarine was able to dive. To dive at all, all of these eight tanks had to be flooded. They have nothing whatever to do with the trim of the boat. The trim, or in other words, the balance, was obtained

*Above: The machinery control console in a modern Swedish* Näcken *Class submarine.*

*Right: The maneuvering console and automatic trim and depth keeping instruments in the* Näcken.

*Far right: The fire control and action information displays in the* Näcken.

when submerged, the upper deck steering wheel being disconnected by means of a simple clutching arrangement. There were also three voice-pipes, through which orders were passed from the bridge to the control-room, and from the control-room to the fore-ends and after compartment respectively. We now crossed over the beam torpedo tubes, of which there were two, one firing through the port side and one through the starboard side. These two tubes were sunk down into a trench so that the tops of the tubes came just about level with the battery boards or deck upon which we walked. Passing over the tubes we saw the wireless cabinet with its one hundred and one gadgets packed into a space little larger than a week-end case.

We now went through the second bulkhead doorway into the third and after compartment. In this compartment were the engines, motors, the stern tube, and the air compressors. The engines were two eight-cylinder Diesel engines, giving a speed of 13.5 knots. These engines not only drove the boat, but also drove the motors to re-charge the battery and the air-compressors to re-fill the air bottles. When the engines were being used in

harbour to charge the battery, the propeller was disconnected by taking out the tail clutch. The engines were for surface use and the motors for use when submerged, the motors being necessary because the engines when working, being internal combustion engines, sucked up the air. The compressed air bottles – large steel cylinders – were to be seen in various out-of-the-way corners of the boat. These air bottles did not contain, as might be supposed, air for breathing purposes, but the compressed air which was used to blow the water from the tanks when rising to the surface. They were connected by an

intricate system of pipes to all the large tanks in the boat, and when air in them ran short they were re-charged by means of the air-compressors.

There was a distinct resemblance between the torpedo and the submarine. Like the submarine, it was divided into compartments, and, like the submarine, it had hydroplanes. The shapes, too, were somewhat similar. The head of the torpedo, being the business end of it, was detachable, so that either a war-head can be fitted or a practice-head. The war-head was practically filled with gun-cotton to a weight of 400 pounds. Right in the centre of the nose was a pit, into which the primer and pistol fitted; this primer was screwed in, within a fraction of an inch of the gun-cotton, so that on striking the object it was driven in and fired the charge, the resulting explosion and damage being sufficient to sink anything less than a modern battleship. In practice, a collision head was used, made partly of lead, and filled with dirty oil and water to exactly the same weight. The idea of dirty oil being used was to mark the spot where, roughly, the torpedo should be, in the event of it sinking, as every torpedo fired in practice was picked up again.

'Next to the head, and in the torpedo itself, was the air-chamber. This was filled with air to a pressure of about 1,800 to 2,000 lbs per square inch. Then came the balance chamber, which contained the weight and valve. These were for the purpose of working the horizontal rudders attached to the horizontal fins on the tail of the fish, the valve keeping the fish to the required depth. If set for eight feet, and the fish sank to ten feet, the pressure pushing the valve in gave rise helm to the rudders, and vice versa if the fish rose to six feet. The weight was to prevent the torpedo from either diving or breaking surface; being attached to the horizontal rudders, it checked the action of the valve in bringing the fish up by preventing the fish from rising at too acute an angle. Next came the engine itself. Torpedoes run either as cold or as hot torpedoes. The engine in the case of a cold torpedo is driven by compressed air, and in a hot fish by oil fuel. The engine compartment was not water-tight, but just the reverse, as the sea, in a cold torpedo, was used to keep the engine warm, and in a hot one to keep it cool. In the tail part of the fish was the gyroscope, which kept the torpedo on its course by working the perpendicular rudders continuously hard over each way. The engine and gyroscope were set going by means of an air lever projecting from the top of the torpedo. When the fish was blown out of the tube a pin (called the tripper) projecting from the inside of the tube knocked back the air lever and opened up the air to engine. The speed of a hot torpedo was about 45 knots, so that it was necessary to see its track some distance away to allow time to avoid it. Incidentally, there was little track to see in the case of a hot torpedo. The adjustments of range and depth at which the fish was to run were set before the torpedo went into the tube. In war, in case the fish should miss its target, it was set to sink.

'The firing of a torpedo was accomplished in the following manner. The torpedo was first entered into the tube, then, before the bow cap through which the fish was fired was opened, the tube was first flooded from the trimming tanks, since if extra water was allowed to enter the boat from the outside, the extra weight would upset the trim of the boat by causing the head to go down, and thus an attack would be rendered impossible. When the tube was flooded the bow cap was swung open, compressed air fired the fish from the tube, the trippers engaged, and away went the fish at 45 knots.

'The crew of such a submarine described would consist of three officers and twenty-eight men. When on war service the submarines worked on ten-day patrols. Leaving harbour, the ship would proceed to the patrol area, and when this was reached the usual routine would be to dive at 4 am to a depth of about 25 feet, which meant that the periscope would be just above water, and then to cruise about on the motors until 9 o'clock at night, when, under cover of darkness, the ship could come to the surface for a renewal of air, and for running the engines to re-charge the batteries. These times were those for summer, the hours varying during the year with the hours of daylight.

'After such a time under water the atmosphere in the boat became distinctly oppressive, since there was no arrangement by which the air was renewed. The longest time known for a submarine to be under water was 36 hours.'

One of the most horrifying pictures of the rigors of submarine life in the First World War comes from the report of the British submarine *E.7* in the Sea of Marmora in 1915. After diving through five minefields off Chanak she entered the Sea of Marmora only to find that some crew-members were ill with dysentery. The disease spread through the 30-man crew rapidly but the captain, Lieutenant-Commander Cochrane, stubbornly maintained that he would finish his fortnight on patrol. Eventually he was too weak to stand, but during that time *E.7* destroyed 20 sailing craft and two steamers by gunfire, torpedoed a steamer

*Above: The PA4 V185 diesel is used in some modern French submarines.*

*Below: The 'heads' of a British World War II submarine with its operating lever and brass plate with the sequence of eight operating instructions.*

and bombarded the Zeitunlik powder mills near Istanbul. There were equally harrowing stories from the U-Boats of bitter weather in the North Atlantic. It is not surprising to learn that tuberculosis was the chief occupational disease, although the high standard of physical fitness tended to offset this hazard.

The sanitary arrangements aboard a submarine were always unusual as a complicated system was needed to equalize the pressure. A British agent taking passage on a submarine to the south of France in 1941 recorded his impressions of the system, and mentioned how easy it was to 'miss the gear-change' and put the whole contraption into reverse. The other hazard was that some vital piece of equipment was located in the WC cabinet, with the result that his morning newspaper reading was rudely interrupted by a rating coming into the cabinet to open a valve. The system only worked at relatively shallow depths, and when in the Second World War U-Boats began to operate at much greater depths it became necessary to design a high-pressure flushing system of such complexity that a special 'Thunderbox Mechanic' had to be trained to handle it. At least one U-Boat was lost as a result of flooding after the CO and his specialist adviser pulled the levers in the wrong order; seawater entered the boat and generated chlorine gas in the battery compartment, and the boat was forced to surface under the guns of an Allied aircraft.

It has already been pointed out that the margin between success and disaster in a submarine is very small. But submarine personnel had one advantage in that they were either alive or dead. Comparatively few submariners were wounded by enemy action; some were taken prisoner but the majority of casualties were killed outright. Medical facilities were limited to first-aid gear; even if a doctor had been carried there was no space for a sickbay or an operating theater. Even prisoners could not be accommodated easily, which is why submarine warfare never stuck for very long to the idealistic rules laid down by the Hague and Geneva Conventions. Naturally the submarines of today differ in detail from all previous submarines, which is why it is convenient to divide them into 'conventional submarines' or submersibles with diesel-electric power, and 'true submarines' which are not forced to surface frequently to recharge their batteries.

The most obvious change is, of course, the massive increase in size, for a nuclear reactor and its shielding occupy a large area. Inside the hull it is possible to have three complete decks and a fourth half-deck, for stores, and so officers and crew can have separate living, eating and recreation spaces. But this scale of accommodation is more necessary than before as nuclear submarines stay submerged for as much as three months at a time. In fact the nuclear submarine's endurance is limited only by the endurance of the crew, in the sense of the stores that they eat and the length of time that a human

being can function efficiently in a totally artificial environment.

The old problem of propulsion does not apply, as the nuclear reactor heats steam to drive a turbine. This means that a modern submarine always has enough power at all times, but a battery-driven electric motor is also installed as a standby. The cost of a nuclear power-plant is very high and it also makes submarines bigger than many submariners

would like, but the tactical value of 20 knots or more underwater *constantly* more than justifies the expense.

The layout of a nuclear submarine is not greatly different from older boats, apart from the enlarged accommodation spaces. Most boats still carry their torpedo-tubes in the forward compartment, and the control room is still amidships. But the side ballast tanks have been replaced by large tanks forward and right

aft, to allow for a fully streamlined hull. The Polaris missile submarines have a large missile compartment abaft the conning-tower, which is now known as the 'fin' or 'sail', but in other respects they are like standard nuclear boats.

To avoid betraying their position to delicate sensors modern submarines have self-contained waste disposal systems. In any case the great depths at which they operate make high-pressure WC exhaust-systems useless, and so all waste goes into a septic tank which is pumped out in harbor.

One visible change which has occurred is the decor. The depressing effect of standard gray paintwork seen under artificial light day in and out soon became obvious; British submarines, for example, were painted white throughout and

*Above: Loading a torpedo on board U.48 early in World War II.*

*Above left: Ratings carry 3-inch shells aboard a 'U' Class submarine from a 'T' Class boat.*

*Right: Loading a torpedo into one of U.124's forward tubes at sea in the spring of 1941.*

*Below: Manning the gun aboard an Austro-Hungarian U-Boat in World War I.*

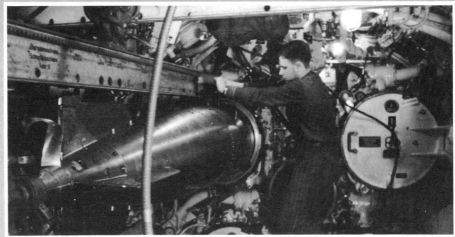

today's submarines have kindlier colors in the living spaces. Submarines used to be a maze of wiring, pipes and controls, but in a Polaris submarine all wiring is concealed for convenience and neatness.

## Torpedoes and Other Submarine Weapons

As we have already seen it was the mating of the torpedo to the submarine which created the full weapon system. The supreme advantage of the torpedo is that it is a 'stand-off' weapon which enables the attacker to choose his moment and

his angle of attack to do the most damage. In one sense it is the oldest guided missile of all, with its gyroscopes and depth-keeping gear to keep it on a steady course.

By the turn of the century the Whitehead torpedo had avanced from the crude and unreliable weapon of the 1870s to a robust piece of equipment which remained unchanged in essentials for another forty years. The Whitehead design was developed by foreign competitors such as the German Schwartzkopf concern but in essentials they differed little. Typical of the latest weaponry available at the turn of the century was the British 18-inch Mark IV, which was 16 feet 7 inches long, weighed 1218 pounds and could take a 171-pound warhead 800 yards. Like all contemporary torpedoes the Mark IV ran on compressed air, but subsequently the range and speed of torpedoes was improved by the introduction of the heater engine. Even in 1901 they were expensive, and so practice torpedoes had a 'crushing head' with a calcium light which ignited when the torpedo came to the end of its run. A safety 'whisker' on the nose prevented the torpedo from exploding if it struck a piece of flotsam outside the torpedo-tube; after a few yards the rush of water unwound it and armed the warhead.

During the First World War submarines were armed with heavier torpedoes, 21-inch (20-inch in the German Navy), but there has been no increase in size since then. By the end of that war German technicians had come up with a brilliant idea, changing the angle of the gyroscope during the torpedo's run. In order to train the tubes it was necessary to swing the whole submarine, and at shorter ranges the rate of turn required was often higher than she could achieve. If the torpedo could be fired at a more convenient angle and then swung onto a collision course the opportunities for a successful attack increased. To do this the gyroscope in the torpedo was set by a hand-cranked spindle for 90 degrees either way before it was put into the tube. In World War II German and American torpedoes had more sophisticated angling systems, but they paid a penalty in reduced reliability. Today's torpedoes are given their setting through an umbilical link from the fire-control computer, and of course there is a new generation of wire-guided or acoustic and magnetic homing torpedoes.

The mine has shared the underwater environment of the submarine and has achieved an equally sinister reputation. It was not long before mine warfare specialists decided to try to extend the idea to the submarine, which could lay a complete field unseen, and thereby enhance its effectiveness. As early as 1908 the Russians, then the world's acknowledged mine experts, started building a submarine specifically equipped to carry and lay mines. In the First World War both sides took to submarine mining on a large scale, and used the mine as an offensive weapon against the submarine herself.

*Two views of the French submarine* Minerve.
*Above: Twin 25mm Hotchkiss anti- aircraft guns on the conning tower.*

*Left: Maintenance on the 400mm torpedo tubes while a mine is loaded in the background.*

Deck guns made their appearance shortly before the First World War, initially as a weapon to overawe merchant ships when trying to force them to stop under the existing Prize Regulations. But as the war progressed submariners realized that a submarine's endurance was directly related to her supply of torpedoes; if she ran out of them she returned to base, even if she had enough fuel to keep on patrol. The U-Boats turned to the gun more and more, particularly against 'soft' targets such as small steamers and sailing ships. The defensive arming of merchantmen by the Allies led the Germans to put bigger guns in U-Boats until the whole idea got out of hand with the 'U-Cruisers' with 5.9-inch guns. The 'cruiser-submarine' idea flourished between the two world wars but died out by 1939. Deck guns continued to be fitted until well after the Second World War, until the dominance of the aircraft was established beyond doubt.

Gunnery in submarines was always a rather crude affair, since there was no fire control and only limited vision from the conning tower. The most that could be done was to calculate range and deflection before surfacing. Rounds of ammunition were passed up through the hatch by hand, and the gunners indulged in a bit of impressive and noisy eye-shooting at a range which was normally as low as 1200 yards. Minelaying, by contrast, was a very scientific business which called for precise navigation. The minelayer had to be equipped with complicated gear for compensating automatically for the weight of mines laid, and the depth of water had to be known precisely to make sure that high tide did not reveal the mines to the enemy. The final development was a torpedo-shaped mine which could be laid by firing it through the torpedo-tube, and when this was perfected the need for special mine-layers disappeared.

In recent years the submarine has been armed experimentally with a series of advanced guided weapons. The earliest of these involved the submarine loitering on the surface to fire them, and the steady improvement of aircraft-borne antisubmarine weapons has put them out of business. Only recently has it proved possible to fire missiles from underwater. But one weapon has succeeded in transforming the submarine into the deadliest weapon ever known. This is the underwater launched ballistic missile with an H-Bomb warhead, which can be fired at any land target in the world. The development of the Polaris missile system brought together existing submarine technology, nuclear propulsion and space technology in one hull, making these submarines the most complex warships ever built. Briefly, the Polaris missile receives flight data from a computer and is forced out of the vertical launching tube by gas-pressure; as soon as it leaves the water the rocket motor ignites to force the missile into a ballistic path covering distances of up to 2500 miles. The advantage of Polaris submarines is their immunity to sudden pre-emptive strikes, for they can move at will anywhere in the world where there is deep water to hide in. Since 1972 Polaris has been replaced by the Poseidon and Trident missiles, functioning in the same way but more efficient.

The awesome power of the Trident submarine, each one of which can fire the equivalent of all the bombs dropped in the Second World War, is matched by the tactical might of the nuclear hunter-killer submarine. With their high speed and maneuverability nuclear submarines have many advantages over surface ships. Although they are not yet ready to usurp all the functions of surface warships, as we shall see they are playing an important part in the evolution of new tactics.

# SUBMARINES IN THE FIRST WORLD WAR

At the outbreak of war in August 1914 the world's navies had nearly 300 submarines between them, with another 80 or more planned. Despite their late start the British and Germans had outstripped the French and Americans, with 77 and 29 boats respectively. Many countries had bought foreign designs and then developed their own improved versions, but the leading submarine-building countries were still Great Britain, France, Germany, Italy and the United States.

Although much lip-service had been paid to the effect of submarines on naval warfare the world's navies in 1914 had little idea of how to use their submarines. All the belligerents and the neutrals regarded themselves as bound by the provisions of International Law and the Hague Convention of 1899 concerning the conduct of war at sea. With no experience later than the American Civil War for guidance it was assumed that a submarine, like any other warship, was not permitted to fire on a merchant ship which was neither armed nor acting in a hostile manner. The submarine would have to stop the merchant ship and examine her

papers to ascertain that she was in fact trading on behalf of the enemy. If her papers indicated that she was carrying contraband the ship would have a prize crew put aboard to sail her to port for examination. The submarine could, of course, sink the ship and forego the prize money, and if the weather was too rough for taking to the boats the crew were to be taken aboard the submarine and become prisoners.

The Prize regulations, as they were called, favored the British and the French with their large merchant fleets, but they took little account of the peculiar nature of the submarine. To stop and search a merchant ship the submarine had to come to the surface, thereby forfeiting her principal advantage. Her tiny crew was too small to allow a prize crew to be spared and there was no room aboard for prisoners. A submarine which endeavored to keep to these rules would either expose herself to counterattacks from enemy warships or would be unable to sink more than one or two ships on each cruise. The Germans had taken to heart the lesson of the great American

*Below: A U-Boat's torpedo strikes home. By 1917 U-Boats were sinking one in four ships around the British Isles.*

*Bottom: U.17, one of the few early U-Boats to survive until the Armistice.*

naval historian Mahan, who pointed out that Great Britain's vast merchant fleet was simultaneously her strength and her weakness, and some thought had been given to using both surface warships and submarines against commerce. On 20 October 1914 *U.17* under Kapitänleutnant Feldkirchner made history by stopping the small steamer *Glitra* off Norway. Although the victim was very small she had a significance out of all proportion to her size.

To most naval officers, however, the enemy's warships were still the true target for the submarine, and the first successes bore out this belief. As soon as war broke out the British and Germans sent out submarines to observe and report on warship movements. The British set up a patrol line in the Heligoland Bight, and acting on the reports from these submarines planned a successful raid on the German light forces late in August 1914. Similarly the Germans sent their U-Boats out on an offensive patrol as far as the Orkneys, for the expected onslaught by the British Fleet had not occurred and they were puzzled to know just what the British were doing.

Both sides were disappointed. The British found that their torpedoes were running under their targets because the warhead was heavier than the prewar practice head, while the Germans found that extended cruising put an unexpected strain on machinery. *U.9* broke down *en route* to Fair Isle and while *U.15* was repairing a fault she was caught on the surface and rammed by the light cruiser HMS *Birmingham*. Another danger was from surface warships shooting first and asking questions later, and in several cases submarines were attacked by their own side. Mines accounted for a U-Boat as early as 12 August, but in the early days of the war the minefields were relatively small in extent. The limited field of vision through a periscope made target identification much harder than anyone had imagined in peacetime, and there were many wrong guesses as to the identity of targets. The early successes against warships were as much the result of the victim's carelessness as the skill of submariners, for the ramming of *U.15*

bred a totally unjustified complacency among surface ship commanders.

The British were given little time to dwell on their success, for on 22 September a single U-Boat, *U.9*, sank three of their armored cruisers, the *Aboukir*, *Cressy* and *Hogue*. These three old ships had little protection against modern torpedoes and carried large crews of reservists. Their vulnerability had been realized by the Admiralty, and the order cancelling their patrols was already drafted, but the senior officer of the squadron contributed to the disaster by assuming that the first ship had been mined. Kapitänleutnant Otto Weddigen was therefore given time to reload his torpedo-tubes and he then worked *U.9* into an ideal attacking position between the two remaining cruisers, with both forward and after tubes bearing. Weddigen's reputation as the first U-Boat 'ace' was confirmed when three weeks later he torpedoed another old cruiser, the *Hawke* off Aberdeen. Yet here again, the British cruiser was lying stopped in the open sea to transfer mail, and there were other examples of ships piping 'Hands to Bathe' or steaming slowly in waters known to be patrolled by U-Boats.

The Anglo-French alliance meant that the bulk of the large French submarine force was stationed in the Mediterranean. The boats were used to watch the Adriatic and the Austro–Hungarian Fleet, but the lack of enemy activity robbed them of worthwhile targets. In December 1914 the *Curie* penetrated the heavily defended anchorage at Cattaro (now Kotor) but she was sunk before she could achieve anything. The Austrian submarines were too few in number to achieve much, but again the careless way in which surface warships were handled gave them opportunities that never recurred. In December the *XII* (Austro–Hungarian submarines originally used Roman numerals, but later changed to arabic) torpedoed the French battleship *Jean Bart* and damaged her severely.

The Royal Navy had moved its main fleet base from the southern dockyards to a new base at Rosyth before the war, but on the outbreak of war the main Grand Fleet moved to Scapa Flow, a large natural anchorage in the Orkneys. The news of the U-Boats' foray to the Orkneys was followed by a submarine scare in the Flow itself, and although no U-Boat got into Scapa Flow throughout the war the fear was enough to paralyze the Grand Fleet. Until Scapa Flow could be defended with nets, blockships, guns and searchlights it was necessary to send the whole Grand Fleet away to the west coast of Scotland. This was the first *strategic* victory scored by submarines, for they had forced an entire fleet away from its chosen area of operations, and had the Germans been in a position to take advantage of it they might have caught the Royal Navy badly off balance. As things turned out there were not enough U-Boats and those that existed were not yet reliable enough to be risked so far from their bases, while the High Seas Fleet adopted a supine attitude and did little to take advantage of the British withdrawal. The chance passed, and once the Grand Fleet returned to the Orkneys it refastened its grip on the German Fleet; its base remained inviolate right to the end.

## The German Submarine Campaign

When war broke out the German Navy had 29 U-Boats (U-Boat = *Unterseeboot*) in service. The original boat, *U.1* had been developed into the *U.27* Class, of which *U.30* was still to complete, and a further 20 boats were on order. This modest program reflects the German High Command's obsession with the surface fleet, and for a long time the admirals continued to think that the main role of their U-Boats was to wage a war of attrition against the British, either by direct attack or by using the surface fleet to draw the British fleet into a 'submarine trap.'

The German Navy's submarines proved to be well-designed for the task

*Below: The French* Curie *was caught in the nets at Pola in 1914, but was later raised and became the Austro-Hungarian* U.14.

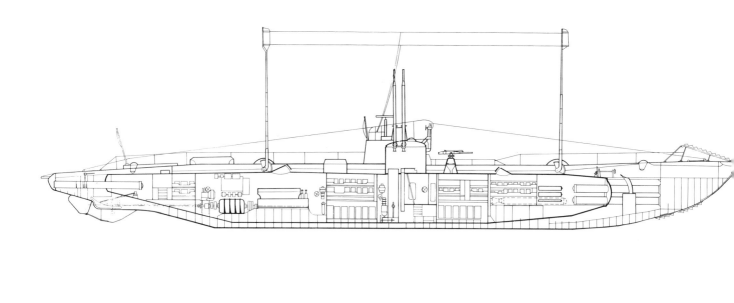

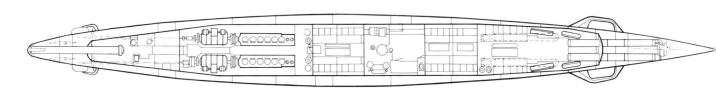

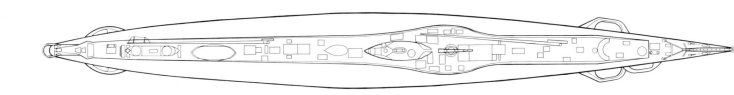

and the current class was put into quantity production. A new small or coastal type, the 'UB' Class was also started to make use of available Körting kerosene engines, and the first minelayers or 'UC' Class were also ordered. The German system used vertical wells inside the forward part of the pressure hull – the mines were loaded from above and dropped out through the keel. The mine and its sinker fell to the sea-bed, and once a soluble plug melted the mine floated free and rose to its pre-set depth. In the early part of 1915 the British were mystified by reports of damage to merchant ships, but in July 1915 a steamer reported that she had collided with a submerged object, and when divers went down they found that the newly completed *UC.2* had blown herself up with her own mines.

The seagoing U-Boat became known as the 'Mittel-U' type, and as the war against commerce progressed it sprouted a number of modifications. For a surprisingly long time the torpedo-armament remained at only two 20-inch (50-cm) bow

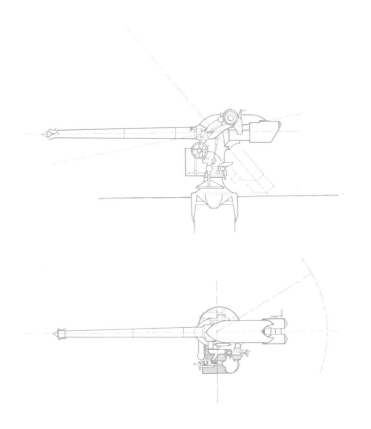

*Above:* UB.42, *a small UB I boat alongside U.35 in the Mediterranean. On the far right a British officer prisoner takes advantage of the chance to get some exercise.*

*Left: The 516-ton UB III Class was the most successful U-Boat design of World War I, and was the basis of the later Type VII.*

*Bottom left: The 10.5cm gun which became the standard U-Boat deck gun.*

tubes and two stern tubes, but the usefulness of the gun for sinking merchant ships led to the replacement of the 3.4-inch (8.9-cm) by the 4.1-inch (10.5-cm) gun. This in turn led to the 'cruiser-submarine' armed with two 5.9-inch (15-cm) guns, despite the fact that submariners indicated that what they really needed was additional torpedoes. By the end of the war the armament of the 'Mittel-U' had been increased to four 50-cm tubes forward and two aft, and the *U.117* Class had external stowage for a further 24 reload torpedoes, in addition to mines. The little 'UB' boats of 1915 were developed into a very effective sea-going type which compared well with the pre-1914 large U-boats, and the 'UCs' underwent a similar expansion. The table shows comparisons of representative U-Boats.

| Type | U.86 | U.161 | UB.1 | UB.48 | U.151 | UC.1 | UC.90 |
|---|---|---|---|---|---|---|---|
| Commissioned | 1917 | 1918 | 1915 | 1917 | 1917 | 1915 | 1918 |
| Length (feet) | 230 | 235 | 92 | 181½ | 213½ | 111½ | 184 |
| Beam | 20ft 10in | 21ft 1in | 10ft 3in | 19ft 4in | 29ft 3in | 10ft 3in | 18ft 2in |
| Draught | 13ft 2in | 12ft 9in | 10ft | 12ft | 18ft 6in | 10ft | 12ft 4in |
| Surface displacement (tons) | 800 | 828 | 128 | 521 | 1512 | 170 | 496 |
| Submerged displacement (tons) | 940 | 1017 | 143 | 657 | 1875 | 185 | 575 |
| SHP of diesels | 2400 | 2400 | 60* | 1100 | 800 | 90* | 600 |
| SHP of motors | 1180 | 1160 | 120 | 760 | 800 | 138 | 600 |
| Speed surfaced (knots) | 16½ | 15½ | 6½ | 13½ | 12.4 | 6½ | 11 |
| Speed submerged (knots) | 8 | 8 | 5½ | 7½ | 5.2 | 5 | 6½ |
| Fuel (tons) | 75 | 107 | 3½ | 69 | 328 | 2½ | 76 |
| Endurance surfaced | 8100 miles @8 knots | 8500 miles @8 knots | 1600 miles @5 knots | 8500 miles @6 knots | 25,000 miles @5½ knots | 800 miles @5½ knots | 8000 miles @8 knots |
| Torpedo-tubes | 2 bow 2 stern | 4 bow 2 stern | 2 bow | 4 bow 1 stern | 2 bow 6 external | none | 1 stern 2 external |
| Guns | one 4.1in | two 4.1in | one machine gun | one 3.4in or 4.1in | two 5.9in two 3.4in | 12 mines one machine gun | 14 mines one 4.1in |
| Complement | 35 | 39 | 14 | 34 | 76 | 16 | 32 |

*Single-shaft Körting engines in place of the more usual two-shaft diesel

*Left: The British* G.13 *alongside the battleship* Queen Elizabeth *at Scapa Flow in 1917.*

*Right: Possibly the best-known photograph of a World War I U-Boat which is nonetheless frequently miscaptioned. It is a UB III type off Heligoland c.1917.*

*Below right: The Italian F.7 at Brindisi in August 1917. Three of this class were later sold to Brazil.*

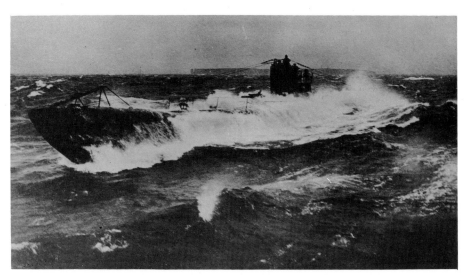

The sinking of the *Glitra* by Feldkirchner encouraged the German Naval Staff in their growing belief that submarines could and should be used against British shipping. The ruthlessness with which Great Britain enforced the blockade also weakened any scruples entertained about violation of international law. For example the British even declared food-stuffs to be contraband, claiming that the German government had commandeered all food supplies. Allied propaganda made good use of any mistakes made by the U-Boats; for example the sinking of the SS *Amiral Ganteaume* by *U.24* off Cap Gris Nez in October 1914 was denounced as an atrocity because she was carrying Belgian refugees, but knowing how little the U-Boat's commander could have seen through his periscope it is more likely that he mistook her for a French troop-ship. The time for a torpedo shot was often limited to a few seconds, during which the submarine captain was supposed to count numbers of people on board, boats, guns and even where they were positioned; guns mounted forward were classed as offensive armament whereas guns mounted aft were defensive, for example.

Even without any flouting of the Germans' self-imposed restrictions the losses were staggering, 32,000 tons of British and 15,900 tons of French and neutral shipping sunk in January 1915 alone. By March the total had risen to 80,700 tons for that month, and two months later to 185,000 tons. Neutral opinion was outraged, and the United States was particularly angry, because the needs of the British and French war economies had opened new markets to all countries exporting war material of any kind. There was a residue of anti-British feeling in the United States, and the blockade did prevent some American exporters from sending goods to Germany, but the vast increase in British and French demands more than replaced the lost German markets. In addition there was a sentimental attachment between France and the USA which went back to the days of Marquis de Lafayette, Admiral de Grasse and the War of Independence. American

public opinion was violently inflamed against Germany by stories of the rape of Belgium, and the deaths of American citizens in torpedoed ships did not help.

On 4 February 1915, Germany announced that a War Zone existed around the British Isles, in which British and French ships would be sunk without warning. The declaration added that it would not always be possible to avoid attacks on neutral shipping; in other words the U-Boats could now sink merchantmen 'at sight' unless they saw a neutral flag. If the neutral countries could have been persuaded to forbid their ships to trade with the Allies the German gamble might have paid off, but the British blockade meant that a refusal to trade with the Allies would mean virtual bankruptcy for most shipping companies as there was not enough trade with other countries to keep everyone in business. It was a fact of life which had brought Napoleon's Continental System crashing in ruins, but in 1915 nobody was very receptive to the lessons of naval history. Apart from munitions, North America's exports were mainly grain and timber to Europe, and both Canada and the United

States were self-sufficient in raw materials and foodstuffs; similarly Europe was the main customer for imports from South America and the Far East.

A great help to the U-Boat offensive was the German Army's conquest of bases on the Belgian coast. After the initial German land advance was held at the Battle of the Marne the front stabilized with its flank resting on the Flanders coast at Nieuport. The German Navy set up a completely new naval base at Ostend, with light forces based there and at Zeebrugge. U-Boats were based at the inland port of Bruges and reached the open sea by canals to Zeebrugge and Ostend. These Flanders bases reduced the distance and increased the time the U-Boats could spend on patrol in the Western Approaches and the Bristol and St George's Channels, their best hunting-grounds. British minefields and net-barriers in the Dover Straits were not effective as the U-Boats soon learned to make the passage on the surface at night, when the chances of being spotted were slim. To encourage the British in their belief that the Dover Straits were blocked U-Boats from German ports making the

*Below: Officers and men of U.35 watch
UB.42 approaching during their
Mediterranean rendezvous in the spring
of 1917.*

*Inset right: UB.70 putting to sea while
two torpedo boats prepare to escort her,
late 1917 or early 1918.*

'north-about' passage around the Orkneys were even ordered to show themselves occasionally to the patrols. Part of the problem was the lack of an efficient British mine, as later experience was to show that minefields were an important weapon against submarines, but above all there was no adequate way of sinking a submarine even if she gave away her presence. The principal tactic for a surface ship was to ram or try to hit the U-Boat with gunfire. Both these methods pre-supposed that the submarine was either submerging or running at periscope depth; once a submarine dived deeper she was not only immune but undetectable.

The Allies' answer to the U-Boat offensive of 1915 was to increase the number of patrols by impressing all manner of warships and merchantmen into service. The battle fleet was screened by destroyers, whose speed and maneuverability gave them some chance of racing to the spot where a submarine had dived. They could then ram or try to hit the conning tower with a lucky shot from her guns. After the initial losses of sitting ducks no major warship moved anywhere without her destroyer escorts, and as a result no battleship of the Grand Fleet was torpedoed by a U-Boat at sea throughout the war, but there were not enough destroyers to spare for escorting merchant ships. A new type of utility warship, the 'Flower' Class sloop was taken off minesweeping and put to work against submarines alongside old destroyers and other obsolescent warships. The Auxiliary Patrol was formed out of the large number of steam yachts, trawlers and drifters not performing any other useful function, and armed with guns they were sent off to the waters around the British Isles to hunt for submarines. However, the Atlantic, even that portion of it around the British Isles, and the North Sea are large, and no matter how many patrols were maintained there was always space in which submarines could hide. The huge volume of shipping in and out of British ports meant that U-Boats merely had to wait for their victims to come to them – if a patrol vessel appeared the submarine could submerge and wait until it was safe to come up and begin the process of destruction again.

Nothing more clearly illustrates how easy this was than the tragedy of the *Lusitania*. Most British transatlantic liners had been taken over by the Royal Navy in August 1914 for conversion to armed merchant cruisers or troopships, but with government approval the *Lusitania* was kept in service running a passenger service between Liverpool and New York. The reasons for this were complex and reveal a lot about government attitudes. First, she was a visible reassurance to the American public that it was still 'business as usual' and that Britain's position as Mistress of the Seas was not even in dispute. Second, the Germans had put up an ingenious answer to the British blockade to the effect that their submarines had imposed a counter-blockade on the British Isles. If this claim had been upheld in international law the Germans would have been justified in sinking *any* merchant ship trying to run the blockade. However, to be upheld in

56

law a blockade had to be 'effective,' and by maintaining a scheduled liner service to New York the British government was quietly keeping its legal options open.

Much has been made of the fact that the *Lusitania* was carrying explosives, according to her manifest 5500 cases of small-arms ammunition and fuse nose-caps, totalling 37 tons. It has even been claimed that she was armed, despite the absence of any evidence other than the fact that she was taken up in August 1914 (along with a number of other liners) for arming as an armed merchant cruiser. In fact she proved to be such a glutton for coal that a month later she was struck off the register of armed merchant cruisers and returned to her owners. No other auxiliary cruiser ever carried passengers in addition to 6-inch guns, for the very simple reason that the passenger-accommodation occupied space needed for ammunition hoists, magazines, accommodation for gun-crews and other purposes; passengers and their requirements were also too much of a fire-hazard to allow liners to operate as carriers of high-explosive. The *Lusitania*'s small cargo (as a passenger liner she had in any case very little cargo-capacity despite her size) comprised the most inert form of munitions in existence, and short of the ship catching fire there was little likelihood of it exploding.

Whatever anybody thought or knew the *Lusitania* was carrying when she lay in New York in April 1915, there was no

*Left: The 800-ton U.81 Class had six 50cm torpedo tubes and a speed of 16.8 knots on the surface.*

*Below: The French Foucault has the dubious distinction of being the first submarine to be sunk at sea by air attack.*

way in which her position at sea could be passed on to a U-Boat at any point. The ship herself would not know her exact position until she sighted land at the other end or took a sextant sighting, and there was no means of communicating with German U-Boats directly from the United States. When in due course on 7 May the *Lusitania* was torpedoed by *U.20* off southern Ireland both sides for their own reasons tried to claim that the sinking had been planned. To the British it was all part of a Hun plot to sink innocent ships, while the Germans claimed that as they *knew* of the *Lusitania*'s cargo their submarine was quite entitled to sink her. What both sides chose to ignore was that Kapitänleutnant Schwieger's own report showed that *U-20* had stumbled on the liner by chance.

The U-Boat had been on patrol in the Irish Sea for some days, but without luck, and so Schwieger moved southward to find more targets. He had been ordered to look out for troopships arriving from Canada and so headed for the Old Head of Kinsale, a popular landfall for trans-Atlantic shipping. Like many other submariners Schwieger was not disappointed, and soon saw smoke on the horizon. He was puzzled by the target's four funnels belching smoke, and assumed that he had stumbled on a submarine's worst enemy, a whole flotilla of destroyers.

Then the 'flotilla' altered course, and to his joy Schwieger saw the massive bulk and four funnels of a large ship in the graticules of his periscope. On the assumption that most large liners were serving either as armed merchant cruisers or troopships, and as no Red Cross markings were carried indicating a hospital ship he ordered one torpedo to be fired. The report made no mention of seeing guns, and as we have already

mentioned, a submariner could see so little through a periscope that he would not have been looking for them, but it did mention a second explosion. This has been held to be the cargo of munitions 'tearing the heart out' of the ship, but any ordnance expert can testify to the fact that 5500 cases of bullets and nose-caps some distance away from an explosion are unlikely to cause a further detonation. Schwieger himself attributed the second bang to boilers, coal or munitions, without further comment. If he was correct in thinking that his torpedo hit level with the funnels the most plausible explanation is that seawater rushing into the boiler-rooms caused an implosion of the boilers. A big liner of that vintage, with her numerous boiler-rooms, was doomed once flooding started on a large scale and the *Lusitania* went down with heavy loss of life.

Among the many dead were 159 American citizens, and the US government reaction was stronger than it had been previously. A note from Washington to Berlin demanded that U-Boats should refrain from torpedoing passenger ships. The Germans did not handle the diplomatic crisis tactfully, and maintained that they had warned passengers of the dangers, thereby giving further credence to the 'conspiracy' theory. The British, who had believed that the Germans would never dare to sink the *Lusitania*, were not averse to making capital out of the incident. Carefully skating around the point about the cargo (the details of the manifest were withheld during World War I), they connived at the idea of a planned sinking, although if anyone had thought about the security implications they would have realized that German agents would have had to control the Cunard Steamship Company or even be in command of the ship herself to achieve such a perfect interception.

The *Lusitania* incident stands out as a milestone in the history of the submarine. She was not the first ship to go down with American citizens on board and not the last, but she was the one which was remembered. It was the point at which America decided that its fundamental sympathies and interests were in favor of an Allied victory, not a German one. The bewildered Schwieger, having returned home to find that he was a hero, was later denounced as a criminal. In fact he was neither, merely a conscientious submariner who acted on the very limited evidence of his own eyes.

The outcry forced the German government to slow down its onslaught on shipping, but in 1916 losses climbed steadily once more, until the *monthly* total reached over half a million tons. The Allies responded with 'Q-Ships,' decoy vessels fitted with concealed guns. The Q-Ship loitered in a likely area with the

intention of luring a U-Boat to the surface for an easy sinking with her deck gun. If all went well a 'panic party' abandoned ship, leaving gun-crews aboard who would open fire as soon as the U-Boat came within range. Although a few spectacular successes were scored the Q-Ship idea was greatly over-rated, and tied up skilled seamen who were needed elsewhere, without sinking enough submarines to justify itself. A variation on the decoy theme was to use trawlers and submarines together to stop U-Boats from shelling the Aberdeen fishing fleet. Among the trawler fleet would be one trawler towing an old, small submarine instead of a trawl. The submarine was in touch with the trawler by means of a telephone link, and could cast off the towing wire. The idea actually worked twice, although each time technical snags nearly ruined everything, and the submarines each sank a U-Boat. News of the sinkings got back to Germany but it did have the desired effect of warning the U-Boats off the fishing fleet.

The Allies also armed merchant ships to enable them to fight off U-Boats. This was seized on by Germany as an excuse for sinking merchantmen at sight, despite the fact that merchantmen had been armed for centuries. In practice the provision of a small gun of obsolescent design on the poop of a tramp steamer did little but boost the crew's morale; however bad the shooting from a submarine's deck-gun the shooting from the average steamer was probably much worse.

In 1916 two important countermeasures were introduced. The first was the

*Above: A German 'egg' mine salved from UC.5 by the British in 1916.*

*Right: The battered minelayer UC.5 lies in dry dock at Harwich after being raised by the British. Note the six vertical mine wells.*

depth-charge, which was simply a 300-pound explosive charge fitted with a hydrostatic valve to set it off at a pre-selected depth. At last it was possible to attack a submerged submarine, but the second invention was even more important, for it enabled a surface warship to detect the *presence* of a submarine. The hydrophone was simply an underwater sound-receiver which picked up noises from a U-Boat's motors, using that property of water which permits sound to travel long distances. Making the hydrophone directional turned it into the first usable instrument for hunting submarines, and although it tuned in just as well to shoals of fish it did put antisubmarine tactics onto a scientific footing at last. A large number of Allied patrol vessels were equipped with hydrophones, and the first kill came in July 1916, when the motorboat *Salmon* sank *UC.7*.

The arming of merchant ships inevitably led the Germans into upgunning their submarines. The 'cruiser-submarine' with her medium-caliber guns had a tremendous moral effect, and in Britain there was even talk of having to arm merchantmen with 6-inch or 7.5-inch guns. What the proponents of big submarine guns ignored was that against the thin plating of a merchant ship a 4-inch shell is as good as a 6-inch, bearing in mind that a submarine had such poor fire control that she would have to approach relatively close to allow her gun-crew to achieve hits. The theory of the cruiser-submarine was that she could drive off small warships by out-ranging their guns, but in practice no submarine was likely to win such a contest. One hit or near miss from a shell could damage the submarine sufficiently to prevent her from diving, whereas the submarine's shooting would have to be exceptionally good to cripple even a small warship.

The first German cruiser-submarines were actually converted from a series of big mercantile submarines, built in 1915–16 to run small cargoes through the blockade. Their purpose was two-fold: to bring in special materials needed for the armaments industry and to prove to neutral opinion that Germany was not being strangled by the blockade. Unlike other submarines the cargo-carrying submarines were named, and the first, the *Deutschland*, left Kiel in June 1916 carrying a cargo of mail, chemical dyes and precious stones for Baltimore. She presented a tricky legal problem for the US Customs authorities but as she was clearly not armed she was entitled to be treated as a commercial vessel. The effect on the Americans was tremendous, and crowds flocked to see the submarine after her arrival on 9 July, and again when she sailed for Bremen three weeks later, loaded with copper, nickel, silver and zinc. Although the size of her cargo would never have made her a commercial proposition the *Deutschland*'s propaganda value to Germany was enormous, but an attempt to repeat the performance backfired.

A second cargo-submarine, the *Bremen*, set out bound for Newport, Rhode Island. She was accompanied by *U.53* under Kapitänleutnant Hans Rose, who had orders to 'blow a path' for the *Bremen* through any British warships which tried to bar her passage. Unfortunately British mines were more effective in doing their job and the *Bremen* disappeared without trace somewhere off the Orkneys, with the result that *U.53* arrived at Newport on 7 October by herself. The US Navy suddenly found itself with a belligerent nation's submarine lying off one of its naval bases, a situation for which the rule book did not cater. While the Navy frantically badgered the

*Above: A U.139* Class 'U-Cruiser.' *This class was armed with six torpedo tubes and two 5.9-inch guns and each boat displaced nearly 2000 tons.*

*Right: The 'commercial' U-Boat* Deutschland *leaving the River Weser on her epic journey carrying cargo across the Atlantic to Baltimore in June 1916.*

State Department and everyone else for instructions, Hans Rose finished the amusing chat that he had been having with the naval officers at Newport and left as quietly as he had arrived. However, what followed undid any goodwill that *U.53*'s visit might have engendered, for the U-Boat started to sink shipping within sight of the Nantucket lightship. Rose was convinced that his mysterious visit had left the US Navy and Government with a deep impression of how powerful Germany's submarines were; before he had left Germany he had been told by Commodore Hermann Bauer (the chief of the U-Boat Arm) that bold action would silence the anti-German party in America and would result in the restrictions on the U-Boats being lifted. The reasoning behind this forecast is hard to follow, and the Germans evidently understood very little of American attitudes. What happened was that the Americans became even more worried about German intentions, while the US Navy started to take the submarine threat seriously indeed. The Kaiser, furthermore, did not feel that the time was right to launch a second unrestricted U-Boat campaign, so the second attempt to break the British blockade was a failure. The *Deutschland* was converted to a military submarine, with two torpedo tubes, two 5.9-inch and two 3.4-inch guns. Six more were ordered in February 1917, and the class

10 in mid-1915 to 30 by the end of 1916. By mid-1917 the figure would exceed 40 U-Boats, with more to come, and with these figures in mind the Germans knew that the time had come to act.

The first results justified all the claims made by the U-Boat Arm. Within weeks the shipping losses rocketed to nearly 800,000 tons (April 1917). The British countermeasures proved quite inadequate, and no matter how many warships, auxiliary patrol vessels and Q-Ships were deployed, one ship in every four that entered the War Zone was certain to be sunk. When the United States entered the war in the same month, Admiral Sims of the US Navy went to London to confer with Sir John Jellicoe, the First Sea Lord, and was appalled to hear that the naval war was being lost, and that food stocks in the British Isles would only last six weeks. Every weapon that could be used against the submarine

was numbered *U.151–157*, the *Deutschland* becoming *U.155*.

Not until February 1917 did the Kaiser give permission for unrestricted U-Boat warfare. It was a gamble, for the High Command knew that it was only a matter of time before the Americans came into the war to rescue the French and British. If they could force the British to sue for peace the attitude of the Americans was irrelevant; with German submarines in command of the North Atlantic the Americans could not intervene in Europe, and Germany could then deal

with France at her leisure. It was an appealing proposition and one that the Navy and in particular the U-Boat Arm favored. The High Seas Fleet knew after the battle of the Skagerrak (Jutland) in May 1916 that it could never win, and that it had been extremely lucky to escape destruction. Thereafter its best officers, petty officers and seamen were drafted to U-Boats and torpedo-boats in increasing numbers. The U-Boats ordered since 1914 were also coming into service, and the daily average of boats at sea was rising steadily from no more than

had been tried, and the Admiralty no longer knew which way to turn.

The most successful U-Boat captain was Lothar von Arnauld de la Perière, who sank 456,216 tons of shipping, mostly when commanding *U.35*. Under all its commanders this boat achieved a staggering total of successes. These broke down as follows:

| | | |
|---|---|---|
| 1915 | 35 ships totalling | 89,192 tons |
| 1916 | 122 ships totalling | 262,832 tons |
| 1917 | 62 ships totalling | 170,672 tons |
| 1918 | 5 ships totalling | 13,204 tons |
| | | 535,900 |

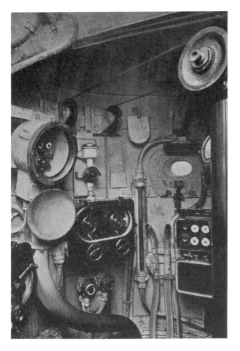

*Scenes aboard the surrendered* U.155
*(ex-*Deutschland*):*
*Above: Voice tube and repeaters in the conning tower.*
*Above right: The control room looking aft, showing electric switches and hydroplane controls.*
*Right: Steering gear compartment.*
*Below right: The two forward 50cm torpedo tubes.*

In the four years of war the total of shipping sunk by all U-Boats was as follows:

| | | |
|---|---|---|
| 1914 | 3 ships totalling | 2,950 tons |
| 1915 | 640 ships totalling | 1,189,031 tons |
| 1916 | 1301 ships totalling | 2,194,420 tons |
| 1917 | 3170 ships totalling | 5,938,023 tons |
| 1918 | 1280 ships totalling | 2,624,278 tons |

These figures do not include the warships sunk, which amounted to 10 battleships, 17 cruisers and nearly 80 minor vessels.

Yet, the oldest weapon of all had not been tried – convoy, the sailing of merchant shipping in groups under the protection of warships. It had been in use from the fourteenth century until the end of the Napoleonic Wars but somehow the impact of nineteenth and twentieth century technology had blinded naval officers to the simple fact that an attack on merchant shipping was easiest to defend against if the merchant ships were concentrated in convenient groups. It seems an obvious statement to make, but the sea is a big area, and individual merchantmen could never conceivably be allocated their own escort. Convoy was the only way in which a limited number of warships could hope to protect the Allies' vast merchant fleet.

There were other factors which made the 1916–17 shipping losses even worse. Virtually all construction of new merchant ships had been stopped in 1914;

after all, it was going to be a short war and warships were more necessary than merchant ships. The result was that even repair work was stopped and damaged merchantmen were often laid up. Nor was there any salvage organization to bring in damaged ships, and in some cases warships sank damaged merchantmen rather than tow them back to harbor. In short the Allies were incredibly improvident and wasted shipping to a dangerous extent. But in the summer of 1916 the British finally realized that the pool of available shipping was drying up, and urgent measures of conservation were put in hand. A salvage organization was set up and civilian repair yards were permitted to undertake work on merchant ships once again. A start was made on new construction, and plans were made to simplify and speed up construction, a foretaste of the Liberty Ship program of World War II. The shipbuilding program did not show any big results until after the crisis was over but the other measures played a most important part in paving the way for convoy.

The argument over who introduced convoy is hard to resolve. The British Prime Minister claimed the idea as his own but it was almost certainly urged on him by the Cabinet Secretary, Maurice Hankey, who in turn listened to influential naval officers in the Trade Division. The Admiralty Board fought against it with all the passion of the bigoted, and ironically it was only French insistence in February 1917 that at least the coal shipments from Britain to France should be convoyed which forced Jellicoe's hand. During the April crisis the French colliers were suffering a loss rate of 0.19 percent as against 25 percent elsewhere. With dire warnings of disaster the Admiralty allowed the first ocean convoy to sail at the end of April, and much to their

surprise a miracle cure occurred. Within a month the loss rate fell from 25 percent to 0.24 percent. By November 84,000 passages had been made in convoy and only 257 had been sunk.

From the U-Boats' point of view convoy meant the end of easy pickings, for it was no longer any use lying in wait for whatever ship might come along. When smoke was seen on the horizon it heralded the arrival of 10–20 merchantmen surrounded by destroyers, sloops and patrol vessels, and often accompanied by an airship. All the U-Boat commanders' reminiscences bear out the fact that the seas suddenly emptied and an important side-effect was that U-Boats could no longer rely on the gun as a cheap and quick means of sinking ships. Now it was numbers of torpedoes carried which determined the endurance of a U-Boat, and this alone helped to reduce the tonnage sunk. Other countermeasures included dazzle-painting, a method of camouflage relying on the disruptive effect of multi-colored irregular patterns. Some U-Boat commanders were so bothered by the lurid emerald greens, pinks and purples used in ships' color-schemes that they had the eye-pieces of their periscopes fitted with color-filters. The main purpose of camouflage was to introduce a slight delay between the first sighting of the target and the order to fire; with luck the target ship might pass out of the danger area while the U-Boat commander was still trying to estimate her bearing.

The British and their Allies took the offensive against the U-Boats in 1917, using a new type of horned mine which was much more effective than the 1914 pattern (the new one was very similar to the highly lethal German 'egg' mine with its electro-chemical Herz horn). Using information gained from cryptanalysis,

the minelayers of the 20th Flotilla assisted by submarines laid mines in the exit-routes from Heligoland and Flanders. As soon as a new route was selected for the U-Boats the minelayers would promptly mine it, and in this way the minelaying UC-Boats operating out of Flanders were finally neutralized. In 1918 an even more sinister weapon was introduced, the first magnetic mine.

The U-Boats kept up the pressure until the end but the combination of convoy and the other measures prevented them from ever getting back to the position that they had enjoyed in April 1917. When the Armistice was signed in November 1918 one of its most important clauses related to the U-Boats, which had to be surrendered in Allied ports. The German Navy had built some 360 submarines during the war, and a further 400 had either been cancelled or lay incomplete in the shipyards. The U-Boat Arm sank over 11 million tons of shipping and damaged a further $7\frac{1}{2}$ million tons, but to achieve this 178 U-Boats were lost, and 5364 officers and men, nearly 40 per cent of the personnel.

One of the most enduring myths of the U-Boat War is the tale of the Haunted Submarine. According to the standard tale, which crops up repeatedly in books of sea mysteries, *U.65* had become a 'magnet for accidents' while under construction. First a girder had slipped out of its slings and crushed two workmen and then three men had died of asphyxiation while working in her engine room. Apparently Admiral Ludwig von Schröder (commanding naval forces in Flanders) investigated the rumor and to dispel any question of a jinx *U.65* was

*Below: Austro-Hungarian UB II type boats lying at Pola after the Armistice.*

launched and went to sea with the rest of her flotilla to exercise off the Scheldt estuary.

When the captain ordered one of his most experienced men to check equipment on the forecastle he is reported to have walked overboard deliberately, but after a complete check of all valves and controls the boat dived without fault. Only when she attempted to surface again did it become apparent that *U.65* was not answering to her controls, and she lay on the bottom for 12 agonizing hours before finally being able to blow tanks and return to the surface. It is claimed that a Lutheran chaplain later conducted a service of exorcism at Bruges and that the boat's first two war patrols passed without incident. In May 1918, however, while she was passing through the Bay of Biscay her gunner went berserk, claiming that he had seen a ghost; he was confined to his bunk but broke loose and committed suicide. That night the engineer broke his leg and shortly after dawn a petty officer either fell overboard or tried to swim away. The U-Boat finally returned to Bruges safely but understandably the commander was relieved and she was recommissioned with a new crew. The final act of the drama occurred on 10 July 1918, when an American submarine is claimed to have sighted a derelict U-Boat off Cape Clear. While the American boat stalked her prey at periscope depth her captain is reported to have seen a ghostly figure on the bows, and immediately afterwards the U-Boat vanished in a mysterious explosion.

That is the popular version, but before it can be swallowed whole some elementary checks reveal that the submarine concerned could not be *U.65*, which was scuttled off Pola in October 1918 when the Austro–Hungarian Navy evacuated the port. The only boat which fits the description is *UB.65*, which was built at Hamburg and entered service in August 1917 under the command of Kapitän-leutnant Scheele. *UB.65* sailed from the Heligoland Bight on 2 July 1918 (still under the command of Scheele) avoiding a torpedo from the British boat *G.6* on the way, but her periscope was sighted off the Fastnet rock by the American submarine *AL.2* at a distance of only 80 yards. Lieutenant Foster was manuevering to attack when he heard an explosion ahead of the U-Boat, followed by the noise of fast-running propellers and then silence. The assumption by modern authorities is that *UB.65* had fired a torpedo (whether at *AL.2* or another target is open to question) which exploded prematurely as it left the tube. As both submarines were submerged during the encounter it is highly unlikely that Foster saw a ghostly figure and his report makes no mention of it. Clearly the facts have not stood in the way of a good story, but the loss of *UB.65* is intriguing enough without ghostly additions. In fact the story appears to have become intertwined with another one, that of a Flanders U-Boat which sank with all hands but was subsequently found floating on the surface with a crew of dead men. It is remotely possible that a submarine lying on the bottom could eventually rise to the surface, if leaking compressed air slowly forced water out of the ballast tanks, and of course she would float on the surface for a while with her cargo of corpses. The only problem with this story is that nobody has ever identified the boat concerned.

## U-Boats in the Mediterranean

After the first timid beginning the submarine war in the Mediterranean took a new turn with the Anglo-French attack on the Dardanelles. The Allies could not get surface warships through the Straits, and so looked to their submarines to achieve something, while the Germans felt that they ought to make some effort to help their new Turkish allies.

The only submarines available were three old British 'B' Class boats and the French *Brumaire* and *Circé*, which had all been sent to the Levant at the end of 1914 to help maintain the blockade of the Dardanelles. On 1 December *B.11* left on a perilous journey up the Straits to see if a submarine could breast the 4 or 5-knot current and dive through the five rows of mines known to exist at Chanak (Cannakale). The tiny submarine had two advantages; her batteries had just been renewed and the depot-ship's workshop had fitted guards to prevent her hydroplanes from fouling the mines' mooring wires. Even so she had an exciting passage through the Narrows but she was rewarded by finding the old armored cruiser *Messudieh* lying at anchor, apparently safe from attack. A single 18-inch torpedo was enough to sink the old ship, hardly an outstanding

*Above: The Australian AE.2 arriving at Portsmouth in February 1914.*

*Below: Hersing's victory at Gallipoli. The old predreadnought battleship* Majestic *heels slowly to port after a single torpedo hit.*

victory but one to offset the recent successes of the U-Boats in the North Sea, and Allied newspapers made the most of it, even upgrading the *Messudieh* to a battleship.

As a direct result of *B.11*'s exploit the British and French sent more modern submarines to the Dardanelles and their arrival coincided with the Allied land-ings. The Anglo-French offensive was not going well and any interference with the Turks' supply-routes through the Sea of Marmora would benefit the hard-pressed troops at Gallipoli. But forcing the Dardanelles was still very dangerous, even for a modern submarine. *E.15* tried it and ran aground off Kephez Point, followed by the French *Saphir* off Nagara Point; the Australian *AE.2* got through on 26 April only to be sunk, but her sister *E.14* followed her a day later. The French *Joule* was mined on 1 May, making the loss rate four submarines for every one

that arrived in the Sea of Marmora. But when the news got through that *E.14* had sunk three ships the Allies redoubled their efforts, and soon another six British submarines and the French *Turquoise* reached the Sea of Marmora.

The German *U.21* under Kapitänleutnant Hersing had also made a safe passage of the Dardanelles from Cattaro. Six of the small UB-Boats and four UC-Boats were sent to the Adriatic by rail to be reassembled at Cattaro, and three of the UB-Boats were sent to the Dardanelles to join Hersing at Constantinople. Two arrived safely but it was *U.21* which scored the first success. On 25 May Hersing spotted the old battleship *Triumph* firing at Turkish positions near Gaba Tepe. He had to wait two hours for a favorable shot, but when it came a single torpedo sent the *Triumph* down, and to escape his pursuers Hersing took *U.21 underneath* the sinking battleship. Two days later he came upon another old battleship, HMS *Majestic*, off Cape Helles. The battleship was at anchor and surrounded by colliers and patrol vessels, but the man who had waited two hours to get the *Triumph* was not easily put off, and eventually a gap opened. Again a single torpedo sufficed to send the *Majestic* over on her beam ends. The obsolescence of the ships was immaterial; they had been sunk in full view of the troops fighting ashore and Hersing's feat was therefore all the more dramatic. The bombarding ships had to be withdrawn to Mudros, and at a crucial moment the presence of *U-21* put fresh heart into the Turkish troops.

Italy joined the war on the side of the Allies on 24 May 1915. Her large surface fleet offered the Austrian and German U-Boats tempting targets, but as she had only declared war on Austria the German submariners at Cattaro were in a difficult situation. The solution was a simple one; the German boats pretended to be Austrian until such time as Italy chose to include Germany among her enemies. *UB.15* and *UB.1* were among the boats reassembled at Cattaro, and they were

*Above: The* Delfino *was the first Italian submarine, built in 1892. Despite her age she was used to defend Venice until 1918.*

*Right: The British 'J' Class of 1915–16 were the first submarines intended to work with the battle fleet. They were provided with long-range radio.*

nominally commissioned as *X* and *XI*, but in October 1915 the Austro–Hungarian Navy adopted the U-prefix with arabic numerals. Among their successes in the Adriatic were the sinkings of the Italian submarines *Medusa* and *Nereide* and the armored cruisers *Amalfi* and *Giuseppe Garibaldi*.

The five small U-Boats sent to Turkey had been formed into a half-flotilla under Otto Hersing as senior officer. He pursued a vigorous policy in the Black Sea and in the Sea of Marmora but he had too few boats to deal with the Russian Fleet as well as the Allied submarines in the Sea of Marmora. The British submarines' campaign against the Turks is a classic of economy of effort, for a handful of submarines was able to dominate both land and sea communications for eight

months. It was discovered that trains could be bombarded with deck-guns, and so British submarines followed the German trend toward heavier guns. *E.20* was even equipped with a 6-inch howitzer, although she never tested it in action, and other submarines sported whatever antique weapon could be dug out of the Malta Dockyard stores. The campaign only ended in January 1916 when the Allies evacuated the Gallipoli Peninsula,

under control just as rapidly as it did in the Atlantic. As an interesting sidelight, it was noticed many years later by an Admiralty historian that the losses of convoyed ships in the Mediterranean were twice those of convoys in Home waters. Only after further research was it realized that Mediterranean convoys

*Left: The Italian* Balilla *was originally ordered for the German Navy as U.42 but was seized in the FIAT San Giorgio shipyard in June 1915.*

*Below: The Austro-Hungarian U.4 and her sister U.3 were built in Germany in 1907–09.*

build Holland-type submarines in 1901. In an effort to transfuse new ideas Scott's were asked to build three boats to the Italian Laurenti design, and Armstrong Whitworth's were asked to build four to the French Schneider-Laubeuf design. As a sop to Vickers' wounded feelings they were allowed to submit their own design in competition, but the experiment proved inconclusive because all three classes were too novel to be adequately tested in wartime. The French and Italian diesels and the unfamiliar layout made the Scott and Whitworth boats difficult to handle, and so they were handed over to the Italians in 1915–16, presumably on the assumption that a Latin navy would know more about them. The Vickers 'V' Class neither disgraced nor distinguished themselves, but as the current 'E' Class boats had already proved to be highly successful nobody was bothered to make any detailed comparisons.

Two other notable experiments were also initiated by the RN at the same time, the first a big ocean-going boat modelled on the German U-Boats and the second a steam-driven boat. The first, Vickers' *Nautilus* was an unmitigated disaster which never even put to sea; she finished her ignoble career as a generating station in Chatham Dockyard. The second, presumably inspired by the French boats, was built by Scott's as the *Swordfish*. She was only a qualified success, and after a year of laborious trials she was rebuilt as a surface patrol vessel. But she had pointed the way to steam propulsion, even if the direction was backwards.

Although the main submarine type in production, the 'E' Class, was highly satisfactory the Admiralty was in an experimental mood regarding submarines, and early in 1915 in response to a request from the Commander in Chief of the Grand Fleet a class of 'fleet' submarines was ordered. Known as the 'J' Class they were intended to accompany the Battle Fleet at sea, which required a speed of 21 knots. However, despite everything that the engine designers could do, there was no diesel available that could drive a submarine at more than 19 knots, even after Vickers had linked three 12-cylinder motors into one gigantic 36-cylinder 'in line' diesel. The chief virtue of the 'J' Class was their long-range radio set, which allowed them to send back reports from the Heligoland Bight without making use of an intermediate 'repeating ship', but nobody was content to leave matters there. Designers have a bad habit of pursuing an idea long after it has been shown to be unnecessary, simply to prove its feasibility, and this appears to be what happened in this case.

In April 1915 Vickers sent Commodore

but in that time submarines had virtually stopped all seaborne communication between Istanbul and the Turkish forces on the Gallipoli Peninsula.

The Mediterranean remained a good hunting ground for U-Boats right to the end. Some of their most notable successes were scored there, including the torpedoing of the battleships HMS *Cornwallis* and the French *Danton*. The introduction of convoy in 1917 brought the losses

averaged only 10 ships as against 20 in the Atlantic convoys, the first statistical proof of a phenomenon noticed during World War II, that the larger the convoy the greater the immunity it enjoyed.

Although the Royal Navy had more submarines than any other navy in 1914 it was nowhere near satisfied with its designs. As late as 1912 the Admiralty had decided to break the Vickers monopoly which dated from the decision to

Hall, who was in charge of British submarines, an outline design for a submarine propelled by geared steam turbines *and* a diesel. The design had not been asked for by the Commodore or the Admiralty, and Vickers had jumped the gun, but after some discussion a 1913 design was resurrected and the best features of both were incorporated in a new version. Instead of 21-inch torpedoes the 18-inch tubes of the 'J' Class were adopted to save time, with beam tubes as in the 'E' Class. Two Yarrow boilers in a single boiler-room with the stokehold between them generated steam for two steam turbines developing 10,000 horsepower. In the original design the diesel motor was to have driven a center shaft but in the final version an 'E' Class 800-horsepower diesel drove a 700-horsepower dynamo to supply power to the electric motors, the first example of diesel-electric drive in British submarines. Two electric motors totalling 700 horsepower were coupled to each shaft at 800 rpm, with 5:1 gearing, and when submerged, current was provided from a 336-cell battery.

The armament was unusually heavy, four 18-inch torpedo-tubes in the bow, another two on each broadside just forward of the boiler-room, and a twin rotating pair in the superstructure. These last were for use on the surface at night, as the 'K' Class were envisioned as acting as surface torpedo boats, in much the same way as Laubeuf's *Narval* fifteen years before. A heavy gun armament was also mounted, two 4-inch quick-firers, replaced by 5.5-inch in the last three boats.

Difficulties with the 'K' Class took two forms. They were very complex and marked a big departure from previous standards, and so it was inevitable that they should have more than their fair share of teething troubles. The biggest problem was one that was inherent in the conception of fleet submarines, for submarines are not cut out to be efficient surface warships. It was once said of the 'Ks' that they handled like destroyers but had the bridge facilities of a picket boat. A 'K' boat was 338 feet long, and if a friendly ship mistook her for a U-Boat on a dark night she was not going to be able to maneuver quickly enough to take avoiding action. To get the two diminutive funnels folded down into their watertight wells took 30 seconds but there were also quadruple mushroom-topped venti-

*Below: The British giant* M.1 *was armed with a 12-inch gun capable of firing an 850-pound shell.*

*Bottom left: The steam driven* K.12 *and her sisters were a bold innovation by the Royal Navy but suffered a series of mishaps.*

*Bottom right:* M.1 *in an unusual camouflage scheme, late 1918.*

lators to be shut before diving, and a small obstruction such as a strop of wire rope was sufficient to jam them open. The 'Ks' had a dismal record of accidents and collisions which earned them the reputation of being under a hoodoo. The worst of these was the 'Battle of May Island,' which still strikes a chill of horror in the hearts of submariners. On the night of 31 January 1918 a large force of warships was leaving the Firth of Forth on an exercise. Two flotillas of 'K' boats were steaming some way ahead of a battle-cruiser squadron when a jammed helm caused two submarines to collide. All might still have been well if the cruiser acting as flotilla-leader had not turned back *through* her own flotilla, in the process ramming and sinking *K.17*. The second submarine flotilla arrived on the scene, and in the confusion *K.6* rammed *K.4* and cut her in half. Only by a miracle did the battle-cruisers sweep through the shambles without sinking any more submarines. To add fuel to the rumors of a hoodoo on the 'K' Class it was later discovered that the catastrophe had been caused by a jammed helm in *K.22*, which was *K.13* renumbered after sinking disastrously on her contractors' trials in 1915. Another unpleasant trick of the 'K' boats was a tendency to dive too fast, using the steam left in the boilers after shutting down, which made them liable to exceed the safe diving depth before they could level off. All in all, the Royal Navy's submariners breathed a sigh of relief when the last of the 'Ks' was sent to the scrapheap after World War I.

The next whim of the Admiralty was for submarines armed with 12-inch guns. Nobody has been able to give a convincing reason for building the 'M' Class, but they may have been intended to bombard shore-targets as submarines had in the Sea of Marmora. There is also evidence of trials against simulated submarine targets, which suggests that they may have been intended for use against the German 'U'-cruisers', but just how is unclear. The 'Ms' were successful in their way, because apart from having a single 40-ton 12-inch gun they were conventional in design, being based on the 'J' Class. Special tactics were evolved for them, known as the 'dip-chick' method of diving, whereby the submarine blew tanks and popped up to the surface, fired a single 850-pound shell at the target, and then went down again, all within 30 seconds! It must have been an impressive sight but no photographs have survived.

A much more interesting development was the 'R' Class, an *antisubmarine* submarine, or as it would be known today, a hunter-killer. They bore a remarkable resemblance to modern submarines as they were fully streamlined and had no deck-gun. An extra-large battery gave them a speed of 14–15 knots underwater, and a single shaft and large rudders gave maximum maneuverability, but as they lacked a good detection device other than the hydrophone, they were to a certain extent 'blind.' Notwithstanding this limitation one of the class claimed a hit on a U-Boat in the Irish Sea in October 1918 but the torpedo failed to explode.

*Above: The British 'R' Class were 30 years ahead of their time, hunter-killers capable of nearly 15 knots underwater.*

*Above right:* L.56, *with two 4-inch guns and six 21-inch torpedo tubes, marked the ultimate expansion of the pre-war 'E' design.*

Apart from these aberrations British submarine developments were logical and safe. The 'E' Class was built in large numbers and was then followed by an improved version known as the 'L' Class. Other classes showed little fundamental variation from the proven formula, although the 'G' Class introduced the 21-inch torpedo to submarines at last. The successful 'H' Class was purchased from America and was developed into a British version. Soon after the outbreak of war the head of Bethlehem Steel, Charles M Schwab, offered to sell the Admiralty a large amount of war equipment, including 10 submarines built to a Holland design. To evade the neutrality laws they were to be delivered unarmed in Canadian waters, and they could then be armed. Material was also to be supplied to Canadian Vickers at Montreal to allow them to build 10 more.

The hands of the State Department were not clean by any means, as a large number of undercover deals had gone through with official connivance, including the shipment of four twin 14-inch gun turrets and armor plates to England, but the submarine deal was too much to swallow. The US government stepped in

*Right: A 15cm (5.9-inch) gun aboard a surrendered 'U-Cruiser' in 1918.*

and forbade Bethlehem Steel to deliver the submarines; in April 1917 the embargo was lifted, but by this time the British had too many submarines, and so they offered them to Chile as part payment for other warships taken over in 1914. The Canadian-built 'H' Class crossed the Atlantic in 1915 (*H.5* established a record for the longest voyage by a submarine to date), and served successfully in the North Sea, Mediterranean and Dardanelles. The Holland Company had also sold the design to the Russians and Italians. Several were delivered to Russia

in 1916; they were known as the 'AG' Class (AG = American Holland in Russian), but after the Revolution the remainder became the American 'H' Class. The Italian boats served successfully until the outbreak of World War II. One British boat was interned in Dutch territorial waters in World War I, and as the Canadian Navy was given two in 1919 the class served in seven different navies.

The success of the German UC-Boats in mid-1915 inspired the British to convert some of the 'E' Class for minelaying, and much useful knowledge was gained

when *UC.5* ran aground on Shipwash Sand on the east coast in April 1916. It was too difficult to alter a submarine under construction and so there was no question of adopting the German idea of mine-chutes inside the pressure hull. However, it was possible to put mine-chutes into the saddle tanks. To compensate for the extra weight the two broadside 18-inch torpedo-tubes were omitted, and the ballast tanks had to be altered to include compensating gear which allowed in the exact weight of water to match that of the mines as they left the chutes. Eight chutes on each side carried two mines vertically, 32 mines in all. Some 'L' Class were also partially equipped as minelayers, and both classes laid many fields in the North Sea.

## The Baltic Campaign

If British sumbarine operations in the North Sea were humdrum the same could not be said about the Baltic, where they equalled their achievements in the Sea of Marmora. The situation was similar to that in the Dardanelles: Russia was under pressure from the German Navy as well as on land, and any diversionary effort by the Royal Navy would take some of the strain off. In October 1914, therefore, two 'E' Class submarines left their east coast base bound for the Baltic via the Kattegat.

Very little was known about conditions in the Baltic, apart from the fact that it was shallow, likely to be crawling with German patrols and certain to be thickly sown with minefields. Their port

of destination was Libau (now Liepaja) but when the two boats arrived they found a scene of utter confusion. The Russians were blowing up ammunition and port installations before evacuating Libau in the face of the advancing German armies. The submarines were given a new base at Lapvik in the Gulf of Finland, and here they were able to repair the minor damage and wear and tear before getting down to business.

The western Baltic had been virtually a German lake, and it was used for training by the High Seas Fleet. The captain of *E.1*, Lieutenant-Commander Laurence, had already shattered this seclusion during his passage through the Kattegat, when he fired at but missed the cruiser *Viktoria Luise*. Lieutenant-Commander Max Horton in *E.9* was more successful when he sank the destroyer *S.120* off Kiel. What shook the Germans was the fact that the attack took place in the depth of winter, when ships were normally iced-in. Horton's only worry had been that his inlet valves might freeze and so prevent him from diving, and once he found that this did not happen he asked the Russians for an ice-breaker to open a passage from Lapvik to the open sea.

German warships were not the prime target for the two submarines, but rather the merchant ships carrying iron ore from Sweden. The Germans were soon convinced that a whole flotilla of boats was operating, and even convinced themselves that a mysterious depot ship was operating in the western Baltic. On one occasion the ominous phrase, 'Horton's Sea' was used by a German naval officer, an indication of the extraordinary dominance achieved by two men, their devoted crews and, it should be remembered, two reliable boats. Eventually the authorities in London realized that the burden was resting on the shoulders of too few people and in August 1915 the first of four reinforcements arrived. Unfortunately one of the boats, the unlucky *E.13*, ran aground off the Danish coast and was hunted down by German destroyers, but *E.8*, *E.18* and *E.19* arrived safely at Lapvik. In addition four of the old 'C' Class were sent as deck-cargo to Arkhangelsk, and then by canal barge and rail all the way down to Lapvik, where they were reassembled.

By October 1915 the nine British submarines were ready to resume the offensive, and with the help of the Russian submarines they inflicted heavy losses. However, the Germans' successes on land were undermining Russian morale and after the Menshevik or 'February'

*Left: Minelayers of the* UC.119 *Class being scrapped in Germany to comply with the surrender terms.*

*Above:* UC.94 *at Gibraltar, after being ceded to the Italian Navy as reparations after the end of World War I.*

Revolution in March 1917 the efficiency of the base support at Lapvik declined steadily. The October Revolution was the final straw, for when the Bolsheviks signed the Treaty of Brest-Litovsk they agreed to surrender the British submarines to the Germans. This the British would not allow at any price, and on 8 April 1918 one of the few Russian ships which was still 'friendly' (fortunately it

was an icebreaker) forced a passage to allow the seven survivors to reach the open sea. By this time the submarines were based at Helsingfors (now Helsinki) and once they reached deep water scuttling charges were detonated. The crews were evacuated through north Russia, but the senior officer, Commander Cromie, remained behind to look after British naval interests. He was later shot while trying to prevent a mob of looters from entering the British Embassy in Petrograd (now Leningrad) but he left behind a remarkable record of endeavor.

### Russian Submarines

Like her surface fleet Russia's submarine forces had been divided between four oceans, 19 boats in the Baltic, one in the Arctic, eight in the Black Sea but the small force at Vladivostok had been withdrawn. The outbreak of war caught the Russian Navy in the middle of an enormous program to replace the losses of the Russo–Japanese War, but submarines came low in the list of priorities. A lot of submarines were planned, but in most cases the motors had been ordered in Germany and were not delivered.

She differed completely from the later German and British minelayers in having a horizontal mine-deck with discharge-ports at the stern. The mines and sinkers were stowed in cylindrical cases which were winched aft by means of a ratchet and chain, a method which was not adopted by other navies for another 20 years. The *Krab* had plenty of teething troubles but she had an active career in the Black Sea and her minefields claimed a number of victims. Two other submarines, the *Ers* and *Forel* were altered during construction to minelayers along the same lines.

The big Lake submarines of the *Alligator* Class had an extremely heavy torpedo armament by the standards of the day, two internal tubes, twin revolving tubes in the casing and two drop-collars. Despite a reputation for unreliability the *Drakon* of this class carried out more patrols than any other Russian sub-

Because they were out of the main theater of operations their work was unglamorous but they had a few brushes with U-Boats. Like the British submarines they used initial class-letters followed by a number, and so to avoid confusion all American submarines on the European side of the Atlantic were temporarily given the prefix 'A'; thus *L.12* became *AL.12* to distinguish her from the British *L.12*.

By the end of World War I the submarine had undergone much the same sort of transformation as the aircraft. From being a rather quaint weapon of limited potential it blossomed into a most advanced and complex weapon of precision. Its special requirements acted as a

*Above:* U.126 *flying the White Ensign while being used for trials in 1920.*

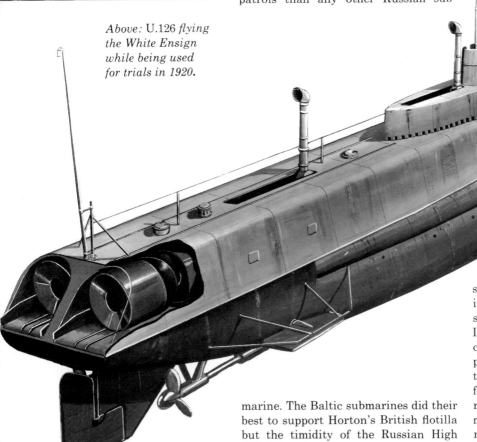

*Left: The Russian* Krab (1908) *was the first minelayer, but did not become operational until 1915.*

spur to industry to improve every item of its equipment, the diesel engine, the periscope and the torpedo to name only three. Its unexpected flexibility as a weapon changed the nature of sea warfare completely; in the Battle of Jutland in 1916 the British tactics were influenced by fear of submarine attack. The submarines' depredations among the world's merchant fleets in 1915–17 nearly bankrupted the British Empire, and certainly hastened its decline, but it had other side-effects. One of their saddest achievements was the virtual extinction of the sailing ship, many of which had been trading profitably in 1914. The blockade of Germany and the U-Boat campaign between them inflicted near-starvation and malnutrition on poor people in both countries, and even neutral Europe suffered from the widespread food shortage. Even today the ruthlessness of U-Boat warfare raises a shudder but in fairness we must admire the courage of the men who took their small submarines to sea in all weathers. Submarine warfare was and will be a mixture of bravery and utter ruthlessness.

In most technical matters the Russians lagged behind other navies, and most of their submarines were obsolescent. They still clung to the Drzewiecki drop-collar in preference to the internal torpedo-tube, but they had introduced a primitive form of schnorkel to reduce the risk of being swamped while running awash. In one way the Russians were ahead of all other navies, for they ordered the first submarine minelayer as early as 1908. This was the *Krab*, but as she did not appear until 1915 she did not make as much impact as the German UC-Boats.

marine. The Baltic submarines did their best to support Horton's British flotilla but the timidity of the Russian High Command did not encourage them. As the Revolution drew nearer the efficiency of the submarine force dwindled, but when British forces entered the Baltic in 1919 Soviet submarines proved once more that they could inflict losses when given the right leadership.

**American Submarines**
The United States had done little beyond improving the Holland designs year by year, apart from a few contracts given to the Lake Company. In 1917 the call from the Royal Navy was for escorts, but American submarines did cross the Atlantic to serve on antisubmarine patrols in the Irish Sea and off the Azores.

# BACK TO THE DRAWING BOARD

The Armistice in November 1918 reduced the fighting forces of the world in total, but as far as the submarine was concerned the end of World War I acted as a spur to development. The belligerent navies could not wait to get their hands on Germany's U-Boats to find out about the weapon which had so nearly defeated the combined industrial and maritime power of the United States and Great Britain.

The conditions of the Armistice included a provision about the surrender of U-Boats, and little more than a week later they began to arrive at Harwich, Gibraltar and other ports as far afield as Sevastopol. Others were immobilized in their home ports, and in a matter of a month or two the whole vast U-Boat force no longer existed. Then the squabbling began, because none of the Allies wanted to see any one country suddenly gain an advantage by getting the most powerful U-Boats. Finally the Peace Con-

ference agreed that the victors could make use of a limited number of U-Boats, but purely for research and trials, after which they had to be scrapped. Only France was able to wring a concession out of the other delegates; she claimed that her submarine building program had been halted in 1914 to release production for the Army, and claimed the right to increase her submarine strength with ex-German U-Boats. There was considerable truth in the French case and so it was agreed at Versailles that the French

Below: The ex-Norwegian U.A was built as A.5 but taken over by the German Navy in 1914.

Navy could retain 10 ex-German submarines. The Royal Navy was allocated no fewer than 105 U-Boat hulls, and ran several of them under the White Ensign during 1919–20; Italy was given 10, Japan seven, the United States six and gallant little Belgium two (the last were a purely political gesture of reparation).

All the progress made in submarine design between 1914 and 1918 was thus dispersed throughout the world's leading navies, although the largest submarine force of all disappeared and while the construction of battleships, cruisers and other surface warships slowed down almost to nothing as the war-weary nations reduced their armies and navies, work on submarine-design actually speeded up. However, in their zeal the designers copied the wrong ideas; despite the demonstrable failure of the cruiser-submarine with its cumbersome guns and its large and clumsy hull, it was cruiser-submarines that the world's navies began to develop. The Japanese and the Americans, both of whom had ambitions in the Pacific, grabbed U-cruisers and incorporated all the ideas into their own versions, the *UEII* type of 1918 being the most influential. The Americans, British, French, Italians and Japanese each had one of this type, *U.117*, *U.126*, *U.119*, *U.120* and *U.125* respectively. The Americans also had the 300-foot *U.140* which inspired the 'V-Series' boats, while the big minelaying boat *Argonaut* adopted the horizontal minelaying system of the *UEII* type. The Japanese modelled their *I.52* on the *UEII* although they copied the American example of building a separate class of minelayers, the *I.21* Class. The British kept very quite about their plans, and in total secrecy launched their biggest submarine yet, the 350-foot

*Right: The American* S.1 *with her floatplane inside its tubular hangar.*

*Below: The floatplane on* S.1's *after casing.*

*X.1.* She was modelled on the uncompleted *U.173* Class of U-cruisers, but had an exceptionally heavy armament of four 5.2-inch guns in two revolving enclosed shields. The Italians designed the large *Balilla* Class to incorporate wartime experience, but wisely kept the size and gun-armament down, in view of the special problems associated with operations in the Mediterranean.

## Aircraft-carrying Submarines

Not all the new ideas for submarines were useless. Early in the war submariners had realized how limited their field of vision was from a low conning tower. The introduction of convoys in 1917 made the problem of locating targets even worse, and after the war designers began to think of ways to give the submarine greater powers of reconnaissance. As early as January 1915 the German *U.12* had flown a small floatplane off the foredeck. The results of this ex-

periment are obscure, but the main purpose was almost certainly to provide better information about targets. Two other experiments in 1915 involving aircraft and submarines were for entirely different reasons. The Norwegian Navy used the submarine *A.4* and others to recover their Farman floatplanes by surfacing gently underneath them when they broke down. The British fitted out *E.22* with a sloping ramp over her after deck-casing to allow her to launch two Sopwith Baby floatplanes; their job was to shoot down Zeppelin airships over the Heligoland Bight. The idea was to compensate for the Baby's short endurance to taking it out to the operational area but in practice the aircraft was not fast enough to cope with a Zeppelin's rate of climb, and the risk to the submarine was too great. The idea of a watertight hangar had been considered earlier, but when *E.22* was sunk the whole project was shelved.

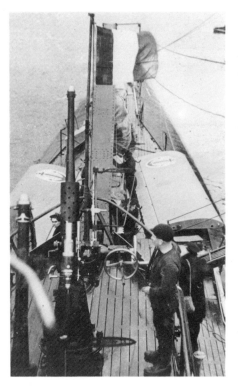

*Above, right and below: Three views of the giant French* Surcouf *at Portsmouth in 1940–41. The drydock picture gives an excellent impression of the size of the submarine while the method of assembling the floatplane is clearly shown right and below. The* Surcouf *also carried two 8-inch guns forward of the conning tower.*

By the end of the war the idea could be taken much further because the design of aircraft had improved so much. In 1923 the Americans designed a small seaplane which could fold down to stow inside a tubular hangar. The submarine *S.1* was chosen for experiments, and photographs show how the aircraft was dismantled to fit inside a very narrow hangar on the after casing. No catapult was provided, and so the aircraft had to taxi on the water before taking off. The obvious weakness of this method of launching aircraft was the length of time taken to open the hangar, extract the fuselage and wings, assemble the aircraft and hoist it out onto the water, to say nothing of the time taken to recover it. While all this was going on an enemy patrol vessel might catch sight of the submarine, and no submarine commander was likely to permit the launching of a seaplane in dangerous waters.

Realizing this weakness, the British decided that a catapult was necessary to speed up the launching process. The 12-inch gunned 'M' Class boats were by now regarded as mere curiosities and so

79

M.2 was chosen for conversion in 1925. She had the size to accommodate a large hangar, and the Parnall Aircraft Company designed a small floatplane known as the Peto. The hangar was box-shaped with a hinged door, and was positioned forward of the conning tower. The Peto was housed inside the hangar on the catapult-trolley with wings folded; the trolley was moved out to the foot of the ramp to allow the wings to be unfolded, and then the aircraft was launched. The whole operation took about 10 minutes, and to speed recovery a heavy crane-arm was mounted on the roof of the hangar.

The Americans did not pursue their experiments after the trials in S.1 although they did get as far as ordering four Martin Kitten aircraft, specially designed for taking off from a runway on deck. The tiny Kitten was unusual in having wingtip ailerons, and had a wheeled undercarriage, which meant that she would have to 'ditch' when her fuel ran out. Another disadvantage, one shared with the Peto, was an extremely cramped cockpit, which meant that aircrew were chosen as much for size as their skill. No Kitten ever flew from a submarine, but one of the four prototypes survives today at the US National Aerospace Museum.

The Japanese persevered with the aircraft-carrying submarine as they felt that the long-range scout plane was essential for all major warships in the vast areas of the Pacific. The 2200-ton I.5 was completed in 1932, basically a modified version of their big Jun-sen Type 1 cruiser-submarine. She had no catapult, and carried the parts of the floatplane in two separate tubular hangars, one on the port side of the conning tower and one to starboard. The decision had been taken to have no stowed item with a diameter greater than 6 meters, and so the fuselage and floats had to be carried in one tube and the wings in the other. This made the process of launching the aircraft so protracted that the next design, the Jun-sen Type 2 (I.5 was the Jun-sen Type IM) was given a catapult similar to the British M.2, except that it was on the after casing, facing aft.

It was left to the French to take the dubious logic of the cruiser-submarine to its limit. This was the 361-foot Surcouf,

which was begun in 1927 and completed seven years later. This monster had a designed surface radius of 10,000 miles at 10 knots, a seaplane and two 8-inch guns, the largest allowed under the 1922 Washington Naval Disarmament Treaty. The twin 8-inch turret guns could range to 30,000 yards with 30 degrees elevation, and a 12-meter range-finder gave her what was almost certainly the most lavish fire control of any submarine ever built. Her torpedo-armament was unusual too, four internal 55-cm tubes forward, four in an external training mount aft and four 40-cm torpedoes in another training mount. External training mounts in the deck-casing were a feature of French submarines of this period, although their drawback was that they could only be reloaded on the surface. The 40-cm (15.7-inch) torpedoes were designed to be used against merchant ships, and ran at 44 knots for only 1550 yards, whereas the 55-cm Model V were slower but had a range of about 11,000 yards.

## Return to Sanity

After the first hectic round of submarine-building was over the world's navies took stock, and with the exception of the Japanese and the French, all came to the conclusion that the super-submarine was not what was required. The medium-sized boat of 750–1500 tons offered much more maneuverability and still had sufficient internal space for fuel and armament.

*Below: Four views of the British M.2 launching her Peto floatplane in the late 1920s.*

Coastal submarines were still needed, but only for shallow or restricted waters which were not favorable to larger boats. Many of the smaller navies, interested solely in coastal defense, found the small submarine very suitable for their needs, but whatever the size of the navy very few found that they could dispense with submarines:

**Submarines in Service 1931**

|  | Large | Medium | Small |
|---|---|---|---|
| Argentina |  | 2 (+1) |  |
| Brazil |  | 1 | 3 |
| Chile |  | 3 | 6 |
| Denmark |  |  | 13 |
| Finland |  | (+3) |  |
| France | 2 (+1) | 33 (+17) | 45 (+10) |
| Great Britain | 1 (+1) | 36 (+5) | 15 (+4) |
| Italy |  | 27 (+11) | 18 (+17) |
| Japan | 17 (+5) | 24 | 26 |
| Norway |  |  | 9 |
| Peru |  |  | 4 |
| Poland |  | 3 |  |
| Portugal |  | (+2) | 3 |
| Russia |  | 4 (+31) | 14 |
| Rumania |  |  | 1 |
| Spain |  | 5 (+1) | 9 |
| Sweden |  | (+2) | 11 |
| Turkey |  | 2 | 2 |
| United States | 6 (+3) | 46 | 29 |
| Yugoslavia |  | 2 | 2 |
| Total | 26 (+10 building) | 188 (+82 building) | 233 (+31 building) |

The French had been the most reluctant of those who opposed the British move to ban submarines at the Washington Disarmament Conference. Far from wanting to limit submarine fleets, some senior French naval administrators had wanted massive expansion. The most outspoken critics took their cue from the post-war utterances of Admiral Sir Percy Scott and Lord Fisher to the effect that the submarine was the capital ship of the future. Admiral Daveluy was supported by the influential chairman of the Naval Estimates Committee, M de Kerguezec. In 1920 Kerguezec had startled the Chamber of Deputies by proposing that the surface fleet of battleships and cruisers should be replaced by a fleet of between 200 and 250 submarines.

The rebuttal of this extreme doctrine by the French Navy makes interesting reading; it was logical and entirely correct, both then and now. Apart from the obvious point that the submarine had recently suffered a massive defeat in a straightforward confrontation with surface warships, the apparent cheapness of submarines was illusory. On a ton-for-ton comparison the submarine was just as expensive as a battleship, and required a large number of highly skilled specialists to build, operate and maintain it. Furthermore, its complexity gave it much shorter effective life; most modern warships have a theoretical life span of 25–30 years, but a submarine is exceptional if she serves for 15 years. One problem peculiar to submarines is that once their equipment begins to wear out they become unsafe to dive, whereas surface warships can operate with elderly machinery and even relatively severe battle-damage. The French Navy rejected the idea, but recognized the need for a large

*Above: The French minelayer* Maurice Callot *(1921) could carry 21 mines in the after casing.*

*Right: The Soviet* Naradovolyetz (D.2) *in the Arctic. The 'D' or Dekabrist Class were the first boats designed after the Revolution.*

fleet of submarines. Two classes were started, a 1500-tonne or 1st Class type for ocean work, and a 600-tonne 2nd Class or coastal defense type.

The only departure from this was the provision for submarine minelayers. Between 1925 and 1930 the annual Naval Estimates allowed for one 761-ton minelayer. The six *Saphir* Class, all named after precious stones, used the so-called Normand-Fenaux minelaying system to lay 32 Sautter-Harlé mines. It was in fact remarkably similar to the saddle-tank wells used in the British 'E' Class in 1915; the mines were guided into each well by vertical rails and then secured by a stop. The depth of mooring was set mechanically from inside the pressure hull shortly before laying, and the mines were released by air pressure gear. As each mine dropped clear automatic compensating gear took on extra ballast. The Sautter-Harlé mine weighed just over a ton with its sinker, and contained 485 pounds of explosive. A further group of four of an enlarged design had just been started when war broke out in 1939, and with another 40 or more submarines they were either cancelled or destroyed in June 1940.

Although French submarines had problems, being rather too lightly built, some foreign navies bought French designs. Greece had six built in French yards between 1925 and 1928 and Yugoslavia had two. At about the same time Poland ordered three, the *Rys*, *Wilk* and *Zbik*. Although built to a Normand-Fenaux design and fitted to lay 28 mines they did not have the same minelaying system as the French *Saphir* Class. Instead they laid their mines horizontally through stern traps, like the original Russian *Krab*.

**Soviet Rebuilds**

Not surprisingly Soviet submarine developments were non-existent for some years after the Revolution, as the work of rebuilding Russia's naval resources did not begin until 1922. Very few submarines had survived the vicissitudes of the two Revolutions of 1917, the British Intervention of 1919–20 and the Civil War which ended in 1921. There were only six in the Baltic, 18 in the Black Sea, eight in the Caspian and one in the White Sea.

The Germans proved helpful, and in 1926 they were asked to provide technical assistance in the design of new submarines. The first of a new class, the six 'D' or *Dekabrist* Class was ordered in 1927, using an Italian design as a basis, but they proved disappointing. So desperate were the Soviet submarine designers that the British *L.55* which had been sunk by Soviet surface ships during the Intervention, was raised in 1928 to see what could be learned from her. Not only was she recommissioned under the same number but a new class based on her design was started, known as the 'L' or *Leninets* Class. Other submarine designs were produced, of which

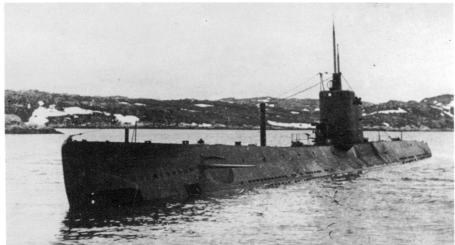

*Below: The Swedish* Uttern *and her sisters were designed in Germany in 1916 but built in Sweden in 1920–22.*

the most successful was the 'S' or *Stalinets* Class. These were based on plans for a UBIII Type supplied by the Germans and were originally known as the *Nemka* Type.

Coastal defense was seen as the primary role of the Red Fleet and so large numbers of medium and small submarines were built between 1930 and 1938. The best known of these were the very small 'M' or *Malyutki* Class, which were built in sections small enough to be transported by rail or canal barge. The 580-ton 'Shch' Class were more successful, and some 100 units were built. The largest pre-war design was the 'K' or 'Kreiser' (Cruiser) Class, also known as the *Katyusha* Type. They displaced 1390 tons on the surface and were armed with twelve 21-inch torpedo-tubes, two 100-mm and two 45-mm guns, and had a surface speed of 18 knots. As far as we know only 13 were completed by 1941, and most served in the Arctic. They represented Stalin's growing awareness of the need for an ocean-going navy, which had replaced an excessively Army-oriented strategy.

On the eve of what was to be called the Great Patriotic War the Red Fleet had 276 submarines in service and a further 21 building: 76 in the Baltic, 45 in the Arctic, 68 in the Black Sea and 87 in the Far East. The Baltic Fleet was in theory already on a war footing as it had been in action against the Finns in the Winter War of 1939–40, but some measure of its readiness can be gained from the fact that its 70-odd submarines sank only four merchant ships and a yacht.

84

## Scandinavian Submarines

The Scandinavian navies had collective experience going back to 1904, when Sweden launched her first boat, the 107-ton *Hajen*. She was a modification of a Holland design, but the next design was bought from the Italians. After World War I German designs were studied, and the Dutch were asked to provide detailed technical assistance. As we will see later, this was in fact German technical help rather than Dutch. The first truly indigenous design did not appear until 1934, when the *Sjölojonet* Class was ordered. These 580-ton boats had a number of unique features. The torpedo-tubes were disposed as follows: three bow tubes, (two over one), a stern tube and a twin rotating deck mount right aft. Instead of the conventional medium-caliber deck gun they had two single 40-mm Bofors antiaircraft guns, which folded down and disappeared into vertical wells at either end of the conning tower.

Norway bought her first submarine, the *A.1*, from Krupps in 1909 but reverted to a Holland Boat Company design for the next class, the six 'B' Class laid down in 1915. Denmark followed a different policy, buying her first submarine, the *Dykkeren*, from Italy in 1909 and then building three to an Austrian Whitehead design. These, known as the *Havfruen* Class were another variant of the Holland design, and their successors of the *Aegir* Class were similar. The first post-war design was the *Bellona* or 'C' class of three units, and these differed in many ways from their predecessors. The three

*Above: The Italian* Pietro Calvi *and other submarines firing a salute on the occasion of Hitler's visit to Naples in 1938.*

*Right: A flotilla of British 'H' Class boats lying at Fort Blockhouse in 1931.*

forward 18-inch torpedo-tubes were disposed vertically, with a swivelling stem-piece acting as a guard when the tubes were not required; another torpedo-tube was mounted on a training mount in the forward deck casing and the fifth fired aft at an upward angle.

The two *Dryaden* or 'D' Class completed in 1926–27 incorporated a number of ideas using German wartime experience. A new *Havmanden* Class was completed in the late 1930s, slightly smaller than the 'D' Class but with higher surface speed and the unusual armament of two deck-mounted 40-mm Bofors guns for defense against aircraft.

## Dutch Developments

The Royal Netherlands Navy bought its first boat from the Holland Company in 1905, but the next four were built in Holland to Whitehead's design. From the beginning they were known as *Onderzeeboote* and given numbers, but boats built to serve in the East Indies Marine had K-prefixes for 'Kolonien', with Roman numerals. Until the early 1930s the O-Boats were coastal types designed to operate in the shallow waters of the North Sea, whereas the K-boats were

the revival of the German Navy.

The ship model tank at Wageningen set up in 1932 was used to re-design the hull lines, achieving a significant increase in speed for a given horsepower. New welding techniques made it possible to weld 80 percent of the hull, and as this was lighter than riveting and gave a smooth external surface it contributed to speed and reduced underwater noise. Nor was this the only respect in which Dutch submarine-design was progressive; hydraulic control was adopted for the rudder, hydroplanes, Kingston valves, vents, periscopes, antiaircraft guns, hoists and even the capstans. The schnorkel (nostril) or air-mast was adopted to allow submarines to run at periscope depth on their diesels, but its main purpose was to improve ventilation, and its real potential was not yet realized.

The first of the new generation boats were O.19 and O.20 a pair of 896-ton minelayers started in 1936. They had the same arrangement of 40-mm Bofors antiaircraft guns in vertical wells already seen in the Swedish submarines of the *Sjölojonet* Class; although the Swedish submarines introduced the idea first it actually emanated from the fertile brain

and *Sep* in 1936–39. On a surface displacement of only 1000 tons they were to have no fewer than 12 torpedo-tubes, 20 knots' surface speed and a submerged endurance of 144 miles at 9 knots. These requirements proved quite a headache to the newly formed Netherland United Shipbuilding Bureaux (Nevesbu) consortium. At the last minute the Polish Navy had cold feet and told the Nevesbu design team that it could reduce the speed to 18 knots and cut the underwater endurance to 100 miles if the specifications could not be met. With a certain degree of wounded pride the Dutch designers announced that they had nearly finished the detailed design work *and* had met all the requirements. These remarkable submarines had four 21-inch torpedoes forward, four aft and two sets of twin tubes forward and aft in the deck-casing. The 4.1-inch (10.5-cm) gun was in an enclosed shield which formed an extension to the conning tower, and at the after end of the tower were two 40-mm Bofors guns on disappearing mountings. The two Sulzer 6QD diesels each developed 2370 brake horsepower at 450 revolutions per minute and the 550 shaft horsepower electric motors produced 9 knots at 265 revolu-

larger to give them greater endurance. In 1937 the K-numbers were dropped as the Dutch had decided to build larger submarines for home defense; from this stemmed the logical decision to make them interchangeable with the Indies flotilla. Dutch submarines compared well with those of bigger European navies and the shipyards were successful in winning export orders. An important factor in this was the expert German team under Dr Hans Techel, formerly of Krupp's Germania Works, which operated as a Dutch ship-design bureau from 1922 until

of Dr Techel. A total of 40 mines was carried in the saddle-tanks. The Dutch Navy used the French Normand-Fenaux system and the Sautter-Harlé mine. The O.21–27 were basically similar but without the mine-wells. Only two were complete in May 1940 but another two were towed to Britain to complete their fitting-out in mid-1940; the last three fell into German hands when German troops captured Rotterdam in May 1940.

Apart from two submarines for Turkey the only submarines built for a foreign navy by the Dutch were the Polish *Orzel*

tions. The two main batteries each had 100 cells, and were sited under the forward accommodation spaces. The diving depth was 263 feet (80 meters) and reloads were carried for the internal tubes, making 20 torpedoes in all.

**British Ideas**
After an experimental period of the early 1920s the British reverted to their previous well-tried formula of modest dimensions and performance. Under the 1923 Estimates the prototype of a new type of overseas patrol submarines was ordered.

Known originally as *O.1* but named *Oberon* before entering service to conform to a new policy of naming submarines, she was based on the 'J' Class of 1915. Like them she had a powerful long-range radio set, but with lower-powered diesel engines she was able to have two stern torpedo-tubes. In place of the clumsy beam tubes the bow salvo was increased to six tubes and an Asdic submarine sonic detection set was fitted to supplement the standard hydrophones. Two 38-foot periscopes were fitted, both $7\frac{1}{2}$ inches in diameter but one bi-focal and the other uni-focal.

One feature of the *Oberon*'s design was undesirable; to increase her range over previous boats larger-capacity oil fuel tanks were fitted in the saddle tanks out-side the pressure hull. As riveted seams were almost impossible to make oil-tight these fuel tanks always leaked, and a submerged submarine thus fitted left an oil slick on the surface which betrayed her position. But other technical faults revealed were corrected, and the 'O', 'P' and 'R' Classes built during the next few years proved reliable. What was more important was the fact that they could dive fast. British submarines of the inter-war period never featured the broad flat deck-casing so beloved of German, Italian, Japanese and American submarine designers, who were aiming for good surface handling characteristics. In contrast British boats had narrow casings, and with the oil fuel carried in the upper portion of the saddle tanks this reduced the diving time. The assumption always had to be made that British submarines would be operating under difficult conditions, hunting defended warships rather than merchantmen, close to the enemy's coastline rather than in mid-ocean, and so seakeeping characteristics took second place.

The third of the 'M' Class, *M.3*, was converted to a minelayer at the same time as the experiments began with *M.2*. But in place of the original vertical minelaying wells tried in 1915, she was given an enclosed mine-deck running for threequarters of her length. Along this deck ran double rails, and 100 mines on their sinkers could be winched aft and dropped over the stern, just as they would be from a surface minelayer. The benefit of this system was that far more mines could be carried than in the saddle tanks, and as the mine-deck was open to the sea or 'free-flooding' there was no need for weighty compensating gear. The experienced gained with *M.3* was incorporated into six *Porpoise* Class minelayers built between 1930 and 1939, each capable of laying 50 mines of the largest type.

The British had one final flirtation with the discredited idea of the fleet submarines in 1929, when they ordered the first of three 'River' Class boats with the high surface speed of 22 knots. Although technically a success in the sense that they reached a designed speed that was only matched by a few Japanese submarines they had the same disadvantage as the 'O' Class, leaky external fuel tanks. They did at least have good endurance, however, and might have proved useful in the Pacific had their high-speed diesels

*Above: The British fleet submarine* Thames *and her sisters were the first diesel-engined boats to exceed 22 knots.*

*Left: The launch of HMS* Perseus *at Barrow in May 1929.*

*Below: The early 'S' Class HMS* Sturgeon *had her 3-inch gun in a disappearing mounting but later the raised casing was removed. She is seen here in 1940.*

been more reliable. However, the most convincing argument against a 'fleet' submarine was the indisputable fact that battleship speeds had jumped from 21 knots to nearly 30 by the time HMS *Thames* was launched in 1932, making it impossible for any submarine to keep up with its own fleet, let alone pursue an enemy battleship on the surface.

At this point the RN called a halt. Clearly it was necessary to cure the nuisance of leaking fuel tanks, and at the same time the growing age of the numerous 'H' and 'L' Class boats which

formed the main strength of the Fleet called for a policy on replacement. It was decided to build two new standard types, a medium-sized 600-ton boat for the North Sea and Mediterranean waters and a 1000-ton boat for foreign stations. Henceforward modest performance and reliability were to be emphasized at the expense of maximum performance, and all fuel was to be carried internally. The first of the smaller type, the 'S' Class was laid down at the same time as the 'River' Class, and twelve had been ordered by 1935, when the first of the larger type, the

'T' Class was ordered. So successful were both classes that in 1939 they were put into immediate quantity production as the standard wartime designs.

The British shipbuilding industry was active in building submarines for foreign navies, and received orders from Chile, Portugal, Turkey and Yugoslavia. In 1936 Vickers-Armstrongs laid down two very unusual boats for Estonia, the *Kalev* and *Lembit*. Not only did they revert to the old 1915 system of vertical minelaying wells but they also had the disappearing antiaircraft gun mounting

peculiar to Dutch and Swedish submarines. The only difference was that the gun used was the Vickers 2-pounder pom-pom rather than the Swedish Bofors. In other respects they resembled the British 'S' Class, but without the heavy bow-salvo of six torpedo-tubes which was standard for RN boats.

## American Ideas

The Americans followed the British tendency to move away from the big cruiser-submarine after trying to take the idea to its limit. Like the British and Japanese

*Above: The USS* Porpoise *(SS.172) was one of the new generation of medium-sized boats which were developed into the outstanding World War II boats.*

*Below: The giant minelayer* Argonaut *(SM.1) was not a great success.*

they acceded to the 1930 London Naval Treaty and accepted a limit of a total of 52,700 tons. This meant that the size of any new submarines had to be kept down as far as possible but not at the expense of fighting qualities. Unlike the British the Americans had to go for larger boats to provide sufficient fuel to operate in the Pacific, while also adopting diesel-electric drive and, eventually, the six-tube bow salvo. Although an experimental pair of 800-ton boats, the *Mackerel* and *Marlin* were ordered in 1939, the standard boat which had evolved was the *Gar* (SS-206), 1475 tons on the surface, armed with six 21-inch torpedo-tubes forward and four aft, and capable of 20 knots on the surface.

A far-sighted diesel development programme was instituted in 1930, and by 1941 private manufacturers had produced a good fast-running but light diesel. The only problem for the US Navy was that it had completed an enormous program of inferior submarines four or five years after the end of World War I. Despite ruthless scrapping, in December 1941 there were still 64 of these obsolescent 'O', 'R' and 'S' Class boats left out of a total of 113 submarines. In this respect the British were luckier, for although their rate of building was lower and they had only 57 boats in service in 1939, only twelve of them were elderly.

## Japan Continues with Big Submarines

The Japanese showed no signs of being influenced by American thoughts, and each year produced more big submarines. Following the trend in their surface warship designs towards superiority over any possible foreign equivalent, Japanese submarines emphasized endurance and armament. The *I.9* or AI Class ordered under the 1937 Fleet Replenishment Law displaced 2900 tons on the surface, carried a floatplane, a 5.5-inch (14-cm) gun and six 21-inch torpedo-tubes, and had a theoretical range of 16,000 miles at 16 knots. They were intended to act as HQ submarines, to coordinate attacks of groups of other submarines, and carried long-range radio equipment. To complement these there were to be 2500-ton BI Type scouting submarines, also equipped with float-

planes, and CI Type attack submarines. Even these last submarines displaced 2500 tons on the surface, were armed with eight 21-inch tubes forward and had a nominal surface endurance of 14,000 miles.

It was not that the Imperial Japanese Navy neglected medium-sized submarines, either. It built these as well, the 1100-ton *RO-35* Class, which were ordered in 1940 to make good the deficiency in this type. They were rather small, but it is significant that Japanese submariners regarded them as the best design of all. The multiplicity of types did little to

help standardize design for mass-production in wartime, and one cannot avoid the conclusion that the Japanese Navy spent far too much time in exploring the fascinating characteristics of their super-submarines while forgetting that reliability and large numbers were the most important goals. A particular problem for the Japanese was that their big submarines proved slow to dive. They also tended to believe their own claims about performance. In the late 1920s *I.1* was

reported to have steamed 20,000 miles (her total endurance was said to be 24,400 miles) and dived to a depth of 260 feet but in 1943 interrogation of survivors from her crew showed that her actual endurance was only 17,000 miles and that her test diving depth was only 246 feet (75 meters); on wartime service she had dived to 294 feet (90 meters), but this was regarded as an exceptional effort made under stress of active service. The uninitiated may wonder how the Japanese managed to build so many submarines within their tonnage allowance under the 1930 London Naval Treaty. The answer was simple, they understated the tonnage; I.1, for example, had an announced standard surface displacement of 1970 tons, whereas it was actually 2135 tons in peacetime condition rising to 2170 tons in wartime.

The worst failure was in the realm of tactics and training, however, and this can be blamed on the Imperial Navy's 'Tsushima Complex.' Briefly, the traditional policy was to allow the more powerful enemy fleet to approach the Home Islands then ambush and annihilate it. This had worked against the Russians, and it was hoped that submarines and light surface forces would be able to whittle down the Americans' superiority to a point where the main Japanese battlefleet could fight on even terms. Implicit in this belief was the need to attack warships and to reconnoiter for other submarines and friendly surface forces. Unfortunately the need to attack warships transcended all else until the Japanese Submarine Arm came to believe that merchant ships were not worthwhile targets. The British also assumed that their submarines would have to attack warships, and designed them for the purpose, but only because they knew that their potential enemies would not be offering them many mercantile targets.

*Below: The Japanese I.68, later renumbered I.168, was the boat which sank the carrier USS* Yorktown *at Midway.*

## U-Boats Once More

No mention has been made of German submarine developments because all work on submarines ceased after the Armistice. The Treaty of Versailles prevented Germany from possessing submarines, so in theory no design work could go on, and all the expert knowledge gathered during four years of submarine warfare and massive building programs was dispersed. This cosy theory failed to take account of the fact that most Germans secretly despised the Versailles Treaty and its provisions as something dictated by the victors rather than negotiated. Anything that outwitted the Inter-Allied Disarmament Commission's inspectors and frustrated their intentions was winked at, and in any case the administrators of the Navy felt it their patriotic duty to preserve as much expert knowledge as possible against the day when it might be needed for Germany's defense.

In 1922 a German-financed 'Submarine Development Bureau' was formed in Holland under the cover-name of *Ingenieurskantoor voor Scheepsbouw* or Shipbuilding Engineering Office. In fact it employed Dr Hans Techel and other designers from the former U-Boat building yards. Its brief was to keep abreast of submarine developments and to prepare its own designs, using secret funds from the Reichsmarine. The bureau worked so well that its designs were accepted by

*Above: U.18 on a training cruise in 1937.*

*Below: U.25 and her sister U.26 were unsuccessful Type IA U-Boats, which were relegated to training duties in 1939.*

the Turkish and Finnish navies, and it began to negotiate for the building of a submarine in a Spanish yard in 1932. This boat was finally sold to Turkey as the *Gur*, but she had served her purpose. She was in fact the prototype of the seagoing class which was planned for the day when the German Navy would resume building submarines. Similarly the Finnish *Vesikko* was built by the German-controlled firm of Crichton-Vulcan at Turku as the prototype of a new coastal type. Much useful research on periscopes was done with Soviet help, in return for help with Soviet submarine designs.

The German naval staff drew up requirements for five different types: (1) a seagoing design of 500–700 tons equivalent to the UBIII class of 1917, (2) an ocean-going minelayer of 1000 tons comparable to the *U.71* of 1918, (3) a U-cruiser of about 1500 tons equivalent to the *U.117* of 1918, (4) a coastal boat of 250 tons similar to the UBII type, and (5) a 500-ton coastal minelaying boat comparable to the UCIII type. By November 1934, with Adolf Hitler installed as Chancellor and fully in agreement with the secret plans of his service chiefs, the German Navy was ready to go into submarine production. Enough material had been secretly bought in Spain, Holland and Finland to start work on 10 hulls. Hitler asked Grossadmiral Raeder, the man who had planned the rebirth of the Kriegsmarine for many years, to wait until the official denunciation and abrogation of the Versailles Treaty the following spring.

Once the go-ahead was given by Hitler progress was rapid, and before the end of 1935 24 U-Boats, *U.1–24*, were under construction. To the British and French Admiralties it must have seemed as if the field sown with dragon's teeth had begun to sprout armed men, although the British Naval Intelligence Division had obtained copies of the plans of the Finnish *Vesikko* in 1933, and knew that new and powerful German U-Boats were planned. In fact the first U-Boats to be built were the Type II coastal submarines, and these proved to be more useful for training than for operational use. The Type I boats, *U.25* and *U.26* were clumsy and poor seaboats, and the design was not continued. Instead a smaller version based on the Finnish *Vetehinen*, the 745 ton Type VII was chosen to meet the need for a seagoing class. The ocean-going type was called Type IX, and was based on the World War I *U.81* Class, but used an important feature of the *U.117* Class, reload torpedoes stowed externally. The requirement for a big cruiser-submarine was dropped in 1939, but the much larger Type X minelayers were substituted for the smaller coastal minelayers originally planned. Like the Japanese the Germans understated the standard tonnage in order to squeeze more boats out of the total tonnage allowed by the Anglo-German Naval Agreement of 1935. As an example, the original Type VII was announced as 626 tons, whereas its true surface displacement was 745 tons.

By the outbreak of war the U-Boat Arm under Admiral Karl Dönitz had achieved a total of 65 boats, made up as follows:

| | |
|---|---|
| *U.1–6* | Type IIA |
| *U.7–24* | Type IIB |
| *U.25–26* | Type IA |
| *U.27–36* | Type VIIA |
| *U.37–44* | Type IXA |
| *U.45–55* | Type VIIB |
| *U.56–63* | Type IIC |
| *U.64–65* | Type IXB |

In August 1939 there were 56 boats in commission, including *U.18* which had already been sunk in a collision with a torpedo-boat in 1936. Five boats (*U.44*, *U.49–50* and *U.54–55*) were nearly ready and *U.56–65* were still fitting out. Once again the world was on the brink of war, but this time the submarine was to be even more deadly than it had been 20 years before.

# HAPPY TIME
# FOR THE U-BOATS

When World War II began in September 1939 both British and German submarines were already at their war stations. The Royal Navy had eight boats based at Dundee, six at Blyth, and a further 16 on training duties, in addition to a pair of old boats being brought forward from reserve, five in the Mediterranean and 15 in the Far East. The Germans had sent 21 U-Boats to sea with the pocket battleship *Deutschland* and *Graf Spee* during August. Their boats were based on Kiel (25 boats divided between four flotillas), 17 boats in two flotillas at Wilhelmshaven and 12 boats for training at Neustadt. The French Navy's *Divisions des Sous-marins* (DSM) had also alerted its flotillas; apart from submarines abroad there were 28 boats based on Toulon, 17 at Bizerta and 12 at Casablanca.

## The North Sea and Western Approaches 1939–41

Both sides were wary, and the Germans in particular had strict orders not to deviate from the Prize Regulations, an international protocol signed several years before in a well-meaning attempt to 'humanize' submarine warfare, or in other words to put the clock back to 1914. Under these regulations submarines were not allowed to sink merchant ships at sight unless they were in convoy or under escort. All other vessels, even if defensively armed had to be stopped,

*Above: Admiral Dönitz (second left) and the bearded Kapitänleutnant Lemp whose U.110 was captured in May 1941. The capture gave important help to British intelligence.*

*Right: The Type VIIB U.101 seen early in World War II.*

boarded and examined to see if they were carrying contraband. It may seem mildly quixotic of Hitler to insist on the observance of such rules after violating almost every other rule of international law but he was well aware of how important it was to give American opinion no opportunity to turn against Germany.

The results were ludicrous, all the more so because the chief beneficiaries of this policy, the British, did not even expect it to be followed. British Merchant Navy captains had been instructed to the effect that a 'sink at sight' policy would be followed immediately, and were told to ignore the Prize Regulations. Yet most U-Boat captains made an effort to carry out their orders. When Kapitänleutnant Lemp, in *U.30* identified the liner *Athenia* wrongly as a troopship he reported his mistake to Admiral Dönitz, who promptly threatened him with a court martial. Unfortunately the Propaganda Ministry then took a hand, accusing the Royal Navy and Winston Churchill of sabotaging the *Athenia* to discredit Germany, and to support this story the U-Boat's logbook and other material evidence was suppressed. Some commanders, like Herbert Schultze in *U.48* went so far as to send messages in clear' to the British to give them positions of lifeboats.

Even when the U-Boats were restrained in their attacks on Allied shipping they sank 114 ships totalling 421,156 tons between 3 September and 31 December 1939. The Prize Regulations were held not to apply in the North Sea from the end of September, and on 2 October U-Boats were given permission to attack any ship sailing without lights off either the British or French coasts. On 4 October the exemption from the Prize Regulations was extended to longitude 15 degrees West and two weeks later U-Boats were given permission to attack all ships – identified as hostile. The last prohibition, forbidding attacks on liners was removed on 17 November and unrestricted submarine warfare was back.

The most spectacular U-Boat successes were, however, against warships in these first weeks of the war. On 12 September *U.29* sank the aircraft carrier HMS *Courageous* which was ironically on antisubmarine patrol in the Western Approaches. A large, fast warship is not an easy target for any submarine, and Kapitänleutnant Schuhart had to wait nearly two hours before the carrier turned into wind to allow her aircraft to land. Had the *Courageous* not detached two of her four destroyers to help a sinking merchant ship *U.29* might still have been frustrated in her attack, but Schuhart was too skilled a submariner to let the chance slip, and at 1950 hours three torpedoes tore into the ship and sent her down with the loss of more than 500 men.

*Above: Kapitänleutnant Günther Prien enjoying his brief career as a U-Boat ace. His U.47 was sunk on 7 March 1941 during a convoy battle.*

Two days later the new carrier *Ark Royal* had a lucky escape west of the Hebrides, when she was missed by torpedoes which passed astern. This time the destroyers detected *U.39* on Asdic and sank her with depth charges, but it was clear to the Admiralty that big fleet carriers could not be hazarded on such dangerous work, and they were withdrawn.

Exactly a month later Günther Prien in *U.47* achieved one of the most outstanding submarine exploits of all time. Knowing from aerial reconnaissance

that 20 years of fierce currents and winter gales had opened gaps between the blockships which had been sunk in Kirk Sound, one of the eastern entrances to Scapa Flow, the U-Boat Command gave permission for an attempt to penetrate the defences. Only two attempts had been made to penetrate the vast anchorage in World War I and both had ended disastrously, so when Prien took *U.47* in on the night of 13 October he was undertaking a mission fraught with danger. His courage was rewarded and after hearing the mooring chains of the blockships rumbling along his U-Boat's sides and touching bottom once, he found himself in the Flow. The main anchorage was empty because most of the Home Fleet was no longer there, but to the north Prien found the old battleship *Royal Oak*. Because one torpedo-tube was faulty he could only fire a bow salvo of three torpedoes, and he was mortified to hear only a small explosion. This explosion was so slight that people aboard the battleship thought it was either a collision or an internal explosion; it may have been a partially 'dud' warhead. Prien turned south to fire his stern tube at the battleship but missed, and was forced to reload his three forward tubes. This time all three torpedoes ran true and exploded underneath the *Royal Oak*'s hull (they were fitted with magnetic pistols); 13 minutes later the 25-year-old veteran of the Battle of Jutland rolled over suddenly and sank, taking 833 officers and men with her.

The triumphant return of *U.47* to Kiel was a great tonic for Admiral Dönitz and his U-Boats. However elderly and out-of-date the *Royal Oak* might be, her loss was a blow to the Royal Navy's prestige and a reminder that the Home Fleet's main

| | U-Boats Sunk | Cause | U-Boats Completed | Total |
|---|---|---|---|---|
| Sept | U.39, U.27 | (E) | U.54, UA | 56−2+2 = 56 |
| Oct | U.12, U.40, U.16, U.42, U.45 | (M) (E) | — | 56+5 = 51 |
| Nov | U.35 | (E) | U.44, U.55 | 51−2+1 = 52 |
| Dec | U.36 | (S) | U.50, U.62, U.64 | 52−3+1 = 54 |
| Jan | U.55 / U.15 | (E&A/c) / (A) | U.63 | 64−1+2 = 53 |
| Feb | U.41, U.33, U.53, U.63 | (E) | U.65 | 53−1+4 = 50 |
| March | U.31* / U.44 / U.54 | (A/c) / (E) / (M) | U.101, U.102 | 50−2+3 = 49 |
| April | U.50, U.49 / U.64 / U.1 / U.21 / U.22 | (E) / (A/c) / (S) / (I) / (A) | U.99, U.102 / U.120 | 49−3+6 = 46 |
| May | U.13 | (E) | U.100, U.121, U.123 | 46−3+1 = 48 |
| June | — | — | U.124, U.137, U.138 | 48−3 = 51 |

Key: (M) = Mine  (E) = Escort  (S) = Submarine  (A/c) = Aircraft  (A) = Accident  (I) = Interned in Norway  *U.31 – later salved

base was not properly protected. The Commander in Chief, Admiral Sir Charles Forbes, was forced to move his fleet to Loch Ewe on the west coast of Scotland, in precisely the same manner as Sir John Jellicoe had dispersed the Grand Fleet in 1914. Once again a single submarine had brought about a major shift of surface fleets and affected seriously the conduct of operations at sea. At a crucial moment the Home Fleet had to move away from its theater of operations and so leave the vital exit route to the Atlantic unguarded. However, the German Navy was in no better position to exploit its victory than it had been 25 years before, and the chance was lost again. Admiral Raeder had planned his surface fleet to act in conjunction with the U-Boats by disrupting the convoy system and so presenting them with a situation like that which had nearly brought about the collapse of the Allies in 1917. When Hitler precipitated war in 1939 the German Navy's plans were still four or five years from completion, and the small fleet of capital ships and cruisers was never big enough to achieve its aim.

The British suffered no such doctrinal doubts about convoy as they had in 1917, and the Admiralty had drawn up elaborate plans for the immediate convoying of merchant ships. All that was lacking was sufficient escorts, and to economize on warships for this purpose 'close' escort was not provided for convoys further west than 15 degrees. In coastal waters constant aircraft patrols were effective in keeping the U-Boats under control, and when the new coastal escorts or 'Flower' Class corvettes began to come into service in the spring of 1940 they proved very effective. To avoid this con-

*Above: The Polish* Wilk *alongside a British depot ship after her escape from the Baltic in September 1939.*

*Below: A further view of the* Wilk. *The boat's number (64N) and the background of the photograph have been deleted by the wartime censor. The* Wilk *was built in France.*

centration of countermeasures the U-Boats moved further west, and as a result the convoy escort limit had to be moved out to 17 degrees West in July, and again to 19 degrees West from October 1940. Similarly on the other side of the Atlantic the Canadians had to extend their convoy limit from 56 degrees to 53½ degrees West, but in between was the 'Black Gap', in which merchant ships had neither air nor surface escorts. But the U-Boats were still far from winning an outright victory because of their own shortage of numbers; many had to be retained for training, others were refitting between patrols, and sinkings by British antisubmarine forces were keeping abreast of new construction.

The respite gave the hard-pressed British and French navies time to develop their convoy organization and to complete and convert more escort vessels. In addition deep minefields were laid in the English Channel to block it to U-Boats and force them to use precious fuel and time on the northern passage to the Western Approaches. In the previous war the Dover Barrage had taken four years to perfect, but this time it worked completely; only one U-Boat got through and three others were mined in the first month.

British submarines were active in the North Sea, but the absence of major targets meant that they could do little more than watch or try to attack the occasional U-Boat on passage. The principal bases for these operations were Blyth and Dundee on the east coast, but in

October 1939 the Admiralty decided to concentrate the submarines temporarily at Rosyth so that they could be better defended against air attack. They were reinforced by two Polish boats, the *Wilk* and *Orzel* (see Chapter 4) which had escaped from the Baltic after the defeat of Poland. Another base was established at Harwich, using the new 3rd Flotilla, created from boats withdrawn from the Mediterranean.

The British flotillas got their chance for action with the opening of the Norwegian Campaign in April 1940. The British Government was anxious about the extent to which German ships were taking iron ore from Norwegian ports. Although the traffic itself was perfectly legal the German ore-ships were able to take full advantage of Norway's military weakness by infringing her neutrality in a number of minor ways. The British finally reached a decision to lay a 'declared' minefield (one whose area and extent were notified to all neutrals) as a retaliation for German breaches of Norwegian neutrality. This move coincided with Hitler's decision to occupy Norway to forestall the British invasion that he felt was inevitable. The result was that British and German naval forces encountered one another in a state of mutual ignorance and surprise.

98

The first intimation of what was afoot came when the Polish submarine *Orzel* sank the German transport *Rio de Janeiro* off Christiansand at noon on 8 April. Yet, although armed soldiers picked up by Norwegian craft admitted that they were on their way to occupy Bergen, and although the Admiralty had this news that evening, nothing was done to alert the 19 submarines in position to interfere with the landing. Even when the submarines were given the vital information they were at first hamstrung by the Prize Regulations similar to those which had hampered the U-Boats earlier. Even to the British Cabinet such hairsplitting was unacceptable; Allied submarines were given permission to sink transports on 9 April, and two days after that they were freed to attack any ship sighted up to 10 miles from the Norwegian coast.

The results were spectacular, for in less than a month 18 transports, tankers and other mercantile vessels were sunk, and the cruiser *Karlsruhe*, the gunnery training ship *Brummer* and *U.1*. In addition submarine-laid mines accounted for another 13 ships, and the 'pocket battleship' *Lutzow* was badly damaged by HMS *Spearfish*. The British losses were not unduly heavy, considering that nearly 100,000 tons of scarce German shipping

*Above: HMS* Severn *in a bleak Scottish anchorage. The 'River' Class were the last British attempt to build a fast submarine able to operate with the main surface fleet.*

had been sunk. The *Thistle* was torpedoed by *U.4*, the *Tarpon* and *Sterlet* were sunk by antisubmarine forces, and the minelayer *Seal* was forced to surrender after she had been damaged by one of her own mines while conducting a 'lay' in the Kattegat. In addition the *Unity* was sunk in collision.

To strengthen their force of submarine minelayers the British Admiralty had asked the French Navy to lend three of its *Saphir* Class before the opening of the Norwegian Campaign. After some discussion only one, the *Rubis* was offered, and she arrived at Harwich on 1 May. Under her commander, Lieutenant de Vaisseau Georges Capanier she laid 32 mines off Egersund on 10 May, and 32 again on 27 May near Haugesund. Twelve other French submarines were also serving in British waters, but unfortunately did not achieve any results. The '600-tonne' type *Doris* was sunk by *U.9* off the Dutch coast in May, however.

By comparison the U-Boats did not do well. The magnetic pistols for their G7a torpedoes were adversely affected by an unforseen change in the Earth's magnetism in the high latitudes off Norway, and so U-Boat commanders were robbed of a number of targets. Most of the U-Boats had been withdrawn from the Atlantic for the campaign, and so the resulting lull took the pressure off the Royal Navy at a crucial time, with nothing to compensate for it elsewhere. The scandal of the torpedoes touched off a searching enquiry into the design and manufacture of torpedoes, and the German Navy was able to eradicate the faults within a short time.

While the Germans were consolidating their gains in Norway their main armies were preparing to invade France and the Low Countries. As soon as news of the German invasion of Belgium was heard on 10 May the bulk of the Allied submarine force was withdrawn from Norway, leaving only the British *Severn* and *Clyde*, the Polish *Orzel* and the French *Rubis* to harass the Germans. All other submarines were redeployed to prevent German surface forces from making any incursion into the southern North Sea in support of their land forces. Although the situation on land quickly deteriorated the German Navy never made any attempt to move; in view of the Norwegian experience this was probably wise.

The fall of first Holland and then France meant that Dutch and French submarines fled to British ports. Strenuous efforts were made to get submarines out of Brest and Cherbourg, and in some cases submarines completing refits or even still under construction were towed away. In all the giant *Surcouf*, the 2nd Class *Minerve*, *Junon*, *Orion* and *Ondine*, the *Narval* and the incomplete *La Créole* reached England but under the armistice conditions agreed by Marshal Pétain French naval officers were ordered to take their ships back to France, where they would be kept out of German hands. Not unnaturally the British, having seen how valid German guarantees were, and knowing just how valuable the French Navy would be making good the deficiencies of the Kriegsmarine, doubted that the French would be allowed to keep their end of the bargain. After Dunkirk the British Government knew that it was fighting for survival, nothing less, and so felt that it dared not gamble once again on a written agreement. Accordingly on 3 July British personnel took over all French warships lying in British ports. The results varied according to the tact and personalities involved. At Dundee Commander Gambier was able to win over the commander and crew of the *Rubis*, and a similar peaceful transfer took place at Fort Blockhouse, Portsmouth, but at Plymouth there was resistance when the *Surcouf* was boarded, and blood was shed. One saving grace was

that the existence of General de Gaulle's Free French movement meant that French naval personnel could retain their uniforms and continue to serve in French warships; it is doubtful if anybody would have cooperated in handing over French warships to be incorporated into the Royal Navy.

Within hours of the fall of France Admiral Dönitz and his staff were ready with plans to exploit the situation. Road transport was commandeered to move heavy equipment such as air compressors and torpedoes from Germany down to the French Atlantic coast. From there, particularly Lorient, Brest and La Pallice, U-Boats could reach the densely crowded shipping routes in the Atlantic quickly, and so could spend more time on patrol. It was the most profound change in the naval situation, for the U-Boats had completely outflanked their opponents; added to this the British had lost the greater part of the French Navy and the large French mercantile marine. To compound their problems the Italians had entered the war as soon as the defeat of France was certain, and in August 1940 they made what they hoped was a significant contribution to the submarine war by setting up a submarine base at Bordeaux. Under the name BETASOM (From *Beta* = B for Bordeaux, and *Som*, an abbrevia-

*Above: Scenes of U-Boat life from the propaganda magazine* Signal *differed little from those taken for similar purposes during World War I.*

tion of Sommergibili) the Italians established a base that by the beginning of 1941 could support a total of 27 submarines.

The new distribution of U-Boats in the Atlantic comprised eight flotillas, all under Operation Area West:

| | |
|---|---|
| 1st U-Boat Flotilla | – Brest (formerly at Kiel) |
| 2nd U-Boat Flotilla | – La Rochelle (moved from Wilhelmshaven) |
| 3rd U-Boat Flotilla | – La Pallice (moved from Kiel) |
| 6th U-Boat Flotilla | – St Nazaire (moved from Danzig) |
| 7th U-Boat Flotilla | – Brest/St Nazaire (moved from Kiel) |
| 9th U-Boat Flotilla | – Brest (new flotilla) |
| 10th U-Boat Flotilla | – Lorient (new flotilla) |
| 12th U-Boat Flotilla | – Bordeaux (new flotilla) |

The other flotillas were distributed in Germany (4th and 5th) and Norway (11th and 13th).

Had the Italian submarines been better suited to Atlantic conditions their reinforcement of the U-Boats might have been decisive, but they achieved comparatively little. Operating mainly off the Azores, they sank about 1,000,000 tons of shipping between January 1941 and September 1943. This was an average of approximately 31,000 tons sunk by each of the 32 boats involved; by comparison the 14 Type IXB U-Boats which operated in roughly the same area sank 40 percent more. But the U-Boats also suffered from problems. The Type VII U-Boat was found to be on the small side for operating so far out into the Atlantic, and special 'milch-cow' U-tankers were designed, the Type XIV boats which could transfer 432 tons of diesel fuel and four spare torpedoes to other U-Boats at sea. Only 10 of these underwater supply vessels were completed in 1941–42, and as all were made the object of special attention by Allied antisubmarine forces they were all early losses. The big Type IX boats had the endurance, but their bulk and slow diving made them particularly vulnerable in the Western Approaches. They were mostly employed away from the main convoy routes, where

the Allied forces were less active. Many of their victims were unescorted. Largely because of this the IXB Class accounted for approximately 10 percent of the entire mercantile tonnage sunk by U-Boats.

Between June and November 1940 British and neutral shipping losses from U-Boats rose to 1,600,000 tons. This was the heyday of a new generation of 'ace' U-Boat commanders, men like Otto Kretschmer and Gunther Prien, who sank more than 200,000 tons apiece. Kretschmer in *U.99* was the leading exponent of a brilliant new tactic, the night attack on the surface. Taking advantage of her low silhouette and relatively high speed on her diesel motors, a U-Boat could actually penetrate the columns of a convoy of merchant ships undetected, from which position her commander could fire his torpedoes with impunity. The escort commanders were on the seaward flanks of the convoy, and unless an exceptionally alert lookout, watching in the least likely quarter, happened to spot the trimmed down conning tower, the

chances of detection were slim. The provision of radar sets was to spell the end of this practice, but in 1940 no convoy escort had a radar set, and the only answer was to provide artificial illuminating rockets known as 'Snowflakes', which could act like starshell and turn night into day.

Even the efforts of the 'aces' were not enough for Admiral Dönitz. Realizing that there would never be time to train a new generation of captains of the quality of Kretschmer, Frauenheim, Schepke and the others, he developed a concept which had been suggested over 20 years earlier by Commodore Bauer. This was the mass-attack or 'wolf-pack' idea (German *Rudeltaktik*), in which a force of 20 or more U-Boats could swamp a convoy's defenses. Briefly the sequence of a 'wolf-pack' attack would be as follows:

1. A 'pack' of U-Boats is disposed in a wide curve across the probable route of a convoy.
2. Any U-Boat sighting the convoy signals its course, speed and composition, as well as its own position to U-Boat HQ.
3. The U-Boat then shadows the convoy without attacking, and merely reports any change in course and speed.
4. U-Boat HQ orders all other U-Boats in the pack to make contact with U-Boat No. 1.
5. When all U-Boats have made contact with the shadower a co-ordinated attack from all sides is made on the convoy, after dark.
6. At daybreak the pack breaks off the attack, leaving one shadower to maintain contact, while the others recharge batteries and load fresh torpedoes etc.
7. At nightfall the pack renews its attack.

The wolf-pack system had the advantage that it made the best use of the newly trained and relatively inexperienced U-Boat commanders and crews, and inevitably it wrought havoc among the poorly escorted convoys of 1940. The new methods were introduced gradually between October 1940 and March 1941, but by then the British had in any case scored such success against the aces that it became obvious to Dönitz that pack-tactics were the only effective method he had left.

In March 1941 the escorts got Prien in *U.47*, and then Schepke in *U.100* and Kretschmer in *U.99*, all sunk while

*Above left: The Italian* Uarsciek *taking on torpedoes early in the war.*

*Left: The conning tower of the* Luigi Settembrini. *Italian submarines were noted for their luxuriously appointed conning towers.*

*Above: The radio room of a U-Boat with the famous Enigma cipher machine (bottom left). The three-rotor machine shown here was used by U-Boats until March 1943 when a more complex four-rotor was introduced. Codebreaking played a vital part in the war at sea.*

attacking convoys. It was a heavy blow to the U-Boat Arm, for these three men alone had sunk 111 ships totalling over half a million tons. They had fallen victim to the new weapons and techniques of convoy escort, for the British had introduced surface search radar, radio direction finding and a series of new weapons and tactics. There were two great weaknesses in the wolf-pack system. All depended on the shadower and communications between U-Boat HQ and the pack, and if any means could be discovered of hindering either of these the defenders could hold their own.

The simplest means of dealing with shadowers was to maintain an aircraft patrol astern of the convoy, as the U-Boat was forced to dive, and could therefore no longer keep up. The most urgent need was to provide air cover for convoys all the way across the Atlantic, but until the end of 1941 there were neither the aircraft nor the aircraft carriers to spare for this.

In mid-1941 the Admiralty began to convert an experimental 'escort carrier,' a small merchant ship with an extremporized wooden flight deck, but she was not ready until the end of the year. In 1917–18 Allied cryptographers had eavesdropped on the large volume of radio traffic between the U-Boats and their bases, but in 1940–41 German codes and cyphers were secure against this. However, the source could be located by a sufficiently sensitive high-frequency receiver. Unknown to the Germans, the British were successful in producing a set small enough to be fitted in a small warship; using it an escort could pinpoint the position of a U-Boat to within a quarter of a mile, and so escorts could drive off shadowers or even sink them.

When the corvette HMS *Orchis* went to sea in May 1941 with the first Type 271 surface warning radar set she was able to detect a conning tower at night at 2½ miles. This was the countermeasure which enabled escorts to deal with night attacks at last, and it was put into quantity production immediately. In May 1941 a British boarding party captured code-books and an Enigma cypher machine intact from *U.110* before she sank, probably the greatest intelligence 'pinch' of the war. Hitherto the German 'B-Dienst' or cryptographic service had enjoyed considerable success in locating convoys, but as soon as the secrets of the *U.110* haul were unravelled the advantage passed to the other side.

In 1941 a number of new antisubmarine weapons were introduced. At last an efficient aerial depth-charge was available, and ships were given extra-heavy depth-charges designed to sink faster. The standard Asdic set could not hold a submarine in its beam directly underneath the ship in which the set was mounted, and so contact was lost in the final moments of an attack. To remedy this the 'Hedgehog' ahead-throwing weapon was devised to hurl 24 small bombs in a pattern forward, while the escort still held the U-Boat in contact. Despite all these countermeasures 1941 saw the loss of more than 2,000,000 tons of shipping, or 432 ships. The British, even allowing for the neutral nations' shipping which was available, could not stand losses of this order. The German attack on the USSR in mid-1941 did little to ease the situation because the Soviets were in no position to offer any naval assistance or draw off any substantial number of U-Boats. All now depended on the Americans, who alone could provide the shipping to offset the huge losses inflicted by

the U-Boats.

The attitude of the United States had been pro-Allies right from the start of the war, but of course as a neutral she could not lend direct support to any belligerent. However, President Franklin Roosevelt was resolved to offer 'all aid short of war,' and had already lent the British 50 old destroyers for escort purposes in return for base-rights in British colonial possessions. The Lend-Lease Act was a fiction to allow war material to be made available 'on loan' to Britain, but however it might enrage Hitler his orders to Admiral Dönitz were to avoid provoking the Americans into a declaration of war. In September 1941 the US President went a step further and ordered the US Navy to escort American merchant ships bound for the British Isles to a mid-ocean

Meeting Point, and warships were given orders to attack any submarines which appeared to be attacking American ships. As the meeting point was near Iceland, where British escort vessels were based, it was not long before incidents occurred between U-Boats and American ships.

On 4 September the old destroyer USS *Greer* picked up a submarine contact on her Sonar (the USN equivalent of Asdic), and following current practice tracked and shadowed it without making an attack. However, the *Greer* was broadcasting in clear and soon a British shore-based aircraft arrived and dropped depth-charges. Under the impression that the *Greer* had attacked him the commander of *U.652* lost his patience, ignored his orders and fired a torpedo at the destroyer. Although it missed the *Greer*, she

went to action stations and counter-attacked, but without success. The next incident was on 16–17 October, when a U-Boat torpedoed the US destroyer *Kearny*, whose silhouette was very similar to the British escort destroyers operating in the area. The *Kearny* did not sink but the attack whipped up anti-German feeling to a new pitch. Worse was to follow, for on 31 October the old destroyer *Reuben James* was sunk, but still the United States was so reluctant to get involved in World War II that President Roosevelt could do nothing but express his indignation. For his part Hitler was adamant in his decision to avoid hostilities with America, and refused to lift the restrictions on the U-Boats. The undeclared war continued without further major incidents until the Japanese

*Above: A* Signal *picture of U-Boats setting out on a mission.*

*Right: HMS* Tuna *showing the flooding holes in the casing to prevent air being trapped.*

attack on Pearl Harbor on 7 December. On 9 December Hitler removed all restrictions on attacks against American shipping, and two days later declared war on the United States. The Battle of the Atlantic was about to enter an even fiercer stage.

## The Mediterranean 1940–43
It has already been described how the Italian Navy had built a large force of submarines before the outbreak of war,

and the Italian High Command or Supermarina had high hopes of denying the British the use of their main base, Malta. With some 90 submarines at their disposal and being very close to Malta, they should have been a decisive factor in the naval war but in fact it was the British submarines which took this honor from them.

When Italy declared war on France and Great Britain in June 1940 the British were in the process of reforming their submarine flotillas after withdrawing all but two submarines for training. With boats transferred from China it was possible to base six at Alexandria and six at Malta, but none could be spared for Gibraltar. Apart from two minelayers, the *Grampus* and the *Rorqual* the remainder were six 'O' and four 'P' Class, and they quickly showed that they were too large for the Mediterranean, apart from being cursed with leaking fuel tanks. Before the end of the first two weeks of operations the *Grampus*, the *Odin* and *Orpheus* were lost. Visibility in Mediterranean waters was so good that an aircraft could spot a submarine 50 feet down in calm weather, and the fact that the three boats lost had recently come from China could have meant that their captains had not yet learned how to cope with these difficult conditions.

The Italian lines of communication in the Mediterranean were vulnerable to submarine attack, and the dangers had to be taken into account if the British were to offset their numerical inferiority in surface ships. The targets were mainly the shipping carrying men and supplies to the North African colonies. But it was not until February 1941 that British submarines were allowed to attack all shipping at sight. In spite of this handicap and poor aerial reconnaissance the British submarine flotillas sank a number of transports and warships, for the loss of nine British boats and the French *Narval*. During the same period Italian submarines achieved very few successes, and sank no warships at all. The reasons for this failure were partly the transfer of most of the top Italian submarines to the BETASOM base in France and partly the design of the boats themselves, which were too large and clumsy for Mediterranean operations.

The British were able to replace their losses in 1941 with new submarines. The 'T' Class proved to be suitable for the Mediterranean despite being on the large side, but the new 500-ton 'U' Class were the most numerous. Three of this small coastal type had been ordered just before the war to replace the old 'H' Class for training antisubmarine forces. They were intended to be unarmed in this role, but common sense prevailed and they were given an armament of six bow torpedo-tubes, which meant that they could also train submariners, but the two external tubes were found to obscure vision through the periscope. In an effort to speed up submarine building in 1939 a further twelve 'Us' were ordered, and the last nine omitted the external tubes. Despite their limited radius of 4000 miles they were so handy in shallow waters that a further 34 were ordered, followed by a slightly improved version with a welded hull, the 22 'V' Class.

By mid-1941 the British submarine strength in the Mediterranean comprised 28 boats:

1st Flotilla – 5 'T' Class, 3 'R', 2 'P', 1 'O',
(Alexandria) *Cachalot*
10th Flotilla – 10 'U' Class
(Malta)
8th Flotilla – various boats working up for
(Gibraltar)   1st and 10th Flotillas etc.

In many ways the campaign now resembled the 1915 campaign in the Sea of Marmora, with the gun being used as much as the torpedo. Submarines were used to land raiding parties and to bombard shore targets such as trains. In the early part of the year British land forces were doing well against the Italians in North Africa, and the depredations of the Malta submarines added to the problems of the Regia Navale in escorting supply-convoys. However, when the Luftwaffe came to the rescue of the Italians they were able to make life much harder for British submarines. Aircraft minelaying caused losses, and heavy air attacks on Malta made it almost untenable as a base. Losses were heavy, but the Axis armies were seriously hampered by the attacks on their supply-lines. Between January and May 1941 the Germans and Italians lost 100,000 tons of shipping to submarines alone, nearly a third of their total losses to surface and air attack, mines and other causes. Between June and September they lost

*Above: HMS* Tribune *(76T) berthed alongside her sister* Trident *(52T). The depot ship is replenishing their fuel tanks.*

another 150,000 tons, but the total fell to half that figure between October and December, reflecting the reversal of British fortunes in the Mediterranean. The Italian merchant fleet was reduced by 30 percent in a year, a rate of decline which would eventually prove to be disastrous.

Until the fall of 1941 there were no U-Boats in the Mediterranean as Admiral Dönitz refused to allow any of his precious boats to be withdrawn from the Battle of the Atlantic. He rightly felt that the war would be won or lost in the Atlantic, and maintained that the Italians should be capable of looking after the Mediterranean by themselves. But the success of the British Mediterranean Fleet and the ceaseless harrying of convoys by the Malta submarines threatened to bring about the collapse of the Italians, and so Hitler over-ruled Dönitz. During September six U-Boats left the Biscay ports, and another four passed successfully through the Straits of Gibraltar in October. Dönitz was resigned to losing them permanently, for the eastward current and thermal layers in the Straits which made it relatively easy for a submarine to get into the Mediterranean made it correspondingly hazardous to get out again.

Not one of the U-Boats left the Mediterranean, for all were eventually hunted down, as Admiral Dönitz had foreseen, but they gave a good account of themselves. On 13 November *U.81* sank the famous aircraft carrier *Ark Royal* near Gibraltar and so robbed the Mediterranean Fleet of its only large carrier. On 25 November the battleship *Barham* was torpedoed three times by *U.331*, and blew up with the loss of 862 officers and men. As Admiral Cunningham ruefully commented, the British antisubmarine forces had become a little rusty as a result of only having to deal with Italian submarines, and the U-Boat had managed to get right through the Battle Fleet's destroyer-screen without being detected. HMS *Barham* was, incidentally, the only battleship to be sunk at sea by a submarine throughout World War II.

Although the U-Boats were sent to the Mediterranean to help the Italian Navy they were never put under the control of Supermarina. Italian training methods were considered too poor, and in any case relations between the two navies were never good enough to ensure maximum effectiveness. Even when the British seemed about to lose control of the central Mediterranean it was because of

*Above: A torpedo mechanic adjusts a G7e electric torpedo in a U-Boat at sea.*

*Left: Two seamen check valves in the control room of the Type IXB U.65, September 1940. The picture gives a good impression of the cramped conditions aboard submarines of this period.*

*Below: Lookouts scanning the horizon on a U-Boat operating in the south Atlantic. The spirals around the search and attack periscopes reduce the 'feather' of spray making it more difficult to sight.*

overwhelming air attack rather than submarine activity. By neutralizing Malta the Luftwaffe and Regia Aeronautica came nearer to victory than the Italian Navy ever did, and the handful of U-Boats achieved all that they could without much support.

British submarines suffered heavily in the summer of 1942, for they were operating in areas almost entirely dominated by hostile air power. Many were sunk and others were damaged in harbor. Malta's situation became so precarious that the submarines had to supply the garrison with such diverse stores as high octane gasoline, kerosene, machine-gun ammunition and glycol coolant for Spitfires. The use of submarines for this vital purpose had started in May 1941, and in some cases conversion involved the removal of one battery to provide more space. It was the big minelayers like the *Rorqual* which carried cargo most easily on their capacious mine-decks, but the *Clyde* carried 120 tons on one trip. All in all some 65,000 tons of supplies were landed by submarines before the crisis was over. Even so the submarines were forced to lie on the bottom of the harbor during daylight, and could only surface at night. However, every submarine engaged on supply-runs was a submarine not available for attacking Italian and German supply-ships. Nonetheless, it is

*Left: Type VIIC U-Boats under construction.*

*Below: Profile and plans of a Type VIIC U-Boat. Although highly successful, the design was rather too small for extended operations away from waters round the British Isles and it could not be stretched to accommodate new ideas.*

quite clear from the German records that submarines accounted for over half the tonnage of shipping sunk in the first half of 1942, and that those losses rose after Malta was relieved by the big 'Pedestal' convoy action in August and after the Battle of El Alamein brought much of the coast of North Africa under Allied control once more.

Between January and July 1942 Allied submarines sank 104,000 tons (38 ships) out of a total loss of 200,000 tons. From August to December the figure rose to 140,000 tons, and by the time Italy surrendered in September 1943, a further 346,000 tons had been sunk. The collapse of Italy meant the virtual end of the Mediterranean Campaign, although submarines continued to score successes

against small craft in the Adriatic and Aegean well into 1944. French submarines from the former Vichy-occupied North African bases were now operating with the Allies, and the *Casabianca* and *Curie* achieved considerable success. Their main job was to maintain standing patrols off Toulon, the last U-Boat base in the Western Mediterranean. Finally in November 1944 the bulk of the Mediterranean submarine force was recalled.

### The Arctic, Black Sea and Baltic
The invasion of the USSR in June 1941 extended the area of submarine operations, first to the Baltic because German naval units moved into the Gulf of Finland to cover the German Army's drive on Leningrad, and later to the Black Sea.

*Above: U.402, a Type VIIC slipped for overhaul in a French base.*

When the British began to run convoys of war material to Arkhangelsk and Murmansk, U-Boats were also sent to northern Norway to add to their woes.

The problem in the Baltic was that operations were circumscribed by the onset of winter but before the Gulf of Finland froze the five Finnish and five German U-Boats tried several times to attack Soviet ships. The Soviets had 76 submarines in the Baltic but German analysis of captured and intercepted information indicates that not a single boat was on station at the outbreak of war and only 25 were operational. The small coastal boats *M.78* and *M.94* were torpedoed by *U.144* and *U.149* in the early days and in 1942 the Finnish boats sank the *Okun*, *Pinsha* and *S.7*, while *U.584* sank *M.175*. In contrast, however, the Finns and Germans soon learned to respect Soviet antisubmarine tactics, despite the lack of Asdic in Soviet escorts.

The Soviets had 51 submarines in the Black Sea, but here the same situation prevailed: no fewer than 17 were trapped in the harbor at Sevastopol on 22 June 1941 by a minefield laid by German bombers. The Germans had no warships in the Black Sea, and their Rumanian allies had only seven destroyers and torpedo boats and a 10-year old Italian-built

108

submarine. The Germans quickly remedied the situation in the same way that they had taken U-Boats to the Mediterranean and the British had sent their 'C'-Class to the Baltic in 1915. Six of the small Type II boats, useful only for the shallow waters of the Black Sea, were stripped down to reduce their weight. Then, lashed on their sides on board road trailers, they were taken from Dresden to Regensburg on the autobahn, and then shipped down the Danube on giant pontoons to Constanza.

The six boats accounted for some 45,000 tons of Russian shipping. In August 1944 *U.9* was sunk at Constanza during a Soviet air raid, but the others survived until the advancing Soviet armies cut off their base. Two were scuttled at Constanza but the other three, like the British in the Baltic in 1918 were removed from the scene to prevent them falling into enemy hands; their crews scuttled them in Turkish waters and surrendered to be interned by Turkey. Italian midget submarines were also active in the Black Sea, and *CB-4* torpedoed *Shch-207* off the Crimea in August 1943.

The Arctic must surely be the worst area in the world for submarine operations. In the winter the seawater was

*Above: HMS* Snapper *returning from Norway on 19 April 1940 after sinking four German ships. British submarines scored many successes during the Norwegian campaign.*

*Right: HMS* Shark *ready to leave Dundee for a patrol in the Kattegat in April 1940. The marks on the photograph were made by the censor.*

often below freezing point, making diving extremely hazardous and life on board uncomfortable, and the bitter cold was dangerous to the boats, and the endless winter nights depressed their crews. In the summer the long hours of daylight were also dangerous because Allied escorts and aircraft were on the prowl. U-Boats did not sink many merchant ships in the Arctic by comparison with the Atlantic, partly because the weather conditions made attacks difficult and partly because the convoys were few but heavily defended. Their greatest success was against PQ-17 in 1942, when the ships were hunted down by U-Boats and aircraft after the convoy had scattered. Aircraft sank 14 ships and the U-Boats torpedoed 10, two-thirds of the total number which had left Iceland. One factor which helped submarines in the

Left: The Soviet 'M' Class coastal submarines were built in sections and transported by rail and canal barge to ports for assembly.

Right: The 600-ton Shcha or Shchuka Class were the first largely original Soviet design.

exploring the edge of the ice cap to see if possible convoy routes existed there.

Soviet submarines proved to be well-designed for Arctic conditions, with enclosed bridges and adequate heating. When the Germans blockaded the eastern Baltic 19 boats were sent by the Soviets through the White Sea Canal to reinforce the squadron in the White Sea. The big submarine K-21 was credited with torpedoing the battleship Tirpitz in July 1942 and thus preventing her from attacking convoy PQ-17. Despite the total absence of any mention of damage in the Tirpitz' War Diary or any other evidence the claim was maintained for many years, and K-21's damage was even said to have made the job of the British X-Craft easier in 1943!

The great value of submarines in the Arctic was for reconnaissance, and the other Allies did their utmost to assist the Soviets in reinforcing their Arctic or Northern Fleet. Four British submarines were transferred, the Sunfish, Unbroken, Unison and Ursula, being renamed B.1–4 and five Soviet boats were transferred in 1942 from the Pacific via the Panama Canal. Unfortunately a lurking Japanese submarine, the I.25, mistook L.16 for an American submarine and torpedoed her, but the others arrived safely in a British dockyard for a refit before going to Murmansk.

Soviet submarines achieved considerable success against the iron ore traffic from northern Norway to Germany. In

Below: The design of the 'S' or Stalinetz Class was worked out by German constructors in Holland and had much in common with the Type VIIA U-Boat.

Arctic was the existence of 'thermal layers,' caused by variations in the salinity of seawater; the differing density often reflected Asdic pulses and so 'hid' the U-Boat from a pursuing escort. The U-Boats were also used for reconnaissance, weather reporting and even for

the Black Sea patrols off the Bulgarian and Rumanian coasts proved costly, and 24 out of 63 submarines were sunk by the end of 1942. Of the 297 submarines ordered for the Soviet Navy before June 1941 over one-third became casualties, including submarines scuttled to avoid capture 18 were lost in the Arctic, 49 in the Baltic, 36 in the Black Sea and one in the Pacific. Precise details of the cause of loss is hard to establish as the Soviet authorities do not choose to make records of the Great Patriotic War freely available to foreign naval historians. However, the German intelligence records which fell into British and American hands in 1945 contain information gathered from interrogation of prisoners and analysis of radio traffic. The list can only be approximate, but it gives some idea of the heavy losses sustained by Soviet submarines. (See table below).

In the opinion of their British allies Soviet submarine crews were brave and well-disciplined, but inadequately trained. The massive expansion that had been started in the mid-1930s had produced hulls faster than the training schools could turn out personnel, and as Stalin's prewar purges had wiped out the heads of the training establishments this problem was still not cured in 1941. Observers noted, for example, that Soviet submarines were prone to maintain a faulty trim, with the result that they popped up to the surface immediately after firing a torpedo. With problems like these it is hardly surprising that the large submarine fleet did not realize anything like its potential for inflicting damage on the enemy. In the three main theaters of operations 128 merchant ships were sunk, 51 in the Baltic, 45 in the Arctic and 32 in the Black Sea. Their most notable success came in January 1945 when the Germans were evacuating troops and refugees from East Prussia in the face of the advancing Soviet armies. Soviet submarines sank the *Wilhelm Gustlov*, *General Steuben* and *Goya* with the loss of 15,000 lives, a terrible example of the havoc which submarines can inflict on unescorted shipping.

## Soviet Submarine Losses

| Cause | Baltic | Black Sea | Arctic | Pacific | Total Sunk |
|---|---|---|---|---|---|
| Mined | 19 | 7 | 8 | — | 34 |
| Escorts | 6 | 6 | 3 | — | 15 |
| Aircraft | 5 | 3 | 3 | — | 11 |
| Scuttled or not completed | 8 | 4 | — | — | 12 |
| Submarine | 4 | 3 | — | 1 | 8 |
| Artillery | 1 | — | — | — | 1 |
| Accident | — | 2 | — | — | 2 |
| Error | — | 2 | — | — | 2 |
| Unknown | 6 | 9 | 4 | — | 19 |
| | 49 | 36 | 18 | 1 | 104 |

# AMERICA COMES IN

Hitler's declaration of war on the United States in December 1941 came as no surprise to the U-Boat High Command for Admiral Dönitz and his staff had felt for some time that it was inevitable. Plans were ready for 'Operation Drumroll' or *Paukenschlag*, and by 25 December 1941, less than three weeks after Pearl Harbor six U-Boats were on their way across the Atlantic to attack coastal shipping off the US east coast.

The US Navy had been in close touch with the Royal Navy and all reports on antisubmarine tactics and equipment were available, yet the fierceness of *Paukenschlag* took the Americans completely by surprise and a total lack of preparedness led to the loss of 500 ships in the first six months. U-Boat commanders had referred to the period June–December 1940 as the 'happy time,' and now they rejoiced at the return of the happy time as they slaughtered ships sailing independently. Destroyers steamed in every direction on 'offensive' patrols, so regularly that they could be timed by the U-Boats, ships broadcast their positions in clear and shore lights gave the U-Boats easy navigational bearings. The US Navy had been suspicious of the efficacy of convoy, despite its deep involvement in the defeat of the U-Boat offensive in 1917–18, and some senior officers felt that the task of escorting a convoy plodding along at 10 knots was too humdrum. It might be right for the stolid British and Canadian character but it did not suit the more dashing American temperament, or so it was claimed. Attractive though this line of reasoning might be, it was totally wrong. Nor was it unique to the Americans; it had been used frequently between 1915 and 1917 by the British to convince themselves that convoy was too defensive a measure for a navy imbued with the Nelson spirit. More important, the developments of Sonar had not kept pace with the British Asdic, and in both tactics and equipment considerable leeway had to be made up quickly by the US Navy. Although the need for a special escort vessel had been foreseen, financial limitations had prevented the Navy from

*Right: On 3 June 1944* U.505 *surrendered to a US hunter-killer group led by the escort carrier* Guadalcanal. *A naval boarding party prepares to take the captured U-Boat in tow.*

placing any orders, but fortunately the British had already placed an order for destroyer-escorts (DEs) under Lend-Lease. The program was immediately expanded from 50 to 250 DEs, and it proved possible for the Royal Navy to transfer 25 Canadian-built corvettes as a temporary measure. The British had also designed a new escort vessel specially for the North Atlantic, the 'River' Class High Endurance Escort (later called the frigate), and an American copy was put into production. All these measures took time, and all the while the U-Boats were adding to their scores.

During 1942 the monthly average shipping loss was 650,000 tons, and in that year the U-Boats sank 6,000,000 tons. By December Admiral Dönitz had 212 U-Boats operational, and the war was entering a critical phase. In simple strategic terms the U-Boats could cut the

United States off from Great Britain and the Mediterranean, and so make it impossible for her to bring her vast resources to bear anywhere in the European Theater. If this had happened, and Dönitz estimated that a monthly average loss of 800,000 tons of shipping would do it, not even the wealth and industrial might of America would be of any use to her. She might have been able to deal with Japan in the Pacific, but her entire eastern seaboard would have been vulnerable to seaborne attack. Thus the Battle of the Atlantic came to mean much more than the survival of Great Britain; it was the decisive theater of the western half of World War II, and the victor in the Atlantic would win the war.

Fortunately there were several factors balancing the enormous losses of shipping. By mid-1942 the American shipyards were able to provide the first escort carriers, and in the fall the first Very Long Range (VLR) Liberator antisubmarine patrol aircraft came into service, and these measures did much to close the 'Black Gap' by providing continuous air cover to convoys. British shipyards were also beginning to turn out larger numbers of escort vessels, and it was possible to form the first support groups in September of that year. These were groups of well-trained escorts, usually destroyers and frigates or sloops, which operated independently of the convoys to break up concentrations of U-Boats and to harry them on passage on their

patrol area. If they sound suspiciously like the old discredited concept of offensive patrolling this is not so, for the support group supplemented the convoy system and was intended to reinforce any convoy that was hard-pressed, as well as hunting further afield. One of the drawbacks of convoying was that an escort which had detected a submarine was often forced to break off the attack prematurely in order to catch up with her convoy. The support group was free to spend hours or even days if needed on a lengthy hunt to destruction.

The climax of the Battle of the Atlantic might have come in the fall of 1942, for all the tactics and weaponry on both sides had been perfected. But political decisions at a high level resulted in the escort carriers and support groups being withdrawn to cover the Allied invasion of North Africa, 'Operation Torch.' The U-Boats were not slow to take advantage of this weakening of the Allied effort in the Atlantic but the effect was delayed by the winter weather, which hampered the U-Boats as much as it did the escorts. Furthermore in the first two months of 1943 the Germans encountered difficulty in locating convoys, due to the Admiralty's success in rerouting convoys to avoid wolf-packs whose position was known.

The first big battle was in March, when two groups of U-Boats tried unsuccessfully to trap convoy SC-121. In a battle lasting five days 13 ships were sunk,

despite the fact that the convoy slipped through the patrol line. Later that month, after the German B-Dienst cracked the current convoy cypher, Admiral Dönitz concentrated 40 U-Boats against the slow convoy SC-122 (52 ships) and the fast HX-229 (25 ships). Both convoys were heading eastward, and on 16 March they were about 120 miles apart with SC-122 ahead. HX-229 was the first to be attacked, and in a space of eight hours 12 ships were torpedoed, *U.338* managing to sink four ships with only five torpedoes. In a desperate attempt to fight off the ceaseless attacks the escorts ordered the two convoys to combine, but even so 140,000 tons of shipping was sunk, and only one U-Boat had been sunk by the escorts. A similar attempt was made against the next Halifax convoy, HX-230, but the weather was so bad that it lost only one straggler, while an American escort carrier helped SC-123 to pass through the gap in the U-Boats' patrol line by using her high-frequency direction-finding gear to locate the U-Boat which was transmitting the sighting reports.

The support groups which had been withdrawn for 'Operation Torch' were now being thrown back into the Battle of the Atlantic as fast as possible, and by the end of March there were five support groups and three escort carriers in the Western Approaches. They were just in time, for Admiral Dönitz had almost achieved his great dream of shattering the convoy system. After the disastrous battle around HX-229 and SC-122 the Admiralty nearly abandoned the convoy organization, for it seemed that the U-Boats had found the answer. Half a million tons of shipping was sunk in the first 20 days of March, far more than the Allied shipyards could make good if losses had continued at that level. But just as the U-Boats sensed that victory was within their grasp it eluded them, and they were overtaken by a stunning defeat.

The reasons behind this dramatic reversal were complex. In an attempt to cope with the growing weight of air attack the U-Boat Command had introduced a radar search-receiver, the Metox, which could detect radar pulses and so warn a U-Boat before the aircraft came into range. So much confidence was placed in the Metox that some U-Boats were even fitted as 'flak traps' with a heavy antiaircraft armament. Although the ruse was successful against the first unwary Sunderlands and Liberators which came in too close it was not long before aircraft took to circling just outside gun-range, while calling up the nearest support group. If the U-Boat tried to break off the action by diving the aircraft immediately switched to the attack.

116

In March a U-Boat reported that she had been attacked at night by a Wellington bomber, and that the Metox receiver had not recorded any radar emissions. It was this action which prompted the order to stay on the surface and 'fight it out' with enemy aircraft, but a month later came a whole series of night attacks which were undetected by the Metox. In response to urgent requests the scientists replied that there was no possibility of an Allied breakthrough in radar. A chance remark by a captured British navigator to the effect that the Metox receiver produced a signal which could be traced by Allied aircraft was sufficient to throw everybody off the scent. Convinced that the Metox was giving away the positions of the U-Boats, the Germans ordered all sets to be removed, whereas this offensive piece of equipment was simply incapable of detecting short waveband (10cm) radar pulses.

A similar error had been made in 1942, when U-Boat commanders had first reported that they were being attacked as soon as they started to transmit their sighting reports. Then they had been disbelieved because the scientists did not think that a high-frequency direction-finding set of such accuracy could be installed in a ship. But this time the lack of liaison between the Kriegsmarine and its scientists proved fatal, and U-Boat losses rose alarmingly.

**Shipping Losses and U-Boat Sinkings July 1942–June 1943:**

| Month | No. of ships | Tonnage | U-Boats sunk |
|---|---|---|---|
| 1942 | | | |
| July | 96 | 476,000 | 11 |
| August | 108 | 544,000 | 10 |
| September | 98 | 485,400 | 11 |
| October | 94 | 619,000 | 16 |
| November | 119 | 729,100 | 13 |
| December | 60 | 330,800 | 5 |
| 1943 | | | |
| January | 37 | 203,100 | 6 |
| February | 63 | 359,300 | 19 |
| March | 108 | 627,300 | 15 |
| April | 56 | 327,900 | 16 |
| May | 50 | 264,800 | 41 |
| June | 20 | 95,700 | 17 |

Above: The smoldering conning tower
of a U-Boat after it has been shelled by
the US Coast Guard cutter Spencer.

Defeat was conceded in late May when the U-Boats were ordered to withdraw for 'regrouping.' There was no disguising the fact that the U-Boat Arm had been shocked by the pounding it had received, and it was necessary to restore morale with new weapons and tactics before committing the U-Boats again. There was also the problem of U-Boat construction to consider, and Hitler and Admiral Dönitz met in a series of conferences to decide on naval policy. In April 1943 it was established that by the second half of the year production of Type VIIC boats would be increased to 27 per month, and that this rate could be maintained even if the more complex VIIC42 design was built. By 1945 it was hoped to increase production to 30 boats per month, but Dönitz reminded the Führer that the program was already using 4500 tons of steel per month for the hulls, and a further 1500 tons for torpedo-bodies.

In June the vexed problem of manpower was discussed, and Dönitz pointed out that even if 40 U-Boats could be delivered each month this would merely exacerbate the shortage of personnel. The current allocation was 102,984 men, whereas the requirements would be for 437,822 men, a shortfall of nearly 335,000. If 634 U-Boats were to be manned 62,000 men would be needed for their crews alone. The Admiral pointed out that since April 1942 the Army had received the major share of manpower, leaving the Kriegsmarine short of an estimated 200,000 men. The officer-candidates who had entered the Navy in the fall of 1939 were now becoming U-Boat commanders, and it would be necessary to transfer officers from the other two services. If the personnel were not found the U-Boat Arm could still function but at the cost of manning none of the new surface craft such as motor torpedo boats which were due to be completed and come into service after January 1944.

In July 1943 Dönitz made the first mention to Hitler of a startling new project, the so-called Electro-submarine. Known as the Type XXI, it was a fully streamlined boat with a novel 'figure-8' hull and enlarged battery-capacity to give it a much higher underwater speed. Another important feature of the design was the provision of automatic torpedo-reloading gear, which enabled a Type XXI boat to fire torpedoes rapidly at a series of targets, unlike the older boats which had to retire to reload, with each torpedo taking half-an-hour to load. This feature alone made the new submarine a lethal weapon against convoys, and Hitler demanded that the *Konstruktionsamt* should try to improve on the November 1944 delivery date for the first. Albert Speer was told to authorize three-shift working in the shipyards in order to get production up to 20 per month, and it was hoped that these new U-Boats would eventually win back the initiative from the Allies.

*Below: Too late. Type XXI U-Boat hulls on the stocks at the Blohm & Voss shipyard in Hamburg in May 1945 after the German surrender.*

*Above and right: Captured U-Boats lying at Lisahally in Northern Ireland late in 1945.*

*Above: Type XXI boats showing the streamlining of the conning tower.*

*Right: Two of the smaller and simpler Type XXIII.*

Another advanced design was in hand, the Walter turbine design known as the Type XVII. The Walter turbine burned enriched hydrogen-peroxide (see Chapter 7) and oil fuel with a catalyst to release sufficient oxygen (from the hydrogen peroxide compound), thus providing a 'closed cycle' to dispense with the need for outside oxygen. This provided very high underwater speed, 20 knots or more, because of the great heat produced during the decomposition of the hydrogen peroxide. The fuel was known as T-Stoff (abbreviation for Trieb-Stoff), Ingolin or Aurol, and proved both difficult and expensive to manufacture. The first catalysts were solutions of sodium permanganate and calcium permanganate (Z-Stoff-N and Z-Stoff-C), but these were replaced by solid catalysts, porous stones impregnated with permanganate. A small experimental boat, *V.80*, ran trials in 1940, and *U.791* (ex. *V.300*) was the first U-Boat to be fitted with a Walter

turbine for trials in 1942. The first production model was the Type XVIIB coastal boat displacing 312 tons, which needed 55 tons of Aurol to run at 21½ knots for 150 miles.

The Walter turbine boats must, however, be judged an aberration, despite their advanced technology. The German Navy was already badly behind in its submarine-building programs, despite all the efforts made in the shipyards, and the Walter boats rank with some of Hitler's tank projects as pipe-dreams which frittered away resources and delayed production of more useful equipment. There is no doubt that 50 Type XXI U-Boats in mid-1944 would have done more to redeem the situation than 200 Walter boats in 1945. To compound the error the shipyards were allowed to continue the construction of the now-obsolescent Type VIIC, and 'diluted' or mixed skilled and semi-skilled labor was used to build the highly complex Type XXI boats. Heavy Allied bombing of shipyards also held up production, and as a result only four Type XXI boats had been completed when Germany surrendered in May 1945. The first, *U.2511*, did not finish her training and work-up until the week before the surrender. A simplified version with a single hull, known as the Type XXIII was also built, and the small numbers of boats completed proved quite successful in British coastal waters but so few were available that they could not affect the outcome of the war.

The only other countermeasures that could be initiated in 1943 were the provision of new weapons and tactics. New acoustic torpedoes were introduced to allow U-Boats to attack escorts, but technical problems made them less dangerous than first thought.

*Right, all three:* Details of the schnorkel on U.889 *showing it raised and folded. The Germans experimented with a range of schnorkel fittings.*

In search for an answer to the danger from aircraft someone remembered the Dutch 'Schnorkel' device which had been installed in the submarines which had been captured in 1940. The first model fitted in the *O-25, O-26* and *O-27* (renumbered *UD.3–5* in the German Navy), was tested, and showed that a U-Boat could run her diesels submerged and thus recharge her batteries under water. The device was by no means perfect, and had to be modified by the Germans because the air induction pipe and the exhaust 10 feet below the surface created a clearly visible wake. This problem was successfully tackled. and the 'Schnorkel' device was soon made a standard fitting for U-Boats.

The schnorkel achieved its aim, but it made life extremely uncomfortable for U-Boat crews. In rough weather the valve shut constantly, and each time the diesels sucked in enough air to create a partial vacuum which made ears and eyes pop. It also had the effect of making the U-Boats 'keep their heads down' for longer periods, so that although they became harder to sink, in turn they sank fewer ships. But the U-Boats never gave up, and they remained dangerous right to the end. More than 32,000 officers and men out of a total of 39,000 died on active service. The balance sheet was grim:

| U-Boats built: | 1162 |
|---|---|
| U-Boats sunk: | 784 |
| Allied warships sunk: | 175* |
| Merchantmen sunk: | 2828* |
| Merchantmen sunk: | 14,687,231* (tons) |

*These figures include sinkings by Italian and Japanese submarines, but they form only a small part of the total.

No figures exist for the total number of merchant seamen lost, because the Allies' merchant fleets included vessels from so many neutral nations, but some idea of the scale of losses can be gauged from the fact that the British Merchant Navy alone lost 30,248 men in action.

On 7 May 1945 Admiral Dönitz, now the Führer as well as Commander in Chief of the German Navy, transmitted orders to all U-Boats to cease hostilities. For the second time in 30 years the U-Boats had failed in their bid to defeat the world's navies and were destined to finish their careers in enemy ports. Some refused to accept the surrender orders and scuttled themselves, while *U.977* went to South America to be interned rather than surrender, but the majority surfaced, hoisted the black distinguishing flag agreed with the Allies, and handed themselves over to the nearest warship to be escorted to port.

## Submarine Warfare in the Pacific

When the Japanese attacked the US Pacific Fleet at Pearl Harbor without warning on the morning of 7 December 1941, it was envisioned that submarines would play their part in supporting the aircraft carrier strike. The Submarine Force was to move to the vicinity of Hawaii in order to provide reconnaissance for the Carrier Striking Force and to attack any US warships which presented themselves. One unit was detailed to launch midget submarines against Pearl Harbor itself, but as we shall see the attack was unsuccessful and all were sunk.

The Japanese submarine fleet at the outbreak of war numbered about 75 operational units. A large construction program was in hand, with 18 boats to be ready by the end of 1942 and a further 11 to be ready by the end of 1943 as follows:

| Ready 1942 | Ready 1943 | Type |
|---|---|---|
| *I.27-36* | *I.37-39* | *I.15* Class |
| *I.176-178* | *I.179-182* | *I.176* Class |
| *RP.100-103* | *RO.104-105* | *RO.100* Class |
| *I.11* | — | *I.9* Class |
| — | *RO.35, RO.37* | *RO.35* Class |

A further 38 boats were to be started in 1942, six *I.16* Class, six *I.52*, six *I.54*, one more *I.9* Class, three more *I.176*, ten *RO.100* and 12 *RO.35* Class. The *I.15* boats were a scouting version of the *I.9* headquarters boats, and were equipped with floatplanes. The *I.176* Class (begun as the *I.76* Class but renumbered in May 1942) were 1800-ton fleet submarines armed with six torpedo-tubes and capable of 23 knots on the surface. The *RO.100* Class were much smaller, only 600 tons, and were ordered as replacements for the obsolescent medium-sized boats built at the end of the 1914–18 War. For the Pacific they were far too small, and could do little more than carry out short patrols in the vicinity of island bases. The *RO.35* Class were more successful as their larger size permitted more fuel to be carried. The *I.16* and *I.52* Classes were large fleet submarines, and the *I.54* another floatplane-carrying type.

By April 1942 the distribution of Japanese submarines was as follows:

| Combined Fleet | 5th Submarine Squadron: *I.56-59\*, I.62\*, I.64-66\** |
|---|---|
| 6th Fleet | 1st Submarine Squadron: *I.9, I.15, I.19, I.25-26* 2nd Submarine Squadron: *I.1-7* 3rd Submarine Squadron: *I.8, I.74-75\*, I.68-69\*, I.71-72\*, I.121-123* |
| 4th Fleet | 9th Submarine Squadron: *RO.33-34, RO.61-63, RO.67-68* |
| Kure District Force | *RO.31, I.52\** (training), *RO.53-55, RO.57-59, I.53-55\** |

*\*I.52-75 renumbered I.152-175 May 1942*

What was lacking was any real grasp of the importance of standardizing and streamlining production, such as the German, British and American navies had already achieved in their submarine programs. The Japanese High Command seemed to be unduly obsessed with the potential of their big boats, but whatever designs were chosen the shipyards were not able to build fast enough. The *RO.35* Class was intended to be a standard medium design, and the first was laid down in October 1941 and completed in March 1943, but 8 out of the 18 ordered were not completed until 1944. A large number of additional boats authorized in 1941 were cancelled in 1943, never having

been laid down. By comparison a typical American *Gato* Class boat, the *Barb* was laid down in June 1941 and completed a year later, and the British were taking 18 months to complete a 'T' Class boat.

### American Submarines

The US Navy had gone to the opposite extreme. Having developed their fleet submarines through a series of logical improvements to the 'T' and 'G' Classes of 1940–41, they were content to put the 'G' Class into quantity production as the *Gato* Class. Then when war experience dictated improvements the new *Balao* Class and their successors the *Tench* Class were kept as similar as possible.

Although only four builders undertook the construction of 73 *Gatos* they proved well able to meet the challenge. Two other yards had to take some of the burden when orders were placed for a total of 366 *Balao* and *Tench* Classes but this does nothing to diminish the remarkable achievement of 228 submarines completed in four and one-half years.

Unlike the Japanese the Americans had no chance to use their submarines in conjunction with the battle fleet. After Pearl Harbor there was no American battle fleet in the Pacific, and the submarines were the only units which could fight back. For a while the attack was blunted because of a high incidence of

*Below: I.58 displaced 2600 tons and was armed with one 5.5-inch gun, a twin 25mm AA gun, and six 21-inch torpedo tubes. She also carried a floatplane and a catapult.*

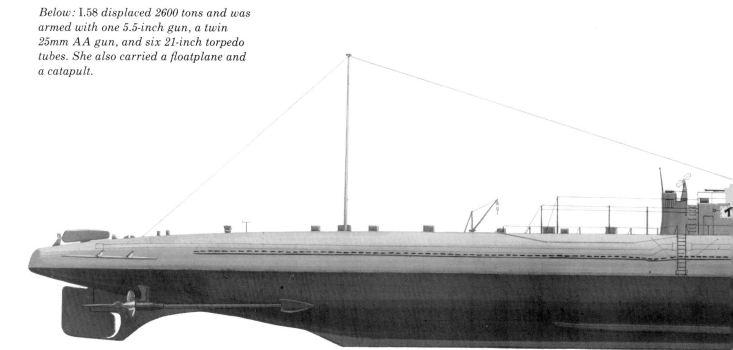

failures affecting the standard Mark 14 torpedo. In some cases the gyroscopes failed, and in others the warhead pistol failed to function, and until these problems were identified and cured the submarine offensive was only partially effective. Once an improved torpedo was available American submarines began to make enormous inroads into Japanese shipping.

Although American submarines did not hesitate to attack warships their cap-

tains were given instructions to concentrate on mercantile shipping, particularly oil tankers. The Japanese had carved a seaborne empire for themselves, and their large merchant fleet was needed to supply the garrisons in all the outlying islands. Furthermore Japan imported 20 percent of its food, 24 percent of its coal, 88 percent of its iron ore, and 90 percent of its oil. Unlike the British the Japanese Navy had not foreseen that this fragile structure could be so vulnerable to a concerted submarine attack, and had failed to devote any resources to antisubmarine warfare. As a result US submarines were not subjected to the full weight of countermeasures that were the lot of a U-Boat in the Atlantic or a British submarine in the Mediterranean. At the end of the war the Americans were amazed to learn that the Japanese claimed to have sunk 486 submarines. The actual losses were: 9 sunk by aircraft, 2 by gunfire, 17 or 18 sunk by depth-charges, 7 or 8 mined, and 23 by miscella-

neous causes such as grounding.

In 1943 American submarines first used 'wolf-pack' tactics against Japanese shipping. Because of the lack of convoying and the poor antisubmarine measures used by Japanese escorts there was no need for the large packs used by the Germans in the Atlantic, and the Americans found that groups of three submarines were suitable. Under such bizarre titles as 'Ben's Busters,' 'Donk's Devils,' 'Ed's Eradicators' and 'Laughlin's Loopers' the packs ranged far and wide across the Pacific in search of targets. Their names derived from the 'aces' who led them, and several boats like *Barb*, *Rasher*, *Silversides* and *Tang* sank over 90,000 tons of shipping. The highest scoring US submarine was USS *Tang* (*SS-306*), with 100,231 tons. By 1945 the Japanese had lost over 4,000,000 tons of shipping.

American submarines were usually able to attack on the surface at night, just as the U-Boats had in 1941 because, unlike the British escorts, the Japanese did not get radar sets until very late. Using their own radar the US submarines could choose their position for attacking, and dodged the escorts with ease. Some daring commanders were expert in the 'down-the-throat' shot, which involved firing a full salvo of six torpedoes at an attacking escort at close range.

As the Japanese came to rely more and more on small junks and coasters for shipping cargoes the big American boats found themselves short of targets but by early 1944 the British and Dutch had established three flotillas in the Far East. Although smaller and shorter on range the British and Dutch boats proved capable of operating within the 10-fathom line. Their most notable successes were the sinking of the cruisers

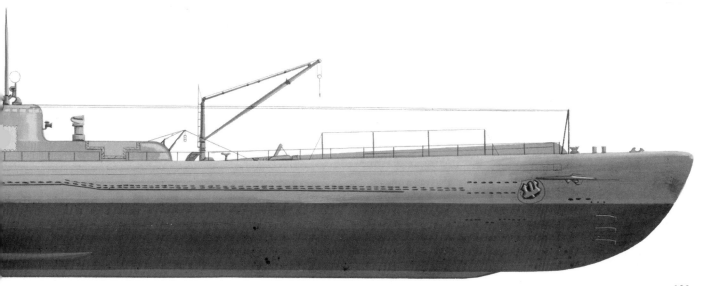

Kuma and Ashigara, but they also achieved the destruction of a large number of minor vessels.

The American submarines, in addition to their onslaught on merchant shipping, performed a vital role in reporting enemy fleet movements. Time and again fleet commanders received vital intelligence from submarines, and it was these patrolling submarines which scored some of the greatest successes of the Pacific War. In 1944, just on the eve of the Battle of Leyte Gulf the Darter and Drum ambushed a Japanese heavy cruiser squadron, sinking the Atago and Maya and damaging the Takao. In June 1944 the Albacore torpedoed the new carrier Taiho during the Battle of the Philippine Sea, causing severe damage which led to her loss, and five months later the incomplete Shinano, a 62,000-ton ex-battleship, was torpedoed by the Archerfish in Japanese home waters.

**The Failure of Japanese Tactics**
The Japanese submarine force, from which so much had been expected, had little to show by comparison. By concentrating on attacking well-defended formations of warships they exposed themselves to the efficient antisubmarine tactics of the Americans, while their neglect of mercantile targets reduced the burden of escorts. American antisubmarine measures were very much better than the Japanese, as demonstrated when a newly commissioned destroyer escort, the USS England, sank six submarines in 12 days. On 19 May 1944 the England sank I.16, 140 miles northeast of Choiseul Island in the Solomons, and acting on the likelihood that the submarine was one unit in a patrol line she moved west. On 22 May she made another sonar contact 250 miles north of Kavieng in New Ireland, which turned out to be RO.106. A day later she sank RO.104 in the same area, followed by RO.116 the day after that, 25 miles south. At about midnight on 26 May, north of Manus Island she caught RO.108, but for her last kill she moved back to the scene of her earlier successes, and sank RO.105 200 miles north of Kavieng.

Against this, credit must be given for some outstanding Japanese successes, particularly the sinking of the damaged carrier Yorktown by I.168 during the Battle of Midway and I.19's destruction of the carrier Wasp south of the Solomons

*Right: The Japanese Patrol Boat No.39 seen sinking after being torpedoed by the USS* Seawolf *on 23 April 1943. The photograph was taken through the periscope.*

*Inset: The USS* Peto, *a Gato Class boat, leaving on patrol in 1944.*

*Above: Various modifications made to the* Argonaut *by Mare Island Navy Yard are circled for quick reference. Note the extra stores aft.*

in 1942. The battleship *North Carolina* was damaged by a hit from *I.26* and paradoxically one of the greatest successes came right at the end of the war, when on 30 June 1945 the heavy cruiser USS *Indianapolis* was sunk by *I.58*. The Americans had become so used to enjoying immunity from submarine attack that they allowed this valuable warship to travel without escort between Guam and Leyte, and even failed to notice that she was missing for three days.

As things got worse for the Japanese they turned to desperate measures. Submarines were sacrified in useless attacks on invasion fleets or used to run supplies of goods and ammunition to garrisons of small islands. Although this misuse of submarines was justified in the case of Malta in 1941–42, the Japanese had so many isolated garrisons that they were forced to use more and more of their submarines for this subsidiary purpose. A special supply-submarine was developed, the *I.361* Class, which could steam 15,000 miles on the surface and carry 82 tons of cargo. Nor did the dispersion of resources end there; the Army started to build its own submarines for supplying its garrisons. By 1945 most of the fleet submarines were converted either to supply craft or transports for *Kaiten* midgets.

The most ambitious project was the *I.400* Class, ordered in 1942. They were the biggest submarines in the world at the time, 400 feet long and capable of operating four floatplane bombers (three plus one in its component parts). The original intention was to bomb the Panama Canal, and the hangar could store four torpedoes, three 800-kg bombs and twelve 250-kg bombs. Only three boats were completed and they fell into Allied hands at the surrender. They displaced 5700 tons on the surface, were armed with eight forward 21-inch torpedo-tubes, a 5.5-inch gun and ten 25-mm antiaircraft guns (three triple mountings and one single). Four German-designed MAN diesels with direct-drive developed 9000 brake horsepower, giving a speed of 18¾ knots on the surface. Two 2400 shaft horsepower electric motors gave an underwater speed of 5–7 knots and an endurance of 60 miles at 3 knots. Although reputed to have a surface endurance of 30,000 miles at their cruising speed of 16 knots, post-war examination by the US Navy showed that they were only capable of 20,000 miles. Nevertheless this still gave them the highest endurance of any submarine in the world.

The *I.14* Class were generally similar to the *I.400* but slightly smaller. They were intended to supplement the bigger type, and could carry two floatplane bombers. As a result of German cooperation later Japanese submarines had schnorkel air-masts and the *I.400* Class had an experimental rubber coating to the hull to absorb sonar pulses, an idea which was also being tried out in Germany. When Germany capitulated in May 1945 a number of U-Boats were in Japanese waters waiting to return to Germany with such valuable cargoes as rubber, tin and wolfram. These were immediately seized and incorporated into the Imperial Japanese Navy.

*U.181* became the Japanese *I.501*
*U.862* became the Japanese *I.502*
*UIY.24* (ex-Italian *Commandante Alfredo Cappellini*) became the Japanese *I.503*
*UIT.25* (ex-Italian *Luigi Torelli*) became the Japanese *I.504*
*U.219* became the Japanese *I.505*
*U.195* became the Japanese *I.506*

*RO.500* and *RO.501* (ex *U.511* and *U.1224*) had been transferred by the Germans in July 1943, at a time when the Japanese were anxious to include some of the German advances in their own boats. *RO.501* was sunk off the Azores in May 1944, one of the few Japanese submarines to serve west of the Indian Ocean.

When World War II ended in August 1945 it also brought to a close the most successful submarine campaign in history. Only 231 Japanese merchant ships survived out of a pre-war total of 2337 ships listed in *Lloyd's Register*. In all 190 submarines were completed for the Japanese Navy by August 1945, but only 55 were surrendered, a loss rate of more than 70 percent. It was a heavy price to pay for so little.

*Below: The Japanese adopted many ideas seen in the German Type XXI. The Ha.201 Class (left) were capable of 13 knots submerged; the I.201 (center) was capable of 19 knots; the Ha.101 Class (right) were for transport duties.*

## Midget Submarines

The Italian Navy was the first in the field with midget submarines in 1912, with two 18-feet boats designed for the defense of Venice. During World War I the Italians asked the French for the plans of their 70-tonne *Naiade* Class of 1903, and built a further twelve midgets for harbor defense. Nothing more was heard of midgets until the mid-1930s, when the Japanese started work on two at Kure Dockyard. The result was the Series 'A,' numbered *Ha-3* to *Ha-44*, 78-foot battery-driven craft armed with two 18-inch torpedoes. They were designed to be carried by seaplane tenders and fleet submarines, and were intended for the penetration of enemy harbors. Their first operation was a disaster, an attack on Pearl Harbor intended to coincide with the main air strike. No midget got into the harbor and four were sunk. An attempt to attack Sydney Harbor, Australia, in May 1942 was also unsuccessful, although a torpedo intended for the US cruiser *Chicago*

Sun was coming ever closer to defeat led to the construction of a new series, the Type 'D' or *Koryu*. A total of 540 were planned but by August 1945 only 115 had been finished. As a counterpart to the Kamikaze tactics of the air force the Imperial Navy produced the *Kaiten* Series, basically the body of a Type 93 24-inch torpedo adapted for one-man control. The prototype could travel 26,000 yards at 30 knots, or as much as 85,000 yards at 12 knots, and had a massive 1½-ton warhead. Later models used a hydrogen peroxide motor in place of the gasoline and oxygen motor, giving a maximum speed of 40 knots, but the shortage of engines meant that many *Kaitens* ended up as fuel tanks. The *Kairyu* midgets were more like the original Type 'A', and carried torpedoes slung underneath the hull. Over 200 were built at Yokosuka Dockyard but like the other types, they did little to stave off defeat.

The Italians revived midget subma-

rines just before World War II, and even entertained an ambitious project to ship one on board a submarine to attack the US east coast harbors. But their most noteworthy achievement was the *Maiale* or 'pig,' a small midget submarine which had two saddle-positions for its crew. Although known as a 'human torpedo' (siluro a lenta corsa = slow-running torpedo) the 'pig' bore no resemblance to the Japanese *Kaiten*; it merely looked like a torpedo, and the 'warhead' had to be detached by the operators and clamped to an enemy ship's hull. In December 1941 three 'pigs' from the submarine *Scire* succeeded in penetrating Alexandria harbor, and disabled the British battleships *Queen Elizabeth* and *Valiant*. In fact the battleships were sunk, and the Italian Navy had eliminated the entire British battle fleet in the Mediterranean, but because they were resting upright on the shallow bottom of the harbor Italian Naval intelligence erroneously assumed that they had only suffered minor da-

*Above: A* Kaiten *human torpedo preserved at Washington Navy Yard. They could run at 12 knots for 85,000 yards and had a 1550-kilogram warhead.*

*Right: A Type 'C' midget loaded aboard a Japanese tank landing ship off Kure, August 1944.*

sank a ferry-boat. An attack 24 hours earlier on Diego Suarez in Madagascar had greater success; two midgets from the submarines *I.16* and *I.20* hit the British battleship *Ramillies* and a tanker. It was also one of the few occasions when submarine-launched aircraft achieved their aim, for *I.10*'s floatplane had scouted the anchorage the day before.

More midgets of the Type 'A' and improved 'B' and 'C' were built, but mainly for local defense, in which role they achieved little. In 1944 the growing realization that the Empire of the Rising

mage, and a great victory was therefore thrown away.

The other success scored by Italian 'pigs' was against shipping in Gibraltar. In an elaborate undercover operation the Italian crews operated from the tanker *Olterra* in neutral Algeciras harbor. Ironically the skill of the Italians was put to best use against their own ships. After Italy negotiated an armistice with the Allies in September 1943 several Italian warships fell into German hands, and Italian crews were used to sink the cruisers *Gorizia* and *Bolzano* at La Spezia in June 1944, an exploit which led to a British admiral pinning a decoration on one of the officers who had led the attack on Alexandria.

The British had shown no interest in midget submarines until the Alexandria attack in 1941 suddenly showed them what could be done. Admiral Horton, the man who had led the brilliant Baltic submarine campaign in 1915, was now Flag

*Above: British 'Chariots' were virtually exact copies of the Italian* maiale *(pigs) captured in 1941.*

*Below: Chariot crewmen wearing their self-contained breathing apparatus. They proved best suited to the warm waters of the Mediterranean.*

Officer Submarines and immediately started work on a series of special underwater assault craft. Two were ideas which had already been put forward, an Army officer's idea for a one-man midget, and a four-man midget proposed by Commander Varley, a former submariner. The third project was a straight copy of the Italian 'pig,' code-named the 'Chariot.' The one-man midget was known as the Welman Craft, and was designed to attach its 560-pound charge to the target by magnetic clamps, the original 'limpet mine.' The Welman was battery-driven, and was capable of being towed by motor torpedo boats, whereas the Chariot was transported in a cylinder welded to the casing of a submarine, as in the Italian submarines *Scire* and *Gondar*.

The large midgets were known as X-Craft, and they differed from all other navies' midgets in not using torpedoes. Instead they were fitted with two 2-ton side charges which were faired into the saddle tanks. Once under the target the X-Craft could release the charges internally and merely drop them on the floor of the harbor; with charges of such a weight there was no need for them to be exploded in contact with the hull to inflict serious damage. Although known merely by numbers, *X-3*, etc., their crews bestowed unofficial names such as *Extant* and *Excalibur* on them. A slightly enlarged version known as the XE-series was built later for Pacific operations, with air-conditioning and other features to improve habitability.

Chariots were used in October 1942 in a daring attempt to cripple the German battleship *Tirpitz*, which was hiding in a fjord north of Trondheim. A Norwegian trawler managed to tow two Chariots past the German outposts, but a sudden squall made them unmanageable, and they had to be abandoned. In September 1943 six X-Craft were sent to attack the *Tirpitz* and the *Scharnhorst* in Kaafjord. One, *X-8* had to be scuttled on the way to Norway and *X-9* dived and was never seen again, but *X-5*, *X-6*, *X-7* and *X-10* left their towing submarines to begin the 50-mile voyage through minefields and nets. Unfortunately *X-10* had to abandon the attack when she was only six miles from the battleship's anchorage, leaving

*Above: A* Marder *midget submarine with its underslung torpedo.*

*Top: The* Seehund *Type XXVIIB midget was the most successful of the large range of midgets produced by the German Navy.*

*Right: A German* Biber *midget. The operator of a* Biber *was normally issued with caffeine-impregnated chocolate but nonetheless ran the risk of being overcome by toxic fumes.*

three to make the final attack. *X-5* came to grief about a mile from the *Tirpitz* but *X-6* and *X-7* laid their charges underneath her giant hull before being scuttled by their crews; both were damaged and had no chance of escaping.

When the charges went off they inflicted heavy damage on the *Tirpitz*, and although she was patched up she was never to put to sea as a battleworthy unit again. In November four Welman craft attacked shipping in Bergen without success. These little midgets were unreliable, and never achieved any results; like the Chariots their operators suffered from the extremely cold temperatures experienced in northern waters, whereas the X-Craft, although uncomfortable, afforded reasonable protection to their crews. In April 1944 the submarine *Sceptre* towed *X-24* to Bergen, where the midget attacked a floating dock and a transport. The transport was sunk, and so *Sceptre* and *X-24* returned for a second time in September; this time the floating dock did not escape.

Chariots were successfully employed in the Mediterranean. In January 1943 five penetrated Palermo harbor in Sicily, sinking the liner *Viminale* and the incomplete light cruiser *Ulpio Traiano* at their moorings. Only prompt action by their crews in removing limpet mines saved the destroyer *Grecale*, the torpedo boat *Ciclone* and the submarine *Gemma* from damage. In the Far East the *Trenchant*'s Chariots sank a transport in Phuket, in Thailand while *XE-1* and *XE-3* attacked the heavy cruiser *Takao* in Singapore in July 1945. It will be remembered that Simon Lake fitted his submarines with wheels to allow them to run on the sea bed because he felt that a submarine should cut cables. This prophesy came true in 1945 when *XE-4* and *XE-5* were used to cut the cables between Hong Kong, Singapore and Saigon.

The German Navy started work on midget submarines or K-Craft (Kleine Kampfmittel = Small Assault Units) as a countermeasure against invasion. As such they were more effective than the Japanese midgets but never played a decisive role. There were several types. The Neger was a one-man torpedo with a torpedo slung underneath, which ran awash with the operator in an open cockpit. About 200 were built, and later models had a perspex dome over the cockpit. The Marder was similar but could run submerged; Negers claimed two patrol vessels off Anzio and a des-troyer off Normandy, while Marders sank the Polish cruiser *Dragon*, four landing craft and four minesweepers off the Normandy beaches. About 300 Biber one-man midgets were built, 29-foot craft armed with two underslung torpedoes. They could be carried on deck by U-Boats and are credited with sinking 95,000 tons of shipping in the Scheldt estuary between December 1944 and April 1945.

The most successful German midgets were those of the Type XXVIIB Seehund Class, which were developed from the XXVIIA or Hecht type. They were 39-feet craft propelled by a single-shaft diesel/electric plant, and when extra fuel tanks were fitted had an operational radius of 500 miles at 7 knots. A swivelling Kort nozzle rudder made them extremely maneuverable, and it was found that depth-charge attacks tended to throw them violently aside without sinking them – an experience which must have been extremely unpleasant for the two-man crew. Seehunds sank the French destroyer *La Combattante* and a British LST in the Thames Estuary in February 1945. Nearly 300 were completed and several served in the Soviet and French navies after World War I.

# SUBMARINE
# RESCUE AND SALVAGE

To the layman the most notorious aspect of the submarine is the miserable fate of men trapped on the bottom of the ocean in a disabled submarine. As far back as 1774 when Lord Sandwich intervened in the operations to rescue Day at Plymouth, no effort, however futile, has been spared to get survivors out of sunken submarines.

The first successful escape was made by Wilhelm Bauer and two seamen from the *Brandtaucher* in Kiel in 1851, and it reflects great credit on Bauer for working out the best method. Knowing that surface ships had already located the wreck with grappling irons, Bauer calculated that the hull might easily be holed, and so persuaded his companions to make a 'free ascent' by flooding the hull until the internal pressure was the same as the external, and then floating out through the hatch.

When the first modern submarines were introduced toward the end of the nineteenth century very little thought was given to the possibility of saving life, although progress was made with the equally difficult problem of salvaging the boat after the accident. There are two main causes of submarine accidents, an error in diving procedure or collision with a surface ship while running on the surface or at periscope depth. Obviously the complicated sequence of operations for diving can go wrong, but submarine crews are usually sufficiently trained to reduce the likelihood. Collision, on the other hand, is always a hazard. A submarine captain has difficulty in hearing a surface ship overtaking if his boat is running at periscope depth, because her propeller noises are masked by his own, and the surface ship has difficulty in spotting a periscope dead ahead. Although stoutly built a submarine is a vessel with low buoyancy and is therefore unlikely to remain afloat for long after a collision.

The first disaster came in March 1904, when the British *A.4* was run down by a passenger liner near Portsmouth. The Royal Navy's lack of a submarine salvage organization came in for strong criticism when the Press learned that it took three

*Right: The Canadian* Ojibwa *and the Vickers Oceanics' submersible L.1 preparing for a rendezvous on the seabed, testing a new rescue system. A picture taken at the British Faslane submarine base.*

days before a German firm's lifting vessel could be chartered to undertake the job of trying to raise the submarine. In 1905 the French submarine *Farfadet* was lost in Bizerta harbor when the conning tower hatch failed to close, and again the lack of a properly equipped salvage organization meant that nothing could be done to rescue the crew. When the *Lutin* suffered a similar accident at Bizerta the following year there was still no salvage organization, although the British sent special equipment from Malta at the request of the French Navy. When the American submarine *F.4* failed to surface after diving off Honolulu on 25 March 1915 she was the US Navy's first submarine fatality. Her recovery from 306 feet by means of 'camel' pontoons established a salvage record, but when her sisters *F.1* and *F.3* collided off the coast of California in December 1917 the hull of *F.1* could not be raised. The US Navy was fortunate that under the influence of two officers, George Stillson and George French, techniques of deep diving had been greatly improved since 1912, raising the record from 211 feet established by the British in 1907 to 274 feet in November 1914. The two experts and four of their best divers were sent to Honolulu as soon as the loss of *F.4* was known. On their first dive they reached 288 feet, breaking the record

134

again, and ultimately they proved able to work at 306 feet.

The first British submarine accident in which lives were saved was the accidental sinking of *K.13* on 29 January 1917. The submarine was still carrying out builders' trials in the Gare Loch, off the Firth of Clyde, and among those on board was one of Fairfield's designers. Under his guidance it proved possible for the survivors to lighten the bows, which allowed the salvage team to cut a hole in the hull, through which they could crawl to safety.

The German Navy tackled the problem of submarine salvage by building a special double-hulled ship, the *Vulkan* in 1907–08. With a docking space 177 feet by 26 feet she could raise a 500-ton hull by means of overhead gantries, but the growth in the size of submarines restricted her usefulness. In 1917 the much larger *Cyclop* was completed, a 297-foot vessel capable of lifting 1200 tons between her catamaran hulls. In 1973 the US Navy revived the idea of a double-hulled rescue vessel when it completed the *Pigeon* and *Ortolan* but there is now no question of lifting the submarine as modern boats are too large. The modern double hull provides a stable platform for lowering rescue equipment over the submarine.

In December 1921 the US submarine *S.48* sank on builders' trials but was salvaged and commissioned in 1922. She ran aground again off Portsmouth, New Hampshire in 1925, but thereafter left her bad luck behind and survived World War II. Her sister *S.51* was rammed and sunk by a liner off Block Island in September

1927. Only three men escaped, but the salvage was accomplished by a man who was to become one of the world's leading experts in this field, Captain Edward Ellsberg. A similar attempt to rescue the survivors of *S.4* off Provincetown, Massachusetts in December 1927 had to be broken off because of bad weather, although the rescuers could still hear tapping from six men alive in the forward torpedo room, only 102 feet down. This is the most heart-breaking part of submarine salvage operations, when the rescuers know exactly where the submarine has gone down but cannot reach the survivors before they exhaust their air-supply.

As a direct result of the *S.4* disaster the US Navy devoted more money and research to improving submarine rescue. The 'Momsen lung' was a self-contained breathing set designed to allow submariners to float to the surface. A special rescue chamber or bell was also developed, which could be lowered onto the hull of a sunken submarine and locked into place over a special escape hatch in the pressure hull. After a diver located the submarine and attached a down-haul wire the two-man crew helped as many as eight men to enter the bell to be hauled up to the surface. The first trial of the rescue bell came in May 1939 when the *Squalus (SS-192)* sank on a test dive off the New Hampshire coast. Using the new bell the rescue ships brought 33 men to safety. The submarine was later raised and recommissioned under the new name *Sailfish* to avoid any suggestion of bad luck. Her crew cheerfully nicknamed her the *Squailfish* and she went on to sink 45,000 tons of shipping in the Pacific.

The *Squalus* salvage operation involved a total of 640 dives to a depth of 240 feet. During the rescue-phase all diving was done on air but during the later salvage work an experimental mixture of helium and oxygen was used with great success. The disaster proved the value of both the Momsen lung and the McCann Rescue Chamber, and as a result the former survived in service until 1956, and the latter is still in use. In theory the Rescue Chamber is usable down to 850 feet, depending on the ability of the operating salvage ship to moor over the wreck.

On the other side of the Atlantic the Royal Navy had suffered its share of accidents, and had devised the DSEA or Davis Submarine Escape Apparatus, similar to the Momsen lung. It derived from diving experience, and comprised a mouthpiece, goggles, oxygen bag and a pressure-release valve. It was first used in June 1931 when the *Poseidon* was rammed by the Chinese coasting steamer *Yuta* off Weihaiwei. The apparatus had just been issued and although the submarine had not yet been fitted with the necessary escape chambers, several men escaped, including a Chinese steward who had no previous training. Although the DSEA saved a number of lives it had several disadvantages; apart from its complicated sequence of operations the oxygen could cause convulsions or loss of consciousness at depths greater than 60 feet.

Post-war research shows that carbon dioxide and nitrogen poisoning begin to take effect on human beings in a confined space after about 12 hours. They become

*Right: The German rescue vessel* Cyclop *was intended to raise a submarine between her twin hulls.*

*Below: Because the Baltic is so shallow World War I U-Boats were pressure tested in this huge floating dock, seen here at Harwich after the war.*

fatigued and dispirited, and eventually almost incapable of performing more than the simplest operations. From what we now know it seems likely that many of the men who died in submarine accidents in the past 50 years exhausted themselves in futile attempts to save their submarine. Had they immediately started to organize an escape they would have been capable of the extra exertions needed, instead of waiting until some men had become too ill or befuddled to operate the apparatus and escape hatch controls. When the new British submarine *Thetis* sank on trials in June 1939 the survivors became very badly affected by carbon dioxide poisoning; two men died inside the escape chamber either because they were unable to operate the hatch control or because those outside the chamber could no longer operate the flooding mechanism.

The loss of the *Thetis* was caused by a remarkable sequence of bad workmanship and ill-fortune. Before opening the rear loading door of a torpedo-tube it is essential to check that the outer door is shut, and for this purpose a spit-cock is

provided on the inner door. Following the prescribed routine the officer responsible checked all six spit-cocks in the forward torpedo-room, and as no sea-water trickled out he ordered the doors to be opened. To his horror seawater rushed in, in such quantities that the forward watertight door could not be closed against the flow. When the wreck was raised the specialists who examined it found that the indicator for the outer torpedo-tube doors had been installed back-to-front, so that the doors were open when the indicator showed 'Shut.' Worse, the spit-cocks on the inner doors had been coated with paint, and so there was no tell-tale spurt of seawater which would have revealed that the tubes were open to the sea. Neither of these small errors of workmanship would have caused the loss of a surface warship but to a submarine they were fatal. Another contributing factor was the complicated series of clips on the watertight door, which prevented it from being secured in time. Today a single '*Thetis* Clip' commemorates the disaster. Like the *Squalus*, which was lost three months earlier,

GERMAN SUBMARINE SALVAGE VESSEL CYCLOP.

Above: U-Boat crewmen practicing with the *tauchretter* *escape gear*.

Right: The wreck of the British M.2 seen on a modern bottom-search sonar.

the *Thetis* was repaired and put back into commission under a new name. As HMS *Thunderbolt* she had a successful war career in the Mediterranean, but was finally sunk off Sicily in March 1943.

After World War II the RN adopted the rescue bell used by the USN, and fitted the submarine rescue vessel HMS *Reclaim* to operate it. Before this, however, the *Reclaim* had to carry out an attempt to salvage the submarine *Affray* which disappeared in the English Channel in 1951. The submarine was lying in a deep trench known as the Hurd Deep, and there was no question of getting men out alive from that depth. It was also too deep for diving, but it was essential to know why a recently built submarine had sunk. The answer was to use a hastily adapted television camera, and so for the first time underwater TV photography was used, and clearly established that the *Affray* had been lost when her snort mast had fractured (snort is the British name for schnorkel). Underwater

TV was also useful in recovering pieces of equipment to substantiate this opinion, and it is now indispensable to submarine salvage work.

The massive size of nuclear submarines does not make them immune to accidents, but the world was shocked on 10 April 1963 to hear that the USS *Thresher* had failed to surface from a deep dive 220 miles off Boston. It was later revealed that the submarine had been crushed by the weight of water when plunging beyond her safe depth after a pipe-joint had collapsed. Five years later another 'nuke,' the *Scorpion* was lost in the

Atlantic, and in April 1970 a Soviet 'November' Class sank about 70 miles southwest of the British Isles.

The risks and complexities of using breathing apparatus have led to the development of 'free ascent' for submariners who are at depths of not more than 300 feet. This means that the only precaution to be taken by the escapee is to breathe out steadily as he ascends, to avoid bursting his lungs when he reaches the surface. Training takes place in a tall diving tank on dry land, with instructors stationed at different levels to give a punch in the stomach to any trainee not breathing out. But with today's submarines operating at depths of 1000 feet or more other methods must be found to rescue men from submarines. When the bathyscaphe *Trieste* dived to 35,000 feet in 1960 it was realized that new methods of submarine salvage and rescue might become possible.

The US Navy bought the *Trieste* in 1958 from its Italian designer, Professor Piccard and then built the improved *Trieste II*. Later the small submersible *Alvin* was bought, capable of operating down to 6000 feet. The *Alvin* first came into prominence when it was used to recover H-Bombs from a crashed bomber off the coast of Spain. From these and other experimental deep-diving vehicles the US Navy developed its two Deep Submergence Rescue Vehicles, *DSRV.1* and *DSRV.2* for the specific purpose of submarine rescue. They can be air-lifted and the nuclear submarine *Hawkbill* has been fitted to carry one on her casing. Each DSRV can carry 24 men in addition to her three operators, and has an endurance of 12 hours.

In 1975 the British firm Vickers collaborated with the Ministry of Defence and

*Above: HMS* Reclaim's *rescue bell above the pressurized chamber into which rescuees can be transferred for decompression.*

*Left: A modern Swedish submarine rescue vehicle, the URF, on a road transporter.*

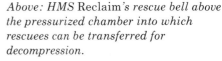

the Canadian Navy by modifying one of its commercial submersibles, the *L.1*, to produce a submarine rescue system. The conventional submarine HMCS *Ojibwa* was modified, with a special hatch on the casing forward designed to mate with a 'mating skirt' fitted underneath *L.1*. To make the exercise realistic the *Ojibwa* was bottomed with a severe list, and men were transferred from her to the submersible. No mechanical hold-down was necessary as the water was merely pumped out of the skirt, and with the pressure inside reduced it proved possible to maintain the watertight seal. In

1978 further experiments were carried out by the Royal Navy, with the SSBN HMS *Repulse* operating the US Navy's *DSRV.2*. To demonstrate the speed of reaction a giant Lockheed Galaxy transport flew the submersible into Glasgow Airport and it was then taken by road to the Clyde submarine base at Faslane. Mounted 'piggy-back' on the after casing of the *Repulse* the *DSRV.2* was then used to transfer men from HMS *Odin* lying 400 feet down. This was the first recorded link-up of two fully submerged submarines, and it demonstrated that DSRVs can be used with any submarine equipped with the right hatch.

Another type of vehicle is the small P-Class submersible developed by the British firm Vickers. Known as 'Pisces' craft they were developed mainly to carry out underwater repair and salvage work, particularly in connection with North Sea oil-rigs. The *Pisces III* displaces 11½ tonnes and can dive to a depth of 3600 feet. She is driven by two 3 horse-power electric motors and can move at a maximum of 4 knots. Endurance depends on the number of operators, but sufficient air is carried for 100 crew-hours and the normal crew is two operators. The potential of these small submersibles was not widely known until 20 August 1973 when the mother ship *Vickers Voyager* broadcast a 'Mayday' call for help. Her Pisces had dived the day before to bury a submarine cable off the southwest coast of Ireland, but just when the operation was over a hatch cover came loose, and the little submersible found herself lying on the bottom at 1575 feet unable to move. The rescue was finally effected by *Pisces II* and *Pisces V*, with the aid of lifting ships on the surface. An American submersible *CURV.III* was also brought in and for three days the world watched a rescue attempt involving naval and civilian ships. Finally both the operators were rescued after 72 hours and their submersible was salvaged.

After saving life the next problem is to recover the submarine if possible, but this part of the operation has always presented peculiar problems. Being complex in their layout it is always important to find out just how many holes there are in the hull, and it may prove impossible to close them all. The weight of a flooded submarine is considerable, and could be 5000 tons or more. Having low buoyancy makes them hard to refloat even if only partially flooded.

One method is the buoyant lift, which can be accomplished by pumping out compartments or blowing the water out by compressed air. It can only be used if the hull is relatively undamaged and all openings are sealed. The more usual method is to use 'camels' or salvage pontoons. These are flooded to make them sink on either side of the submarine, and

*Far left: The American Deep Submergence Rescue Vehicle (DSRV) perched on the after casing of the nuclear submarine HMS* Repulse.

*Above: The* Avalon *(DSRV.2) showing the chamber underneath designed to lock onto the submarine's escape hatch.*

*Left: A Vickers Oceanics Pisces III submersible, designed for industrial use.*

then linked by chains or wires passed underneath her hull. As the camels are pumped out they rise and slowly lift the submarine between them. With a mechanical lift the load is raised by special lifting vessels or cranes. With either method the slings have to be placed carefully to prevent the submarine from moving during the lift. A tidal lift can be done in shallow waters by moving the camels or lifting craft inshore with each tide. It has the advantage of not requiring the same lifting power as a straight mechanical lift.

The problems of rescue and salvage have been getting greater in recent years. Not only are submarines going deeper but the use of nuclear propulsion has raised the specter of radiation affecting both rescuers and rescued. It remains to be seen if the new methods of rescue will be effective. So far nobody has escaped from a deep submarine disaster.

# POST-WAR DEVELOPMENTS

As soon as German resistance ceased in May 1945 teams of American, British and Soviet submarine experts converged on German dockyards and shipyards. They had only one aim, to locate and recover as much information as they could on the new German U-Boat designs, particularly the Type XXI and the Walter boats. The British and Americans each raised a sunken Type XVIIB boat, and the Soviets certainly recovered at least one.

It was 1918 all over again, with the victors almost coming to blows over their shares in the loot. Everybody knew how far the Germans had progressed with their revolutionary designs, and it was solely a question of who got there first. In the end the British and Americans got the lion's share as they occupied the principal yards and harbors well to the west of the advancing Soviet armies. A share of the British tonnage was, however, later handed over to the Soviets in 1946. The following U-Boats fell into Allied hands intact and were used for trials:

| Type | Number | Fate |
|---|---|---|
| XVII | U.1406 | To USA |
| | U.1407 | To Royal Navy as HMS Meteorite (N.25) |
| | U.795 | To RN |
| XXIII | U.2326 | To RN as N.35, then to France |
| | U.2353 | To Soviet Union as N.31 |
| | U.4706 | To RN, then to Norway as Knerter |
| XXI | U.2513 | To USA |
| | U.2518 | To RN, then to France as Roland Morillot |
| | U.2529 | To Soviet Union as N.27 |
| | U.3008 | To USA |
| | U.3017 | To RN as N.41 |
| | U.3035 | To Soviet Union as N.28 |
| | U.3041 | To Soviet Union as N.29 |
| | U.3515 | To Soviet Union as N.30 |
| | U.3538-3542 | Captured incomplete by Soviets and completed |
| | U.3543-3695 | Some of this series completed by Soviets |

| Type | Number | Fate |
|---|---|---|
| VIIC | U.249 | To RN as N.86 |
| | U.471 | To France as Mille |
| | U.712 | To RN |
| | U.766 | To France as Lanbie |
| | U.776 | To RN as N.65 |
| | U.926 | To RN and then Norway as Kya |
| | U.953 | To RN |
| | U.995 | To RN and then Norway as Kaura |
| | U.1023 | To RN as N.83 |
| | U.1057-1058 | To Soviet Union as S.81 and S.82 |
| | U.1064 | To Soviet Union as S.83 |
| | U.1105 | To RN as N.16 |
| | U.1108 | To RN |
| | U.1171 | To RN as N.19 |
| | U.1202 | To RN and then Norway as Kynn |
| | U.1305 | To Soviet Union as S.84 |
| IX | U.123 | To France as Blaison |
| | U.190 | To Canada |
| | U.150 | To France as Bouan |
| | U.1231 | To Soviet Union |

It was the Walter hydrogen peroxide engine which interested everybody, despite the problems associated with it. Both the British and Americans succeeded in making their captured boats work, and the British even built two improved versions subsequently, but the Soviets are believed to have abandoned their efforts after a lengthy period of trials. Looking back now it can be seen as a waste of time and money for the unstable nature of the fuel combined with its bulk made the submarine the dangerous and short-legged weapon that it had been before the introduction of diesel engines. Nevertheless it was the only means at the time of producing the high speed needed to counter the ascendancy of anti-submarine tactics.

The basis of the Walter system was the chemical hydrogen peroxide ($H_2O_2$), a relatively unstable compound which breaks down easily into water ($H_2O$) and oxygen ($O_2$), the breakdown being accompanied by the generation of considerable heat. In the normal industrial use a 35

*Above and below: In 1947 the USS* Cusk *(SS.348) was fitted with a tubular hangar and a launching ramp for the 'Loon' missile. This copy of the VI 'buzz bomb' was the first naval cruise missile.*

*Above: The British* Alderney *and* Alaric *lying at Gibraltar post-war, with a pair of 'T' Class alongside the depot ship HMS* Forth *in the background.*

percent solution, known as Perhydrol, could be produced, but any greater concentration needs stabilizers, which form protective layers around any contaminating particles such as dust or rust. High Test Peroxide (HTP) was the name given to very high concentrations of hydrogen peroxide, with the 78–85 percent solution needed by the Walter turbine being the maximum which could be achieved in a factory under safe conditions.

The HTP which resulted was a colorless liquid considerably more viscous than water, and liable to explode if its temperature rose above 200 degrees Fahrenheit (93 deg C). As the decomposition which was a necessary part of the process produced great heat, and as minute impurities such as rust particles produced spontaneous decomposition it can be imagined that operating a Walter-engined submarine was like driving a tank loaded with nitro-glycerine across a battlefield. To make matters worse a fire could not be put out by smothering it with foam or even sand, as the oxygen in the compound was sufficient to maintain combustion. The only way to deal with a fire was to dilute the HTP with water and so stabilize it, and an essential precau-

142

tion was to store the fuel in sterile conditions with special venting and spraying equipment.

Despite all these problems the British pressed on with their two HTP-fuelled boats, the *Explorer* and *Excalibur*, built in 1952–58, but they proved to be expensive freaks which were not worth the trouble. They ended their careers as 27-knot underwater targets, acting as stopgaps until the commissioning of the first British nuclear submarine could give antisubmarine forces similar target-speeds.

The influence of the Type XXI design was ultimately far more important than that of the Walter boats. As we have seen the Type XXI boats were dispersed among various navies as soon as they had been evaluated by the major navies, and their characteristics were incorporated in new construction as fast as possible. The Russians designed their 'W' Class and its later variant the 'Z' type to incorporate everything possible including the rudder faired into the stern. Other navies, notably the American, adapted the design as far as possible to fit in with their own ideas. In 1946 the US Navy began its 'Guppy' program, named from the acronym for Greater Underwater Propulsive

Power; as an alternative to building large numbers of new submarines nearly 50 of the 200 wartime submarines of the *Gato*, *Balao* and *Tench* Classes were rebuilt to incorporate Type XXI characteristics.

The basic approach in the 'Guppy' program was to streamline the hull and in-increase the underwater power. The prototypes *Odax* and *Pomodon*, were first intended to provide fast targets for training surface antisubmarine forces, and to cope with an expected improvement in Soviet submarines' performance. They lost their conning towers and instead were given a streamlined 'sail' which enclosed the periscopes and schnorkel mast. The characteristic buoyant bow was replaced by a round bow and every conceivable piece of equipment likely to cause resistance was either removed or made rectractable, down to deck-cleats. Internally it was much harder to find space for a bigger battery as the wartime fleet submarines were by no means spacious. The solution was to move the auxiliary diesel-generator from the after engine room and to take advantage of the fact that gun-ammunition was no longer needed.

An important improvement had to be made to the batteries to achieve the much higher output required. By accepting a shorter life (18 months) and designing a smaller battery-cell it was possible to provide four main batteries of 126 cells each, as against the previous two batteries. This brought fresh problems, for high-capacity batteries generated much more heat and hydrogen than the older type. After experimenting with a closed-cell system the US Navy reverted to a water-cooled open-cell system, and the boats' air-conditioning equipment was increased by nearly 300 percent to 23 tons to handle the load. Other minor improvements were made and apart from the inevitable teething troubles the two

'Guppy I' boats proved a great success.

A program had been undertaken simultaneously by Portsmouth Navy Yard (New Hampshire) to cure the worst faults of the schnorkel. Basically the difficulty was that exhausting gases underwater imposed much greater back-pressure on the diesels than they had ever been designed to take. In particular the American two-cycle diesels suffered from pressure-fluctuations when the float valve closed in rough weather whereas the German four-cycle diesels were not badly affected. Although some components of the General Motors and Fairbanks-Morse diesels were redesigned to cope with the stresses the real answer was to replace the float valve with an air-actuated head valve designed to operate more rapidly and positively. The opening and closing of the valve is controlled by

three electrodes located near the head of the schnorkel, and when a wave breaks over them they complete an electrical circuits which directs air to shut the valve. As soon as the electrodes are free of water they reverse the process, and to make the opening and closing as rapid as possible the valve is assisted by six springs. Any water which accidentally enters the mast is removed by a water separator.

The exhaust mast was designed to be raised with the induction mast and to ride about 4–8 feet below the surface of the water. The exhaust port was fitted with baffles to reduce the amount of smoke and haze reaching the surface. A similar telescopic schnorkel to the German Type XXI boats was developed but the first installation in the USS *Irex* in 1947 threw up an excessive plume of spray. The American boats, being so much bigger than the U-Boats, needed to have a much bigger schnorkel head and mast to draw in sufficient air, and it was necessary to redesign the head to reduce the amount of spray thrown up. Three types of schnorkel were developed, the original 'Guppy' type, a simpler version for the older fleet boats and a sophisti-

*Left: The* Balao *Class* Springer *(SS.413) was partially streamlined along 'Guppy' lines. She is seen here in a later guise as the Chilean* Capitan Thomson.

*Below: The Brazilian* Rio Grande do Sul, *formerly a US Navy Guppy II.*

cated fast-attack type. Even nuclear submarines continue to be fitted with the device, for it is the only quick way to rid the interior of a boat of the various contaminants which cannot be absorbed by the air-purification system.

The success of the *Odax* and *Pomodon* led to a further 22 *Balao* Class boats being converted, but because of a number of improvements all 24 were regraded as the Guppy II type. There was even a 'Pearl Harbor Guppy' a simple conversion undertaken at the Pacific Fleet base which involved removal of deck guns and platforms and crude streamlining of the periscopes. In 1950 a cheaper and faster conversion, the Guppy 1A was authorized for 10 more *Balao* Class. With only two 126-cell batteries, but of a more powerful type known as the *Sargo II*, they were all in service in January 1952. The Guppy IIA program, authorized in 1951, allowed for 16 boats to be streamlined but without the same emphasis on high underwater speed. Instead a massive, powerful sonar was installed, with its processing equipment replacing the forward set of machinery.

The 'Guppy' configuration became standard for submarines throughout the world. The British converted their 'T'

and 'A' Class boats similarly, and even when navies could not afford the expense of a full conversion the hitherto standard deck gun was sacrificed and the conning tower became a slender fin. The snorkel or 'snort' (its British name) also became a standard fitting but with many improvements over the original German version. The British copied the German folding type, but after a disastrous accident which caused the loss of the *Affray* when her snort tube fractured, they turned to the American telescopic type.

In addition to its large Guppy program the US Navy experimented with novel uses for fleet submarines. In 1946 the *Requin* and *Spinax* went to sea with large radar antennae on deck and processing equipment below, to act as radar pickets capable of detecting hostile aircraft and directing defending fighters. They were never popular with the Fleet on account of endless problems with flooding of electrical circuits, and the enquiry into remedies was known appropriately as Operation Migraine. The two existing boats and two more, the *Tigrone* and *Burrfish*, were modified but they were never popular as they were crowded, and the complex electronic equipment was difficult to maintain. A

*Above:* U.22 *(nearest the camera) and* U.23 *on dry land at Kiel show how small the Type 206 submarines are.*

*Right:* Agosta *Class submarines in the covered building dock at DCAN Cherbourg.*

further six *Gato* Class and even three nuclear radar pickets were built before the idea was finally abandoned in 1959.

Nothing had come of a German project late in World War II for U-Boats to tow submersible rafts across the Atlantic to act as launching pads for V-2 rockets, but the US Navy pushed ahead with the idea of firing guided missiles from submarines. In 1947 a submarine fired the first surface-to-surface cruise missile, the KUW-1 Loon. This small missile, an improved version of the German V-1 'doodlebug,' could be carried in a watertight 10 feet by 30 feet canister on deck, much like the old aircraft hangars of the 1920s, and then launched from a collapsible ramp by a rocket booster; it was assembled on deck and then 'flown' by radio signals, either from its parent submarine or another boat to its target.

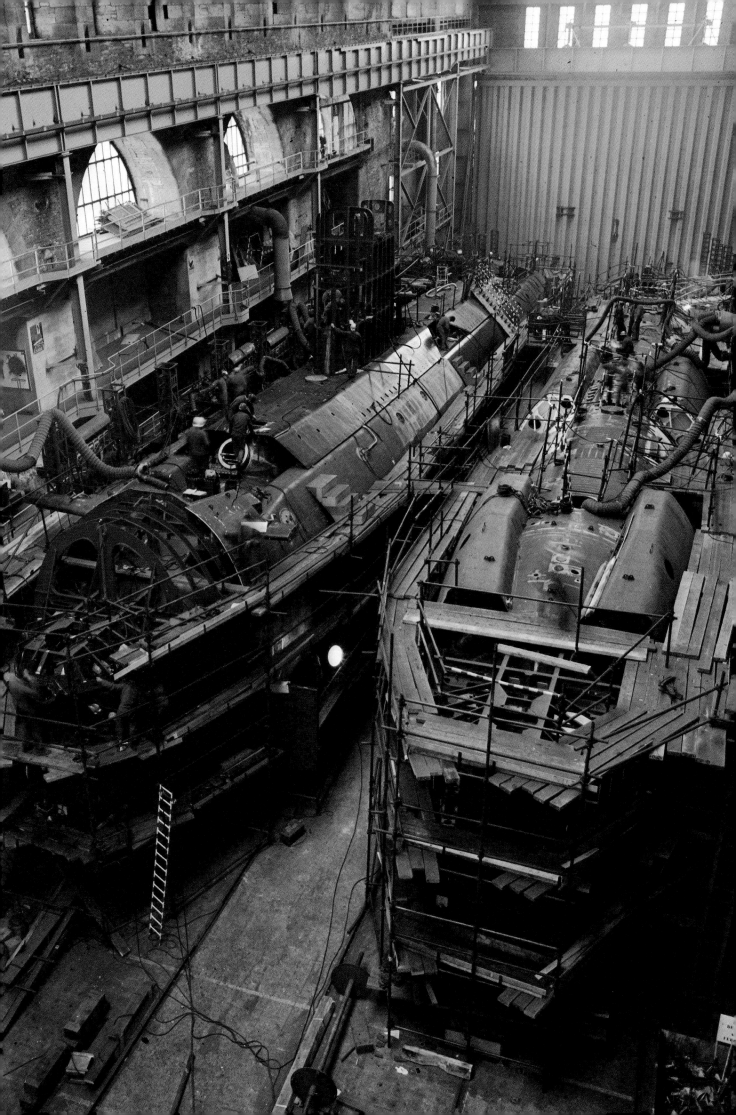

*Below: Lockheed P2V Neptune and Grumman S2F Tracker aircraft fly overhead, a US Navy HS-1 helicopter 'dunks' its sonar with the diesel-electric submarine USS Darter (SS.576) and anti-submarine ships behind during a demonstration of ASW tactics in 1960.*

*Below:* A US Permit Class nuclear hunter-killer boat loading a subroc tube-launched missile down the forward hatch.

*Above: The Spanish* Delphin *(S.61) on trials. She is one of the four French* Daphné *type which have been built under license in Spain.*

*Left: HMS* Dreadnought, *the first British nuclear submarine, was fitted with an American reactor.*

Although a crude weapon in that it could be jammed or even shot down by existing antiaircraft defenses, the submarine-launched Loon (later redesignated LTV-N-2) was the forerunner of the most lethal submarine weapon of all, the underwater-launched ballistic missile.

The culmination of the program was the conversion of the *Gato* Class *Carbonero* and *Cusk* in 1946, and on 12 February 1947 *Cusk* launched her first Loon off Point Mugu, California. An even more important achievement was on 3 May 1950 when the *Cusk* launched her Loon and then submerged to periscope depth and proved that she could track the mis-

sile for a distance of 105 miles, using her AN/BPQ-2 guidance equipment. It was the birth of the cruise missile, and the US Navy was quick to exploit the possibilities. Development of an improved Loon, the SSM-N-8A Regulus had started in 1947; it made its maiden flight in 1950 and production began in March 1953 at the same time as the first Regulus submarine, the *Tunny*, commissioned. She and her sister *Barbero* were fitted with a hangar capable of accommodating two Regulus rounds and they were given Guppy streamlining as well. The purpose of Regulus was strategic, and during the 1950s a force of five submarines was assigned to the Pacific to counter any threat from China. Two large conventional boats were built, the *Grayback* and *Growler* and the nuclear *Halibut*.

The flight-path of the missile was pre-selected and fed into its on-board computer, but this did not prevent course-corrections and evasive maneuvers from being given. After launching the sub-

marine submerged and started to transmit guidance details to the missile, or handed it over to the control of another submarine fitted with the AN/BPQ-2 control gear. In this way Regulus could fly a maximum of 500 miles, although half that was more normal. On arrival over the target it accelerated from a cruising speed of Mach 0.87 and dived at Mach 1.1.

An improved version, Regulus II (SSM-N-9A) started development in 1952 and the first firings took place from the *Grayback* in September 1958. She and her sister had been designed to take the missile as had the nuclear boat *Halibut*, but when the Regulus II program was abandoned in December 1958, only three months after the successful trials, all three were armed with Regulus I. With a range of 1000 miles and a cruising speed of Mach 2 it promised to be a formidable weapon and it was hoped to build four more *Permit* Class nuclear submarines to serve with the *Halibut* and the *Grayback* Class but money was more urgently

151

needed to develop an even more deadly system, Polaris. Although supporters of the Regulus system pooh-poohed the dangers of remaining on the surface it was clear that such a practice would prove as difficult and dangerous as it had been for the aircraft-carrying submarines of the 1930s. What finally killed the Regulus program was the absurd discrepancy between the cost and the results. Even the 3850-ton nuclear-powered *Halibut* could only accommodate two 57-foot Regulus II missiles – at a cost of $45,000,000 without the missiles!

Apart from experimental conversions of older *Gato* Class boats to such exotic functions as cargo carriers, underwater oilers and amphibious transports the other major effort the US Navy was forging ahead with was the most revolutionary idea of all, the use of nuclear propulsion. Work on a reactor capable of harnessing the immense power of nuclear fission at a controllable rate had started in January 1948. Known as the Submarine Thermal Reactor (STR) this was developed by Westinghouse into the STR Mark 2, later designated the S2W type in collaboration with the Argonne National Laboratory. Development of the associated technology was in the hands of a group of scientists and engineers at the Naval Reactors Branch of the Atomic Energy Commission, led by a Captain Hyman G Rickover of the US Navy. The penalty for failure would be immense for not only was a large amount of money involved but also the

prestige of the United States, but Rickover and his team never showed the slightest hesitation.

On 12 December 1951 when the Navy Department was satisfied that the time had come to order the hull it announced that the name chosen would be *Nautilus*. This commemorated not only two previous US submarines but also the mythical boat of Captain Nemo in *Twenty Thousand Leagues Under the Sea.* Her keel was laid on 14 June 1952 by President Truman at what had now become the Electric Boat Division of General Dynamics, the birthplace of the Hollands. Work progressed rapidly and the *Nautilus* (SSN-571) was launched by Mrs Eisenhower on 21 January 1954 at Groton, and she was commissioned on 30 September only eight months later. She was an immediate success, and in her first year steamed over 62,000 miles. Apart from the streamlining of her hull she was very conventional in her design, with two shafts driven by steam turbines using superheated steam provided by a single nuclear reactor. An electric motor

*Left: A Federal German Navy U-Boat, U.18, exchanging information with a Sea King helicopter.*

*Below: The* Porpoise *Class were the first post-war patrol submarines built for the Royal Navy and proved a great success.*

and batteries were provided for emergencies; by a strange quirk of history steam propulsion had finally justified itself in submarines.

From the moment at 1100 hours on 17 January 1955 when she slipped her moorings and signalled to the Submarine Force Commander 'Underway on nuclear power' the *Nautilus* began to set records and to break many long-standing ones. On her shakedown cruise she made the longest submerged cruise at the highest speed, 1381 miles to Puerto Rico, at an average speed of 16 knots. By 27 November the same year she had logged 25,000 miles, and Rickover, now a Rear-Admiral for his services, could claim that 'The *Nautilus* is not merely an improved submarine, she is the most potent and deadly submarine afloat. She is, in fact, a new weapon. Her impact on naval tactics and strategy may well approach that of the airplane.' And yet, technically, she was no more than an enlargement of the previous *Tang* Class, with six 21-inch bowtorpedo-tubes and a big BQS-4 passive sonar in the bow. Yet the figures speak for themselves: in April 1957 when the uranium core of the reactor was replaced she had logged 62,562 miles, while the second core lasted another 91,234 miles. She was credited in the Press with staggering speeds, as much as 30 knots underwater, but never exceeded 20 knots. Her worst fault was noise, for the cooling pumps could be heard 10 miles away, it was reported.

Of all the exploits of the *Nautilus* none

caught the world's imagination like her voyage to the North Pole. On 23 July 1958 under her captain, Commander William R Anderson, she left Pearl Harbor, passed through the Aleutians and the Bering Sea and surfaced only when she reached the shallow Chukchi Sea. She submerged again when she spotted deep water alongside the pack ice and headed north along the 12,000-foot deep Barrow Sea Valley. Two days later Anderson told his crew that *Nautilus* had reached 90 degrees North, the exact site of the North Pole, but there could be no flags or landing parties for the submarine was underneath a 35-foot thick roof of ice. Film of the adventure gives an impression of a translucent cloud of fantastic shapes, dimly lit by the 24-hour sunlight above. Only on 5 August, two days after reaching the Pole, could Anderson announce to the world '*Nautilus* Ninety North.' She had been submerged under the polar ice for 96 hours and had traveled 1830 miles.

It had been a risky business, and had only succeeded after five attempts between August 1957 and June 1958. There was the obvious risk of collision by surfacing underneath the ice pack but much more serious was the risk of colliding with unknown hazards in the deep Arctic channels. These were totally uncharted waters and the *Nautilus* was traveling virtually blind, with no navigational aids beyond echo-sounders and a TV camera to allow the captain to look up at the ice. If she had been badly holed by a

*Three examples of modern Soviet submarines:*
*Top: A nuclear-powered 'Victor' Class attack boat, seen in the South China Sea.*

*Center: An 'Echo I' Class nuclear attack boat pictured in 1975.*

*Bottom: One of the numerous 'Foxtrot' Class diesel-electric boats photographed from an RAF Nimrod reconnaissance aircraft in the Atlantic south of the Faroes.*

pinnacle of rock or had damaged her propellers far under the ice cap there was no other submarine in the world capable of reaching her, and her crew would have shared the fate of a previous generation of polar explorers.

Four more experimental nuclear submarines followed, the 268-foot *Skate* and *Swordfish* (SSN-578 and *579*) and *Sargo* and *Seadragon* (SSN-583 and *584*), intended to evaluate different types of reactor. A fifth, the giant 5450-ton *Triton* (SSN-586), broke all previous records by having *two* reactors; in 1960 she made an incredible underwater voyage around the world lasting 84 days. She submerged off Long Island on 16 February and proceeded to the St Peter and Paul Rocks where she began the circumnavigation on 24 February. The round the world voyage was completed on 25 April but she did not finally surface until 10 May. The early nuclear submarines continued to make records; *Skate* surfaced at the North Pole in 1962, and later that year *Seadragon* and *Skate* both arrived at the Pole. The purpose of these Arctic exploits was to test the new inertial navigation system, which was the only accurate method of navigating at the Pole.

The early nuclear submarines did not have the most efficient hull-forms for underwater speed, largely because they were derived from existing ideas on streamlining. At about the same time as the final designs for the *Nautilus* were being prepared work started on a small submarine designed to test new hydro-dynamic principles. She was the *Albacore*, and when she appeared at the end of 1953 her appearance caused a great deal of surprise. She had a whale-backed hull with no deck-casing, and even the streamlined 'sail' had given way to a much thinner dorsal fin. Her two propellers were contra-rotating on a single shaft, and she bore a noticeable resemblance to the original British 'R' Class of 1918, with a hull made up of tapering circular sections, much like a small airship or 'blimp.' In fact many of the ideas tested by the *Albacore* derived from earlier aerodynamic research on dirigible shapes. Refined into the now-standard 'tear-drop' form, the new hull-form provided significantly higher speed and maneuverability for the extra power available.

**The Rise of the Soviet Navy**

The Soviet Navy had been very impressed by the massive U-Boat campaign in the Atlantic and spent the years after World War II in building up a large fleet to replace the one which had performed so dismally in World War II. The lessons of the German Type XXI and Type XVII boats were absorbed, but the HTP experiments were discontinued after some years of abortive efforts. Like the Americans the Soviets grasped the potential of nuclear power, and in 1958 they completed the first of 14 'November' Class, 3500-tonners. The only known designations for Soviet submarines are their NATO code-names, although it is known that they have hull-numbers like US submarines, and the fleet submarines are known as *bolshaya* or large boats. The 'Novembers,' for example, are the 627 Class, just as the American *Skipjack* Class are the SSN.585 Class, and the so-called 'Foxtrot' Class are the 641 Class. The 'Victor' Class which appeared in 1967–68 were much quieter than the 'Novembers' and are believed to be capable of 30 knots underwater.

The only other countries to embark on the construction of nuclear submarines were Great Britain, France and possibly the People's Republic of China. The British and French both have surface fleets of considerable size, and wished to develop the nuclear submarine as a defense against Soviet nuclear submarines, and also to give their antisubmarine forces proper experience. It is becoming more and more obvious that the hunter-killer submarine is not only the only craft which can catch another 'nuke' but also the ideal Sonar platform. During operations in the Arctic in the Second World War, Allied escorts noticed that U-Boats were often able to hide under 'thermal layers' formed by layers of water of differing temperatures. When water changes temperature it changes density, and this can deflect sonar pulses. Surface ships have to be equipped with variable-depth sonar to avoid this effect, whereas a submarine simply changes

depth. She is also relatively unaffected by rough weather as there is virtually no wave effect below periscope depth.

The 'tear-drop' hull design became standard, but another problem had to be overcome, that of noise. The first nuclear boats like the *Nautilus* were very noisy, partly because of the shape of hull, and also because of the turbulence caused by the inevitable holes in the casing and the design of propellers. Propellers 'sing' from the effects of cavitation, and today a computer can scan the recorded 'signatures' of all types of ship to give a quick identification of ship-type and the speed at which it is traveling. Soviet submarines have the reputation of being very noisy, the old 'Whiskey' type being compared to an express train passing in the

*Below: The launch of the* Trafalgar, *first of a new class of British hunter-killers, at Barrow-in-Furness in July 1981.*

distance. Sound travels far underwater, and the *Nautilus*, for example, could be heard ten miles away when using pumps to cool her reactor. Great emphasis is placed on propeller-design to eliminate cavitation, but the need to let water into ballast tanks means that a submarine must have a number of holes in its outer hull.

## Modern Conventional Boats

However impressive the tally of nuclear submarines building by the two superpowers it would be wrong to assume that there is no future for the conventional submersible. Not only are the 'nukes' expensive to build, they also make demands on skilled manpower which all navies are finding hard to meet. The inevitable bulk of the reactor and the steam machinery needed for high speed makes the nuclear submarine very big, yet there are areas like the Baltic, the North Sea and Mediterranean and Black Sea where a 3000-ton submarine is at a severe disadvantage on account of her draft and size. The Soviets are rumored to be considering a new conventional class for defense and the smaller navies still rely on them to defend their coasts.

It is hardly surprising that the nation which has made the most original contribution to conventional submarine design is Germany. Although the Federal German Navy was not permitted to build submarines when it was first formed as part of NATO in 1954 this restriction

was soon waived to permit 350-ton boats. The Federal German Navy had no need to repeat the effort of the 1920s to conceal its researches, for NATO gave its blessing to a rapid reforming of a U-Boat Command under Kapitän zur See (later Admiral) Otto Kretschmer, the former ace of 1940–41. He was assisted by another World War II submariner, Kapitän zur See Topp. Two Type XXIII U-Boats which had been scuttled in the western Baltic were raised in 1956. As the *Hai* (Shark) and *Hecht* (Pike) they were recommissioned in 1957 for training. At the same time a Type XXI boat, the former *U.2540* was raised and put back into service as a non-operational trials vessel under the distinguished name *Wilhelm Bauer*. The *Hai* was lost off the Dogger Bank in 1966 and the *Hecht* was scrapped in 1968. Two even smaller boats were built in 1965–66, the 130-ton *Hans Techel* and *Friedrich Schurer* but neither was commissioned into the Bundesmarine.

The first U-Boats of the new generation were *U.1–3* of the Type 201. They had a novel arrangement of torpedo-tubes, with eight disposed in a semi-circle in the bow. Although there were problems with corrosion of the hulls the designers were anxious to use non-magnetic steel to reduce the danger from magnetic influence torpedoes and mines. All-electric propulsion was used, and the boats had to return to harbor to recharge their batteries. The next group, *U.4–8* had a slightly longer hull to accommodate

more electronic gear, but again the problem of corrosion called for urgent attention. This class, the Type 205 was divided into magnetic and non-magnetic types.

The Norwegian and Danish Navies showed great interest in the German developments. Two *Narhvalen* Class were built in the Royal Dockyard at Copenhagen to Type 205 plans but with Danish equipment, while the Norwegians ordered 15 *Kobben* Class to a slightly enlarged design. In June 1969, with the limit now increased to 450 tons the German Navy placed orders for the first of 18 Type 206 boats, *U.13–30*. They differed in having a much greater array of electronic gear in the bow, and in having wire-guided 'See schlange' torpedoes. Their 21-man crews are composed entirely of officers and petty officers, and as they are not intended to be lived in the internal space is packed with gear. To load torpedoes the bow is trimmed up and the torpedoes are loaded tail-first into the tubes.

In 1966–67 three German firms, Ferrostaal, Ingenieurkontor Lubeck and Howaldtswerke formed a consortium to exploit the knowledge gained in Germany to date. Many of the smaller navies which had been given old American *Gato* and *Balao* Class boats by the US Government were now looking for replacements, but the US Navy was now so firmly committed to nuclear propulsion that American submarine builders had virtually given up the construction of conventional boats. Another incentive to the

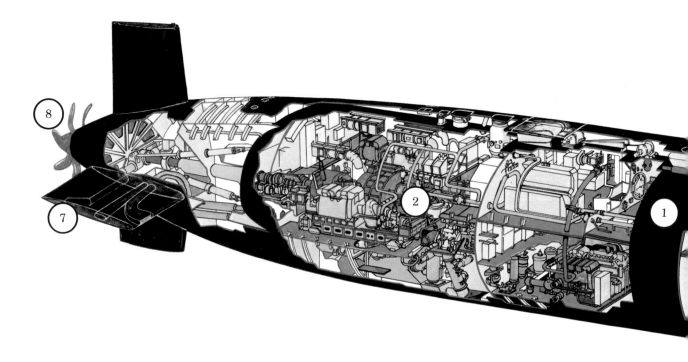

consortium was the certain knowledge that the Federal German Navy had all the submarines it needed for some years.

As a result the Germans were able to produce a highly successful Type 209 1000-ton export design which embodied all the technical advances of the boats built for the German Navy but using the extra tonnage to produce boats which were more suitable for work on the oceans. The man behind this new design was Professor Ulrich Gabler, the founder of Ingenieurkontor Lubeck, a company which had assisted in designing the Types 201–206. Professor Gabler had previously worked on the development of the Type XVII and Type XXI boats during World War II. The Type 209 has become one of the most popular submarines for countries unable to build their own:

### Export Sales of Type 209

| | | |
|---|---|---|
| Argentina | (2) | *Salta* and *San Luis* completed 1974 |
| Colombia | (2) | *Pijao* and *Tayrona* completed 1975 |
| Ecuador | (2) | *Shyri* and *Huavancila* completed 1978 |
| Greece | (8) | *Glafkos, Nereus, Proteus, Triton, Possidon, Amfitriti, Okeonos* and *Pantos* completed in 1971–78 |
| Indonesia | (2) | *Cakra* and *Candasa* completed 1980 |
| Peru | (2) | *Islay* and *Arica* completed 1974–75 |
| Turkey | (4) | *Atilay, Saldiray, Batiray* and *Yildiray* completed 1975–80 |
| Venezuela | (2) | *Sabalo* and *Caribe* completed 1976–77 |

*Above:* U.10 *in dry dock, showing the single 5-bladed propeller and the stubby hull of modern U-Boats.*

*Below: The British* Swiftsure *Class resemble other nuclear hunter-killer submarines in layout. Key – 1 nuclear reactor, 2 steam turbines and diesel generators, 3 control room, 4 periscopes, snorkel mast, radar etc, 5 bow sonar compartment, 6 torpedo tubes, 7 after diving planes, 8 7-bladed propeller.*

In addition IKL and Howaldt in 1971
signed a contract with the British
Vickers Shipbuilding Group, the leading
submarine builder in the United King-
dom. This led to a contract the following
year to build three 500-ton submarines at
Barrow for the Israeli Navy, the Gal,
Tanin and Rahav. The secrecy surround-
ing this contract was such that it was
almost impossible to get the builders to
admit that the boats were being built!

Two other countries have specialized
in submarine-building for export. France
has sold a number of her Daphne and
Agosta Class abroad, usually to countries whose regimes excite hostility in

the West. Spain, Portugal and Pakistan
have either bought Daphnés or built
them locally, while South Africa has
bought three Daphné Class and intended
to buy two of the more modern Agosta
Class (the sale was embargoed in 1979).
The British have been more successful in
selling their 1500-ton Oberon Class to
Australia, Canada, Brazil and Chile.

The United States Navy's submarine
force has become more and more involved
with nuclear power, to the point where
the capability of designing and building
a diesel-electric boat has all but disappeared. But the conventional boats did
not disappear overnight, and there was
still a useful role for them to play as the
new construction programs lagged behind and the dwindling numbers of boats
began to worry defense planners. In
Fiscal Year 1962 nine Guppy IIs were
approved for modernization to stretch
their hull-lives for another five years or
more. Known as Guppy IIIs these boats

*Above: The Swedish* Näcken *was lowered into the water at Malmö in 1978 as against a conventional launch.*

*Left: The* Agosta *Class are the latest French diesel-electric boats. Inset, sections of* La Praya *being assembled.*

were cut in half and given a new 15-foot section for electronic fire-control and accommodation. As in other navies new materials were introduced, mainly glass-reinforced plastic for the sail and parts of the casing. By moving the sonar room back abaft the control center it was possible to provide up to 18 reloads for the torpedo-tubes, a much-needed improvement to their fighting power.

Externally the Guppy III boats could be recognized by a much longer sail, extended to cover the lengthened conning tower containing fire-control and sonar consoles. In addition there were three shark-fin protrusions from the deck casing, passive hydrophone arrays for

the PUFFS passive underwater fire-control and ranging equipment. None of the boats are in service with the US Navy now, but since 1973 they have been turned over to foreign navies and will continue to serve for some years yet. With the remaining *Tang, Darter* and *Barbel* classes they are the last diesel-electric boats left out of the huge fleet which existed a quarter of a century ago.

Sweden's latest submarines show how the best of foreign developments can be combined with native innovations to produce a radical solution. When a new submarine design was projected in the late 1960s and early 1970s by the Swedish Naval Staff and Kockums Shipyard at Malmo there were three inescapable limitations. The first was on size, for the shallowness of the Baltic precludes large submarines. The second was on cost, for the spiralling cost of new warships was eating into the funds available. The third factor, which could be ignored but only at great peril, was the military necessity

to have performance equal to the job of defending Swedish territorial waters in wartime. Taken together these factors put a great burden on the design team but they were able to limit cost as well as size by resorting to a high degree of automation, while attention to detail design resulted in a more efficient hull-form.

The boats which resulted, the three *Näcken* Class, owe a lot to the previous *Sjöormen* (sea serpent) Class, using the same X-form tailplanes and a similar hull-form. But manpower has been cut by a third, with automated machinery control and opening and closing of all valves and hatches. Improvements in the hull-form mean that only half the power is required for the same speed, so that on the same fuel-supply range is increased considerably.

The British, having tried to go all-nuclear in the 1970s, have had to get back into the conventional game again to provide the more discreet surveillance possible with conventional boats. The

*Below: At the end of 1981 a Soviet 'Whiskey' Class diesel-electric submarine caused a diplomatic rumpus by running aground in a restricted area near the Swedish naval base at Karlskrona.*

result is the Type 2400, so called from its standard metric tonnage. The announcement was made in September 1979 that this new type of diesel-electric boat would be ordered as a replacement for the *Oberon* Class. From details of the design published it appears to be a smaller version of the latest nuclear type, the 4000-ton *Swiftsure* Class, with five torpedo-tubes capable of launching both torpedoes and missiles.

The design has been criticized for being too large, as compared with, say the 1000-ton Type 209 or the *Näcken* Class, but those two examples are boats intended for operations in restricted waters. The Royal Navy, if it is to be able to use its diesel-electric boats for extended patrols must provide them with adequate endurance and spare torpedoes. An added problem is that a long-range missile system such as the American

Sub-Harpoon or a heavyweight torpedo-system requires bulky fire control and processing equipment, and this pushes up size. A good example of the difference made by internal volume is the operators' verdict on a popular export design of the 1960s, the French *Daphné* Class. On a displacement of 850 tons they have proved too short-ranged even for the Spanish Navy. Their chief competitor, the British *Oberon* Class, displaces nearly double the tonnage and even the next French design, the *Agosta* Class displace 50 percent more, despite having only four torpedo-tubes.

Some idea of the continuing importance of conventional submarines can be gauged by the fact that there are over 140 modern boats in service with European navies, compared to 80 in the Soviet and Warsaw Pact navies. From 1951 onwards the 1000-ton 'Whiskey' Class was seen in growing numbers, and it is estimated that about 240 of this class were built by 1957. The original design showed some signs of Type XXI influence, particularly in having light antiaircraft guns at both ends of the conning tower but the full impact of knowledge gained from the Germans was felt in the 2000-ton 'Zulu' Class, 28 of which were built in 1951–55.

All submarines age and Soviet submarines are no exception. As the 'Whiskey' Class were transferred in large numbers to friendly navies and the remainder were used for a weird variety of guided missile and radar picket conversions it was necessary to build replacements.

The 'Quebec' Class were 420-ton coastal boats and they were followed by the 1400-ton 'Romeo' and 2900-ton 'Foxtrot' Class. The 'Foxtrots' are the best known of recent Soviet boats because they have been built in large numbers and transferred to such countries as India and Libya. The latest design is the 2100-ton 'Tango' Class, the first of which appeared at the Sevastopol Review in mid-1973, and the existence of these and the 'Foxtrots' and 'Romeos' has enabled the older 'Whiskey,' 'Zulu' and 'Quebec' Classes to be laid up in reserve. If these boats are still in existence their only role can be in providing static training, for the resources of the Soviet Navy could not run to overhauling some 100 worn-out boats.

# WEAPONS OF ARMAGEDDON

The US Navy's early experiments with cruise missiles launched from submarines proved abortive, but submarine-designers were still fascinated by the possibility of mating the awesome destructive power of the inter-continental ballistic missile (ICBM) with the nuclear submarine's phenomenal underwater endurance. The United States' government was particularly worried throughout the 1950s by the idea of a preemptive strike by Russian missiles and bombers against its ICBM launching sites. It was therefore reasoned that if part of the nuclear deterrent could be launched underwater it would be immune to attack from ICBMs and bombs, and could act as a second strike weapon to be used if an enemy attacked.

There were formidable technical problems to be solved, but certain factors were known to favor the idea. For one thing, water is incompressible and so a rocket could use the surface of the sea as a launching pad. A second bonus point was that a submarine-launched ballistic missile need only be of intermediate range (IRBM) size since no place on earth is more than 1700 miles from the sea. Against these advantages there was the difficulty of sustaining life in a submarine for months on end and the virtual impossibility of fixing her position accurately enough to plot the co-ordinates for accurate firing of a ballistic missile. These problems were common to the existing nuclear submarines but they were crucial to a ballistic missile-armed submarine. To maintain an effective deterrent she must remain totally out of sight for as long as possible, and cannot afford to surface to get a sextant sighting or even pick up a radio-transmitted 'fix.'

In 1956 the Secretary of the Navy authorized the US Navy to begin work on the new system, to be called 'Polaris.' Scientists shook their heads and prophesied that the US Navy would not be able to make the idea work before the 1970s, but President Kennedy sanctioned the expenditure of extra money to speed up

*Right: The USS* Henry Clay *(SSBN.625) fires an A-2 Polaris on the surface during trials off Cape Kennedy in 1964. The slight list to port is deliberate and the debris consists of adaptors holding the missile in its launch tube. The tall mast is a temporary fitting carrying monitoring equipment.*

Polaris. On 20 July 1960 the submarine *George Washington* (*SSBN-598*) fired two A-1 Polaris missiles from underwater off Cape Canaveral (Cape Kennedy), a distance of 1200 miles, and received the message, 'From out of the deep to target. Perfect.' This news set the seal on the work of Admiral Rickover, the man who had planned the US Navy's nuclear submarine program from the beginning. Within 12 months the second Fleet Ballistic Missile Submarine (SSBN) *Robert E Lee* had set a new record by logging 68 days underwater.

Two important technical advances had made this possible. The Ship's Inertial Navigation System (SINS) provided for the first time a method of accurately computing the submarine's course, without reference to Magnetic or True North. Using accelerometers and gyroscopes SINS plots all drift and movement in relation to a known point, and although its accuracy improves if it can be given additional fixes from time to time it is good enough to provide coordinates for a Polaris missile-system's fire control computer. The habitability problem had been cured by the development of 'scrubbers' which cleaned and filtered air in-

166

side the submarine, and allowed it to be re-breathed by the crew. The research also produced incidental evidence about the urgent need for non-toxic paints in submarines, since minute traces of paint vapor were found in the filters.

The working of Polaris relies on six main components:
1. The SINS, which maintains a constant plot of the submarine's position, both for navigation and fire control.
2. The fire control computers, which receive information from SINS about the relative bearing of True North and the submarine's position. They compute continuously a trajectory for each missile to reach its target, for transmission to the missile's 'memory.'
3. The Missile Test and Readiness Equipment (MTRE), which checks the readiness of the missiles and associated equipment.
4. The launcher control, which prepares the 16 tubes for launch, including equalizing the pressure to ensure that the tube remains free of water until the missile is launched.
5. Each missile's memory, which receives and stores trajectory data from the fire control system before launching.

*Above: The SSBN* George Washington *was adapted from an attack submarine of the* Skipjack *Class by installing 16 Polaris tubes abaft the sail. She is seen here shortly after her launch in June 1959.*

*Right: The awesome sight of a Trident missile rising from the ocean depths.*

6. The Missile Control Panel, which reflects the status of all 16 missiles. The firing sequence is chosen and the final launching circuit is closed after the captain gives permission to fire.

The firing key is closed in the final sequence and then the gas generator ignites to form exhaust gases which eject the missile upwards from the tube. After it leaves the tube the solid-fuel motor ignites and the missile leaves the water. Once launched its inertial guidance system keeps it on course without external control and it functions like any other ballistic missile.

That in the simplest terms is Polaris, in its day the most deadly weapon system ever taken to sea. One Polaris boat with its 16 hydrogen bomb warheads can deliver more explosive power than all

the high explosive dropped in World War II. In 1966 the A-1 Polaris was replaced by the A-3, with a range of 2880 miles, giving even more flexibility to the system, and in 1970 the *James Madison* fired a new missile, the C-3 Poseidon. Despite its greater diameter this missile has no more range than the A-3 Polaris because it is designed primarily to incorporate three more sophisticated Multiple Independently Targeted Re-entry Vehicle (MIRV) warheads. This produces a shotgun effect of warheads which can be directed at different targets to confuse and saturate Anti-Ballistic Missile (ABM) defenses.

While all this was going on the Soviet Navy was not idle. Although taken by surprise by the speed with which the Polaris missile was tested and introduced the Soviets were quick to provide an answer. In 1958 they commissioned a hurried conversion of a conventional 'Whiskey' boat armed with two SS-N-3 Shaddock cruise-missiles. They were, however, only experimental and crude conversions, and they were followed by a variant with SS-N-3 launchers faired at an angle of about 30° into the fin. The 16 'Juliett' Class which followed were the first proper SS-N-3 submarines, and they appeared in 1962–67 with four launching tubes which folded horizontally into the casing, two forward of the fin and two aft. The 28 'Echo' Class had double the armament, but however impressive these boats were they were still armed only with the tactical Shaddock missile, which bore no comparison with the ballistic Polaris as it only had 300 miles range and had to be launched on the surface.

In 1961 the first 'Golf' Class appeared, still a diesel-electric submersible, armed first with the SS-N-4 Sark but soon rearmed with the 650-mile SS-N-5 Serb. Although only three of these ballistic missiles were carried in vertical tubes inside the fin they could be launched underwater. The 3700-ton 'Hotel' Class were a nuclear-powered version of the 'Golf' with the same armament, but the 33 boats of the 'Yankee' Class completed between 1967 and 1971 were true ballistic missile submarines like the American SSBNs. The SS-N-6 'Sawfly' has a reputed range of 1300 miles, and each 'Yankee' carries sixteen.

The British and French followed an altogether more coherent policy when they came to build their own SSBNs. When in 1962 the United States Air

*Left: Poseidon (C-4) was the successor to the A-3 Polaris using a wider body to accommodate improved penetration aids. Older SSBNs were converted to Poseidon by enlarging their launch tubes.*

*Above: The Soviet 'Juliett' Class carry long range cruise missiles in external folding launchers.*

*Left: The Soviet 'Yankee' Class follow the configuration of Western SSBNs.*

*Below: An SS-N-4 Sark missile being loaded at the Soviet submarine base at Nakhoda in the Far East.*

Force decided to drop its proposed air-launched Skybolt ballistic missile the British Government was forced to make a decision about continuing to maintain the RAF's airborne deterrent. The development of a new generation of bombers was prohibitively expensive and developing a British equivalent of Skybolt was out of the question, whereas Polaris was available and British shipyards already had the knowhow to build nuclear submarines. Accordingly the momentous decision was made to transfer the responsibility for Britain's nuclear deterrent from the Royal Air Force to the Royal Navy, and the keel of the first boat, *Resolution*, was laid in February 1964. Less than three and one-half years later she started her trials and she began her first patrol the following year. The hull and reactor were totally British in design, but the missiles, their tubes and the associated fire control equipment are all either made in the USA or British-made under license. When HMS *Resolution*

commissioned the missile compartment carried a notice reading, 'You are now entering the American Zone.'

The French Navy had hoped to build a force of Polaris boats but a quarrel between General de Gaulle and the United States led to an embargo on the sale. Determined to maintain French independence de Gaulle sanctioned an expensive programme to design a French equivalent, the *Mer-Sol-Ballistique-Stratégique* (MSBS) M-2. Five SSBNs were authorized, starting with *Le Redoutable* in 1963 and they came into service between 1971 and 1980.

Known as *Sousmarins Nucleaire Lance Engins* or SNLEs, they are based at Brest on the Atlantic coast, and like the British and American SSBNs they are manned by two crews. The idea of this is to maintain a constant patrol, avoiding too much strain on the officers and men but taking full advantage of the high endurance afforded by nuclear power. This means in effect a very short turn-around time between patrols, with the second crew (Blue and Gold in the USN, Port and Starboard in the RN) taking over while minor running repairs are carried out. A visit to HMS *Resolution* at Faslane leaves the onlooker with a vivid impression of electrical leads and powerlines snaking through the confined spaces, and a frantic urgency normally absent from a surface warship about to recommission.

In 1979 it was revealed that under the code-name 'Chevaline' the Royal Navy had produced a new 'semi-MIRV' warhead to update the A-3 Polaris to improve its ability to penetrate anti-ballistic missile defenses. Basically Chevaline is a triple warhead which can be programed to hit three targets up to 40 miles apart, whereas the original British A-3 warhead did not have this facility.

## Bigger and Better SSBNs?

To understand the next step in submarine developments it is essential to look at submarine weaponry and antisubmarine warfare. Naturally the growing might of the nuclear submarine led at first to stunned dismay, when navies felt that there was no answer, then to a vigorous pursuit of countermeasures. And today,

nearly 30 years after the *Nautilus* first put to sea on nuclear power, it must be said that nuclear submarines do not have it all their own way. For one thing their high speed is best used to break away *after* an attack, for it generates too much noise for a surprise attack. Ambush tactics are still the best for any submarine unless she happens to encounter a target of opportunity. Another disadvantage is the size of the nuclear boat, which limits the areas in which she can maneuver freely.

Right: Spare torpedo stowage in a French Redoubtable *Class* SSBN. Modern submarines can reload much faster than was possible during World War II.

Below: View along the casing of HMS Renown.

Bottom right: A helicopter winching crew members off the after casing of HMS Resolution.

The biggest danger facing the modern submarine is the helicopter-carried weapon and its more sophisticated variant the antisubmarine missile. The range of modern sonar systems, particularly when used passively, that is to 'listen' rather than 'ping' actively, is measured in miles, thanks to the distance traveled by sound through water. Older antisubmarine weapons such as rocket-fired depth-charges and homing torpedoes have nothing like this range, and so there is a gap between detection-range and attacking range. Obviously it is desirable to attack a submarine at the earliest opportunity, before she can approach her target. The helicopter is able to take off and land on small flight decks, and is therefore able to carry a homing torpedo rapidly (90 knots or more) to the area of a submarine contact. The next step was to develop a sonar set light enough to be carried in a helicopter for 'dunking' in the sea, and so extend the range of the shipborne sonar set.

The US Navy tried in the late 1950s to develop a remotely controlled 'drone' helicopter, but the so-called DASH (Drone Anti-Submarine Helicopter) was an expensive failure. The subtle techniques of landing a helicopter on a pitching deck were beyond the capabilities of the guidance system, and some 60 percent of the drones were lost. DASH

operations were attended by risk to personnel as well; on several occasions the drone 'ran wild' or flew upside down, complete with its load of armed homing torpedoes, straight back at the ship. Finally the US Navy turned its back on the whole costly fiasco and adopted the LAMPS or Light Airborne Multi-Purpose System, a rather pompous term to describe a manned helicopter. Navies like the British and French had always maintained that a human pilot was a far more reliable guidance system, and that the risk of losing one was outweighed by the reduced risk of landing accidents, a point of view which has been vindicated by the success of the RN's Wasp helicopter operations from frigates.

Big helicopters like the American SH-3, its British development the Sea King, the French Super Frélon and the Russian Kamov Ka-25 'Hormone' can accommodate both sonar and weapons. This gives them more flexibility but limits their employment to larger ships, although the Royal Canadian Navy has followed a separate line of development by operating two of the very bulky Sea Kings from destroyers. Long-range maritime aircraft carry much bulkier equipment which allows them to use sonobuoys. These passive receivers are parachuted into the sea to cover a wide area, and their signals are analysed

*Above: Crewmen of a Soviet 'Foxtrot' preparing to retrieve a NATO aircraft's sonobuoy.*

*Right: The Vickers SLAM (Submarine Launched Airflight Missile) was an attempt to provide submarines with a defense against helicopters. Six Blowpipe missiles were mounted on a retracting head with a TV camera.*

electronically aboard the aircraft to provide data for an attack with homing torpedoes or depth-charges.

The eternal problem with the shipboard helicopter is mechanical realiability. It is virtually impossible to guarantee that a single aircraft of any type will be ready to fly all the time, and the workshop provided in a small warship can cope with no more than running repairs and maintenance. To avoid this difficulty the US Navy developed the Asroc system, while the British and Australians followed with their Ikara. Both systems are the same in principle as they employ a rocket-propelled homing torpedo which flies at high speed to the contact area and then drops free of its 'carrier' to track the submarine. Asroc is a ballistic weapon which is fired much like a gun from an 8-tube launcher; the rocket is jettisoned and a parachute opens when the projectile is over the target to allow the torpedo to make a 'soft' landing. Asroc can also be used with a depth-charge as a warhead, in which case it makes a normal entry into the water. Ikara differs in being a small delta-winged aircraft which can be redirected to conform to any change of the target's position and speed; once over the target the 'carrier' breaks into three parts to release the homing torpedo. The French Malafon system is similar, but the carrier glides at a fixed height using a radio altimeter. All three systems have the great advantage of being immediately available in all weathers.

What defense has the submarine against all these weapons? As might be expected, a countermeasure against helicopters has been designed. Known as SLAM (Submarine Launched Airflight Missile), it is a cluster of six small missiles around a 'head' containing a TV camera and the guidance control. The operator is in the control room of the submarine below, whereas the SLAM-launcher is extended above water like a snort mast. When not in use the launcher folds down into a watertight container in the fin. The missile itself is a development of the Blowpipe system used on land, and although only 1.35 meters long can travel a distance of 3000 meters. Helicopters are extremely vulnerable, and a hit from even a small missile will cripple one, but there remains the danger of

loitering at periscope depth merely to take revenge on a helicopter – every submariner's instinct must be to forget the helicopter and make his getaway as soon as possible. In fact apart from the trials boat HMS *Aeneas*, only one Israeli boat, the *Rahav* was fitted for the SLAM system and the missiles are not installed.

Another way of hitting back at submarines is to identify 'choke-points' through which they must pass to reach their target areas. One such choke-point is the Greenland-Iceland-UK Gap, the so-called GIUK Gap, through which Soviet submarines from Murmansk must pass to attack shipping in the North Atlantic. For the past decade the seabed of the GIUK Gap has been sown with passive arrays of sensors known as SOSUS Barriers (Sound Surveillance Underwater System), which can triangulate the position and speed of a passing submarine from its sound-effects. Using modern methods of micro-processing shore stations can scan the computer memory electronically to identify not only the class of submarine but even individual boats within that class. No two propellers are identical and no two hulls generate exactly the same noise, so that sound-analyzers can distinguish these minute variations. What is more important is that this information can be fed back to an antisubmarine frigate or a maritime patrol aircraft within seconds,

enabling the target to be attacked quickly.

The Straits of Gibraltar form a similar chokepoint, and as the shallow, clear waters of the Mediterranean are historically lethal for submarines it is not surprising to learn that Soviet SSBNs do not like to operate there. But the limitations on range of the first generation of Submarine-Launched Ballistic Missiles (SLBMs) mean that SSBNs must get reasonably close in order to be able to strike at selected targets. This means, for example, that British and American Polaris and Poseidon SSBNs must operate in the Barents Sea and Soviet 'Yankee' boats must get into the mid-Atlantic. However, the growing sophistication of ASW on both sides means that these areas are now much more dangerous to SSBNs than they were before, and in order to maintain the credibility of SLBMs as a strategic deterrent it is necessary to provide them with much greater range. This requirement led the US Navy to its latest addition to the catalog of acronyms, ULMS or the Underwater Long-range Missile System, while the Soviet Union went ahead with its massive SS-N-8, known in the West for a time as the 'Extended Sawfly.' This missile is credited with a range of 4200 miles, while the progeny of ULMS, the UGM-96A Trident will have a similar range and the D-5 version will reach out to 6000 miles.

To accommodate Trident the US Navy has ordered seven giant *Ohio* Class SSBNs and plans to build 4 more. Each one is 170.7 meters long and displaces nearly 16,000 tons on the surface. The reason for the huge increase in size from the 7250-ton *Lafayette* Class is simply the need to replace 41 Polaris and Poseidon SSBNs, carrying a total of 656 missiles, by building 11 boats carrying 264 Tridents. Under the second Strategic Arms Limitation Treaty (SALT II) the number of seaborne launch vehicles is limited to 1320, and the total has to take account of the number of actual warheads carried in each missile. Each A-3 Polaris carries three Multiple Independent Re-entry Vehicles (MIRVs) and a Poseidon carries 10, so that the American SSBN force deploys some 5000 warheads, or about 55 percent of the total strategic deterrent. A smaller number of SSBNs carrying bigger missiles will spend less time off-station, and although their size will inevitably make the *Ohio* Class clumsier than older boats the colossal range of Trident II will enable them to cruise in waters well away from hostile antisubmarine forces.

The *Ohio* Class break new ground in many ways, not merely because they are the largest submarines built in the west. General Dynamics spent $150,000,000 on developing a 10-acre Land Level Sub-

*Below: The* Ohio, *first of the 560-foot long Trident SSBNs, dwarfs the attack submarine* Jacksonville *(Los Angeles Class).*

marine Construction Facility, including a 617-foot long pontoon graving dock for launching and dry-docking the submarines. The building method is quite different from the traditional method of building submarines, being a modular process with cylindrical hull-sections moved about on a grid network of rail tracks and transfer cars. By 'end-loading' major components into the hull it has been possible to build faster and therefore keep cost down. Another feature is 'station loading;' by dividing the facility into 13 stations it is possible to break down the building process by function. Thus on 7 April 1979 when the USS *Ohio* was named by Mrs Rosalynn Carter the

hull of the *Michigan* (SSBN.727) was lying outboard of the *Ohio* in the graving dock. On the same day sections of the third boat were already being assembled and the first section of the fourth, to be called *Georgia* was about to be laid down. The new method is much faster than before; whereas it took 39 weeks to get a complete hull assembled on the inclined ways at Groton the *Ohio*'s hull was assembled in 15 weeks and it is hoped to get the time for future Trident hulls down to as little as 9 weeks.

At the Quonset Point facility hull-cylinders are fabricated on four unique machines, one making frames, the second making cylinder shells, the third instal-

ling frames and the fourth pairing the cylinders. Each machine incorporates massive jigs and fixtures for precise control of dimensions and uses automated welding to ensure a uniform quality of weld. Six radio-controlled cranes and a motorized ground transporter move the components from machine to machine and when the hull-sections are complete they are shipped by barge to Groton. One of the most important features of nuclear submarine design is the standard of welding, for in the first nuclear boats, so-called 'hairline' cracks were found in the welds. It turned out that these cracks had always been likely to appear but had only come to light through the new

practise of X-raying the welds. Today the use of special HY80 steel is standard and so is examination of the welding, so that accidental loss such as that of the *Thresher* or *Scorpion* is less likely.

The Trident force will be based at new facilities built at Bangor, Maine. The new Naval Submarine Base has been built on the Kitsap Peninsula, with re-fitting berths, dry docks, workshops and extensive re-supply facilities. As far as possible upkeep will be by replacement of faulty equipment, so that a Trident boat will be able to return to sea while the original equipment is being repaired. Quite apart from the range advantage of Trident over Polaris and Poseidon, the fact that the Trident boats are based in the United States rather than in Rota, Spain or Holy Loch, Scotland, makes them less vulnerable to a preemptive strike and much cheaper to operate.

The layout of the *Ohio* Class is similar to previous SSBNs but they are significantly bigger:

| | |
|---|---|
| Displacement: | 18,750 tons (submerged) |
| Length: | 560 feet |
| Beam: | 42 feet |
| Draught: | 35 feet 6 inches (surface trim) |
| Machinery: | single-shaft S8G nuclear reactor, 60,000 shaft horsepower |
| Speed: | 20 knots |
| Complement: | 154 officers and enlisted men |

In addition to her Trident missiles she carries four 21-inch torpedo-tubes forward of the sail, capable of firing the long-range wire-guided Mark 48 torpedo, Sub-Harpoon or Tomahawk missiles. In all recent US submarines the torpedo-tubes have been positioned abaft the bow compartment to leave room for a spherical sonar dome, and these four tubes are angled out. Four deck-levels are incorporated in the massive hull.

The US Navy is also pushing ahead with a Sea-Launched Cruise Missile (SLCM), which could deliver a nuclear warhead against strategic targets up to 1500 miles away, or a conventional warhead against ship-targets up to 300 miles

*Below: France's first three SSBNs,* le Redoutable, le Terrible *and* le Foudroyant *exercising off Brest.*

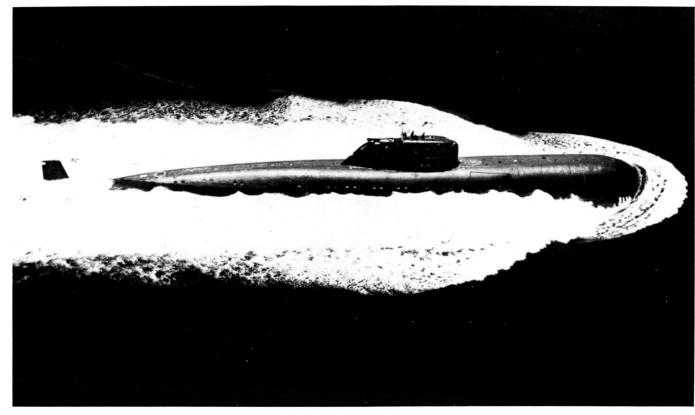

away. Known as Tomahawk, it follows an electronic 'map' of the terrain, flying at low altitude and because it is considerably cheaper than a ballistic missile it will be available in larger numbers. The best argument for Tomahawk is that it can be fired from a torpedo-tube and so does not require a specially designed (nuclear) submarine. One suggestion has been to replace the A-3 Polaris missiles in the older SSBNs by vertically-launched Tomahawks but equally it can be fired from torpedo-tubes in the normal hunter-killer SSNs. The same method is used for launching the Sub-Harpoon antiship missile and a very similar system is used for the French SM-39 version of the Exocet missile, which started trials in 1981.

All this activity was sparked off by a Soviet innovation, the SS-N-7 underwater-launched cruise missile. In 1968 the first of a new class of 4000-ton nuclear attack submarines was spotted, with eight large hatches on the forward casing. Although at first alarmist reports indicated a huge range, subsequent estimates of the SS-N-7's range came down to 25 miles, but even that gave a formidable advantage to submarines in attacking surface ships for if they can slip inside the ASW screen of a task force the target has very little time to react. The first warning is when a missile jumps out of the water, as little as 10 miles away, its rocket motor ignites and then it locks on to the nearest radar target. These 'Charlie' Class boats have been followed by the similar 'Papa' Class but have not been built in large numbers, 15 'Charlies' and only one 'Papa' according to the

178

*Above: The Soviet 'Charlie' Class are credited with being able to fire eight anti-ship missiles at a range of 30 miles.*

*Right: The Soviet 'Delta' Class carry twelve 4000-mile range ballistic missiles.*

most reliable reports received by Western intelligence sources.

The Soviet Navy has taken development of the nuclear submarine as far as any Western navy. After the eight 'Hotel' Class commissioned from 1958 to 1962, armed with three 300-mile SS-N-4 'Sark' missiles (replaced by 700-mile SS-N-5 'Serbs' in 1962–67) the Soviet Navy built 34 'Yankee' Class. Instead of carrying three missiles in the fin these 7800-tonners resembled the US *Ethan Allen*, with 16 SS-N-6 'Sawfly' missiles in the after part of the hull. Then came the 19 'Delta' Class from 1973 to 1977, an early version with only 12 SS-N-8 tubes but followed by 15 enlarged 'Delta II' and 'Delta III' boats with 16 missile tubes. The problems of maintaining and manning 76 SSBNs are just as acute in the Soviet Union as they are in the United States, and it is interesting to see that the next class of SSBN announced was the 24,000-ton *Typhoon* Class, reported to have 24 tubes for the SS-N-8 'Extended Sawfly' and to be 480 feet long and 57 feet in diameter.

There has been much speculation about the use of titanium for the hulls of the new 'Oscar' Class, and also for the 'Alpha' attack type. There have been reports in Western newspapers of 'Alphas' tracked at 40 knots at depths down to

3000 feet, far in excess of anything claimed for the latest *Los Angeles* Class in the US Navy. In support of these figures it is claimed that the Soviet Union has a virtual monopoly of titanium and that the deep diving qualities of the 'Alpha' enable it to make a rapid transit from base to operating area, thus out-flanking satellite reconnaissance, SOSUS barriers, ASW ships and aircraft. Even if the figures are correct, and it must be remembered that all submarine performances have been exaggerated for the past 30 years (the *Nautilus* was at one time claimed to have done 30 knots underwater but only reached 20) there is very little that a submarine can achieve at such a depth. All experience with torpedo-launching and homing systems indicates that from 3000 feet down a submarine could not hope to attack anything, simply because of the excessive pressure. In other words, although a hull can be made strong enough to withstand the pressure and a nuclear plant can be built to drive it, it can only use that facility to evade pursuit, in much the same way as interceptor aircraft cannot

fight and maneuver at anything like their maximum speed.

The 'Alpha' type has been followed by the 'Oscar' Class, reputed to displace as much as 10,000 tons. Here again, allowing for hyperbole and over-reaction in the West, it could have a new 200-mile underwater-launched cruise-missile (tentatively identified as SS-NX-19) which would pose a much greater threat than the 25-mile SS-N-7 in the 'Charlie' Class. It must, however, always be remembered that bigger does not mean better where submarines are concerned, particularly in the case of SSBNs, whose purpose is to carry a specific number of strategic weapons, not to fight one another. Man's ability to exploit technology is unlimited but sooner or later sheer practicality must impose some limits.

The underwater battleground of tomorrow is both fascinating and horrifying to contemplate. To the naval strategist it has the advantage that forces can be deployed across the oceans with much the same freedom as admirals once enjoyed before the introduction of air power. Without direct surveillance from

aircraft and satellites it is theoretically possible to fight with a measure of freedom long since banished from surface warfare. But that is an over-simple view for despite all the advances of technology submarines are still largely deaf and blind in the vastness of the ocean. Great advances have been made in ultra-low frequency communications and passive sound-analysis can be achieved at phenomenal ranges but water remains an intractable medium and there is no direct parallel to the freedom of communications which surface ships enjoy.

If such a conflict occurs we know from experience in the two World Wars that a submarine-versus-submarine engagement will be one of bluff and double-bluff, testing the nerves of the rival commanders and their men to the utmost. As always the penalty for a mistake will be sudden and complete destruction. It will be a matter of stalking a quarry, sudden decisions based on electronic analysis of the quarry's propeller-noise and a measure of intuition.

Today the United States Navy maintains a force of 13 aircraft known as

TACAMO ('Take Command and Move Out'), whose job is to maintain round-the-clock communications with the Polaris and Poseidon submarine fleet. Not only must routine operational instructions be given to the SSBNs but in the event of an attack on the United States Presidential authority has to be given to each commander to fire his nuclear missiles. The modified Hercules EC-130G and EC-130Q aircraft each transmit a 200kW signal which can be picked up by a submarine trailing a buoyant towed antenna.

The next step was to go to an Extra-Low Frequency (ELF) system which allowed a land-station to broadcast directly to the SSBN without an airborne link. Known as Seafarer, the program ran into opposition from environmentalists who feared the physiological effects of ELF transmissions on human beings. An alternative proposal is the

*Above: A Trident missile lifts off during testing in 1977. Trident became operational in 1980 and the early version will be followed by the larger D-5.*

use of blue-green lasers transmitted by satellite, a proposal which might eventually lead to a new method of detecting submarines. The problem with such high technology is cost, and current thinking in the United States is that blue-green laser communications with submarines will not be available until the late 1990s at the earliest, whereas ELF technology is available now. Whatever the outcome an answer is needed urgently for the TACAMO fleet is now elderly and cannot last forever. More important, the awesome firepower of the Trident missile must be kept under tight political control: without some direct means of communication it could be used accidentally to destroy civilization on this planet.

*Above: Preparing to load the Poseidon launch tubes on the USS John C Calhoun at Charleston Navy Yard, South Carolina.*

*Left: A Tomahawk cruise missile in flight. Two versions exist, a nuclear warhead carrying strategic version and a conventionally armed 250-mile version for use against ship targets.*

*Far left: A Tomahawk flies clear of its underwater-launched capsule.*

# MEMORIES

It is just over two centuries since the *Turtle* made her attack on HMS *Eagle*. The submarine has taken nearly the whole of that time to develop from an interesting toy into the deadliest of warships. Even 30 years ago the submarine was still little more than a torpedo-boat which could submerge for short periods, whereas today it is a capital ship in every sense of the word. The nuclear submarine and her ballistic missiles make up the most complex piece of machinery on earth. She represents both a threat to civilization and a means of its preservation, and every branch of science has been explored to find ways of neutralizing her. Sadly, it is only now that submarine

technology is beginning to be used for peaceful purposes. Throughout their history submarines have been manned by the bravest of men, and whatever doubts we have about the misuse of human ingenuity and their prodigious cost we should honor the memory of those who have given their lives to perfect the submarine.

So rapid is the pace of advance that in 1980 two of the first Polaris SSBNs, the *Theodore Roosevelt* and *Abraham Lincoln* were decommissioned at Mare Island Naval Shipyard for scrapping. Another sign of the march of progress was the decommissioning of the USS *Nautilus* for the last time in March 1980. Although

the ceremony was also held at Mare Island she is to be spared the ignominy of being cut up for scrap. To commemorate her distinguished career spanning 25 years and the contribution she has made to science she is to be preserved as a permanent public exhibit at Washington Navy Yard.

Submarines do not lend themselves to preservation in quite the same way as surface warships, partly because they are usually small and cramped internally. But an equally important reason is their reputation, which in the public mind ranges from mildly unsavory to downright evil. Yet a surprisingly large

number of boats have survived as memorials and museum exhibits, a testimony to a growing public interest in the technical ingenuity and bravery embodied in undersea craft.

The oldest preserved submarine is the Confederate CSS *Pioneer*, which was completed in 1862 at New Orleans but had to be scuttled in order to avoid capture by Admiral Farragut's forces. The hulk was salved many years later and now lies in the Louisiana State Museum. Her Federal contemporary, the *Intelligent Whale*, built a year later, was sold to the Navy Department in 1869 and now lies in Washington Navy Yard. Appropriately John P. Holland's *Fenian Ram* is preserved at Patterson, New Jersey.

Visitors to Cartagena in Spain can see Isaac Peral's 1887 prototype outside the entrance to the Naval School, while in Sweden the original *Hajen* was preserved ashore at Karlskrona after being taken out of service in 1922. The Royal Netherlands Navy honored its early pioneers

*Below: A U-Boat on the beach of an English resort after breaking her tow on the way to the breakers, c.1920.*

*Above: The small Italian submarine*
CM.1 *waiting alongside the* Atropo.
*Both boats were scrapped in 1947–48.*

*Right: The restored hull of Germany's*
*first U-Boat* U.1 *is now in Munich's*
*Deutchesmuseum.*

by preserving the conning tower of the
quaintly named *Luctor et Emergo*. Commissioned as *O.1* in 1906, she was taken
out of service in 1920 and her diminutive
conning tower can be seen at Den Helder,
the headquarters of the Dutch submarine
squadron.

Not until after World War II were any
more submarines preserved. When the
*Sailfish* (formerly the *Squalus*) reached
the end of her successful career in 1945
her conning tower was put ashore at
Portsmouth Naval Dockyard to serve as
a memorial to all who died in the *Squalus*
accident. Other US submarines' conning
towers preserved in this way are the
*Flasher*'s at the New London Submarine
Base and the *Balao*'s at Washington
Navy Yard. In 1954 the Greek Navy
chose to commemorate the wartime
successes of the *Papanikolis* in a similar
way. Much later several complete submarines were preserved in the United

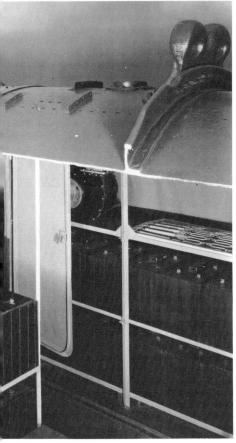

*Above: The cramped forward casing of an American 'C' or Octopus Class boat, c.1909. The signalman right forward is using semaphore flag-signals. The officer in the middle is possibly the future Fleet Admiral Chester Nimitz.*

States, notably the *Cobia* at Manitowoc, Wisconsin, birthplace of so many wartime submarines, the *Drum* at Mobile, Alabama alongside the battleship *Alabama*, the *Cavalla* at Galveston, Texas, and the *Batfish* and the *Bowfin*. In 1970 it was announced that the Royal Navy would preserve one of the 'A' class, *Alliance* at the Submarine Base at Gosport, HMS *Dolphin*. In 1981 the wreck of the Royal Navy's first submarine, *Holland No. 1* was found off Portsmouth. She had been sold for scrap in 1913 but had foundered in tow. The hulk has now been raised and there are plans to preserve her at HMS *Dolphin* alongside the *Alliance*. It is believed that several World War II submarines are preserved as war memorials in the Soviet Union.

Being much smaller than fleet submarines midgets have not been preserved to the same extent, although a number of German midgets were put on display after World War II. There is, for example, a *Seehund* at Washington Navy Yard, a *Biber* at the Imperial War Museum, London and another at the South African War Museum in Johannesburg. Recently a British X-craft was exhibited at the National Maritime Museum in London. Several Japanese and German midgets still exist in the United States.

There are of course many museums and memorials to the men who served in submarines, notably the Submarine Museum at New London, Connecticut, its British equivalent at HMS *Dolphin* and the German U-Boat Museum at Laboe, outside Kiel. The U-Boat memorial was built before World War II and dedicated in 1938. It was rebuilt in 1962 and since then has been extended. In 1963 the Norwegian Navy paid off one of three ex-Type VIIC U-Boats, the *Kaura* (ex-*U.995*), which had been surrendered in 1945. The Norwegian Navy was aware of her historical importance and took care that the old U-Boat was sold to German interests, but the fear of being accused of neo-Naziism made the West German Government reluctant to get involved in any preservation scheme.

*Left: The razor bow of U.995, the last operational Type VIIC U-Boat.*

*Below: Giant salvage cranes bringing U.995 to Laboe near Kiel, her last resting place.*

ULRICH HARMS

However the objections were finally overcome and the *U.995* was put ashore at Laboe, where she is now open to the public. Only one other World War II U-Boat is preserved, *U.505* (a Type IXC) at the Chicago Museum of Science and Industry; she was captured by an American task force off the Azores in 1944. By a series of lucky coincidences Germany's very first U-Boat, *U.1*, has also survived. She had been used purely for trials and training and was stricken from the effective list in 1919, but she was then bought by Krupp's and refitted as an exhibit. Later she was acquired by the Deutschesmuseum in Munich and although badly damaged by bombing during World War II is now fully restored.

These memorials commemorate the thousands of forgotten submariners who served in the two World Wars, but nothing can equal the fame of the aces. It is interesting to compare the various scores of these outstanding commanders, for they reflect the different conditions under which each navy's submarines operated. It is hardly surprising that the Germans hold the record; *U.35* (WWI) was far and away the most successful, sinking 224 ships totalling 535,900 tons gross, but the aces of the other navies must be judged by the number of targets available to them. Kapitänleutnant Lothar von Arnauld de la Perière in *U.35* and *U.139* sank 196 ships totalling 456,216 tons gross, while Kapitänleutnant Dr Walther Forstmann in *U.12* and *U.39* sank 147 ships, a total of 385,124 GRT. The most successful Austro-Hungarian submariner was Leutnant Baron von Trapp (of 'Sound of Music' fame), whose ex-French *U.14* sank 11 ships totalling 44,595 GRT.

In World War II the pickings were not so easy but Korvettenkapitän Otto Kretschmer was able to sink 35 ships totalling 268,000 tons. The top Italian ace was Capitano Gianfranco Gazzana, who sank 12 ships of 94,356 tons gross in the *Leonardo da Vinci*. The most successful boat was *U.48*, which under the three aces, Schultze, Rösing and Bleichrodt achieved the staggering total of 51 ships (310,007 GRT). Against these figures the Allies could field Lieutenant-Commander David Wanklyn of HMS *Upholder*, with 98,947 GRT, while the *Flasher*, *Rasher*, *Barb* and *Tang* all sank over 90,000 tons of Japanese shipping each, and the Soviet Navy's *K.21* sank an estimated 115,000 tons. The top Japanese boat was *I.27*, which under four commanders sank 14 ships of 77,620 GRT.

Undoubtedly the most successful campaign of all time was the American submarines' onslaught against Japanese shipping, which sank 1113 ships of 5,320,094 tons gross. Although dwarfed by the German scores of 6000 ships in World War I and 2779 ships in 1939–45, the American campaign was the only one to succeed in its objective. American submarines also trumped the German score against warships, sinking 201 including a battleship, nine aircraft carriers, 15 cruisers, 22 submarines and 46 destroyers, virtually a quarter of the pre-war Imperial Japanese Navy. The U-Boats, which had sunk 94 warships in 1914–18, did even better in 1939–45 with 148 warships: two battleships, six aircraft carriers, six cruisers, nine submarines and 52 destroyers.

Today the submarine still casts its menacing shadow over the naval scene. Whether we think of the nuclear hunter-killer with its high speed and ability to stay down for weeks on end, the SSBN with its awesome power of destruction or the silent-running diesel-electric boat, every navy fears them. Every year that goes by sees their capabilities growing, and the day may not be far off when they· take over from all but the smallest surface warships.

*Right: A vanished breed. U-Boat crewmen during the First World War.*

*Below: A new British 'U' Class, probably the famous* Upholder, *running trials on completion in October 1940.*

# INDEX

*Page numbers in italics refer to illustrations.*

# INDEX

*Page numbers in italics refer to illustrations.*

# Acknowledgments

I wish to thank all those who have been helpful in providing material and locating obscure facts and figures for this book. In the process I tracked down large numbers of official drawings and technical records of submarines, despite the understandable tendency for navies to treat submarines as a security-sensitive subject.

Among individuals who deserve special thanks are the following: Arthur D Baker, David Brown (Head of Naval Historical Branch), the late Gervais Frere-Cook, Alan Pearsall, David Lyon and George Osbon (National Maritime Museum), Geoffrey Edbrooke, Rod Vennell, John Lawson, Cdr Eriksen (Royal Danish Navy), Cdr Richard Compton-Hall (Submarine Museum, HMS *Dolphin*), Samuel L Morison, Richard Groves, Sir Ian McIntosh, Jacques Mordal, Alan Raven and John Roberts. I am also indebted to Cdr D W Waters, Deputy Director of the National Maritime Museum, whose articles in the *Naval Review* contain so much useful information on the evolution of convoy doctrine.

The following institutions have given a great deal of help: the National Maritime Museum, Greenwich; the Imperial War Museum, London; the Submarine Museum, HMS *Dolphin*; Ministry of Defence (Navy), Whitehall and Bath; US Navy Historical Center; Museum of History and Technology, Washington; Kockums AB, Sweden; Bibliotek für Zeitgeschichte, Stuttgart; Bundesarchiv, Freiburg; Central Naval Museum, Leningrad.

I would also like to thank Alan Gooch of Design 23 who designed this book, Ron Watson, who compiled the index, John A. Roberts and Helen Downton for their artwork, and Donald Sommerville, the editor. The following agencies and individuals kindly supplied the illustrations.

**AEW, Haslar:** 30
**Alsthom-Atlantique:** 41 top
**Associated Press:** 92
**Marius Bar:** 6–7, 9, 22, 26 top, 26–27, 56–57, 134
**John Batchelor:** 61, 62 all four, 71 bottom, 128 top
**Empresa Naçional Bazán:** 150–151
**Bison Picture Library:** 99, 102–103, 106, 114 main pic, 136 top, 189
**BLT Karlskrona:** 162–163
**Brazilian Navy:** 143 lower
**Chas E Brown:** 142
**British Official:** 32 top & bottom, 86–87, 103, 104, 109, 115, 118–119, 120 both, 129 top
**Bundesarchiv:** 1, 43 top & right, 60–61, 94–95 both, 101, 105 all three
**Canadian Public Archives:** 36 lower, 121 all three
**Central Press:** 97 both
**Chilean Navy:** 143 upper
**Stephen Cribb, Southsea:** 4–5, 65, 66–67 bottom, 70, 71 top
**Deutschesmuseum, Munich:** 184–185
**Directions Techniques Constructions Navales:** 145, 180 inset
**HMS *Dolphin* Submarine Museum:** 19, 32 center, 41 lower, 69
**Helen Downton:** 13, 30–31, 50, 107, 122–123
**ECPA:** 18 top, 27, 44, 45, 79 all three, 160 top, 171 top, 176–177
**K P Exner (U-Boat Museum):** 186–187 both
**Federal German Navy:** 144, 152
**Flight International:** 80–81 all four
**Fox Photos:** 98
**Aldo Fraccaroli:** 18 bottom, 66–67 top, 100 both, 184
**General Dynamics Electric Boat Division:** 158, 174–175
**General Dynamics Pomona Division:** 180 bottom, 181 bottom
**Goodyear Aerospace:** 148–149
**Robert Hunt Library:** 8, 64–65
**Imperial War Musum:** 14, 35, 48–49, 51, 53 lower, 54–55, 63, 66, 67, 82 center, 92–93, 96, 107, 110, 111, 114 inset, 128 bottom, 130 top, 131, 185
**Hansgeorg Jentschura:** 23, 123 top left
**Humphrey Joel:** 52
**Kriegsarchiv Vienna:** 42–43
**Kockums:** 2–3, 40 all three, 137 bottom, 161
**Norbert Krüger:** 28–29
**London News Agency:** 108
**Lockheed:** 180
**Ministry of Defence (Navy):** 37, 38 lower, 39, 138, 139 top, 150 (HMS *Neptune*), 152–153, 154 bottom, 170–171, 172, 178–179
**Musee de la Marine:** 15, 16–17, 82–83
**Naval Photograph Club:** 68–69, 87 center, 188
**National Maritime Museum, London:** 22–23, 24–25, 42, 46–47 bottom, 55, 58–59 both (Gunn Collection), 72–73, 74, 76–77, 129 bottom
**Peter Newark's Western Americana:** 11
**Norwegian Naval Museum:** 26 center, 36 top
**PPL:** 31, 33, 34, 46–47 above, 53 top, 56, 74–75, 130 lower, 135 both, 182–183
**Popperfoto:** 68, 123 top right
**John A. Roberts:** 75, 156–157
**Eberhard Rössler:** 157
**Scicon Industries:** 10
**Science Museum, London:** 12
**Scott Lithgow:** 158–159
**Swedish Navy:** 83 bottom
**TASS:** 169 bottom
**C & S Taylor:** 38 top, 137 top
**Ufficio Storico:** 84
**US Air Force:** 181 top
**US Navy:** 20–21, 78 both, 88–89 both, 90–91, 110–111, 112–113, 116–117, 122, 124–125, 126–127 both, 140–141 both, 146–147, 154 top & center, 164–165, 166–167 both, 168, 169 top & center
**Vickers Oceanics:** 132–133, 139 bottom
**Vickers Shipbuilding and Engineering:** 155, 156–157, 173
**Waverley Electronics:** 136 bottom
**Wright and Logan, Southsea:** 85, 87 top